INTERNATIONAL ENERGY AGENCY

BLACK SEA ENERGY SURVEY

IN CO-OPERATION WITH
THE ENERGY CHARTER SECRETARIAT

INTERNATIONAL
ENERGY AGENCY
9, rue de la Fédération,
75739 Paris, cedex 15, France

ORGANISATION FOR
ECONOMIC CO-OPERATION
AND DEVELOPMENT

The International Energy Agency (IEA) is an autonomous body which was established in November 1974 within the framework of the Organisation for Economic Co-operation and Development (OECD) to implement an international energy programme.

It carries out a comprehensive programme of energy co-operation among twenty-four* of the OECD's twenty-nine Member countries. The basic aims of the IEA are:

• To maintain and improve systems for coping with oil supply disruptions;
• To promote rational energy policies in a global context through co-operative relations with non-member countries, industry and international organisations;
• To operate a permanent information system on the international oil market;
• To improve the world's energy supply and demand structure by developing alternative energy sources and increasing the efficiency of energy use;
• To assist in the integration of environmental and energy policies.

*IEA Member countries: Australia, Austria, Belgium, Canada, Denmark, Finland, France, Germany, Greece, Hungary, Ireland, Italy, Japan, Luxembourg, the Netherlands, New Zealand, Norway, Portugal, Spain, Sweden, Switzerland, Turkey, the United Kingdom, the United States. The European Commission also takes part in the work of the IEA.

Pursuant to Article 1 of the Convention signed in Paris on 14th December 1960, and which came into force on 30th September 1961, the Organisation for Economic Co-operation and Development (OECD) shall promote policies designed:

• To achieve the highest sustainable economic growth and employment and a rising standard of living in Member countries, while maintaining financial stability, and thus to contribute to the development of the world economy;
• To contribute to sound economic expansion in Member as well as non-member countries in the process of economic development; and
• To contribute to the expansion of world trade on a multilateral, non-discriminatory basis in accordance with international obligations.

The original Member countries of the OECD are Austria, Belgium, Canada, Denmark, France, Germany, Greece, Iceland, Ireland, Italy, Luxembourg, the Netherlands, Norway, Portugal, Spain, Sweden, Switzerland, Turkey, the United Kingdom and the United States. The following countries became Members subsequently through accession at the datesindicated hereafter: Japan (28th April 1964), Finland (28th January 1969), Australia (7th June 1971), New Zealand (29th May 1973), Mexico (18th May 1994), the Czech Republic (21st December 1995), Hungary (7th May 1996), Poland (22nd November 1996) and the Republic of Korea (12th December 1996). The Commission of the European Communities takes part in the work of the OECD (Article 13 of the OECD Convention).

FOREWORD

In 1998, the International Energy Agency published *Caspian Oil and Gas*, highlighting the Caspian Sea's potential as a main energy source for both Europe and Asia. We follow that study now with this *Black Sea Energy Study*, for the key to moving Caspian oil and gas to market in Europe is the politics and economics of the complex Black Sea region.

World oil demand is expected to continue to grow, with prosperity and the relentless spread of motor and air transport. The Caspian Sea region is one of the great potential reserves of petroleum – not nearly so vast as the Middle East's pool, but comparable to North Sea reserves. How the riparian states resolve the problem of energy through and along the coast of the Black Sea will be of high importance to Europe and the world over the next two decades.

This study describes the extreme variety of conditions in the states involved – from rapidly-growing and gas-hungry Turkey to oil-rich Azerbaijan. Bulgaria and Romania, together with three republics of the Former Soviet Union, are still undergoing the difficult transition from Communism to a market economy. All need foreign investment to support the expensive energy projects before them. Several have yet to create the stable and predictable investment climate needed to attract such investment.

In the current volume, the IEA seeks to render a service to the countries of the region as well as to future investors and clients. Facing up to the political, economic and geographic problems of the region, we offer some proposals on how they may be met. Among the key issues dealt with is, of course, that of alternative transit routes that will safely deliver oil and gas while avoiding congestion in the Turkish Straits.

Robert Priddle
Executive Director

ACKNOWLEDGEMENTS

The IEA wishes to acknowledge the very helpful co-operation of the Energy Charter Secretariat, the OECD Nuclear Energy Agency, and Hagler-Bailly Services Inc.

Thanks are due to the following experts for their valuable comments: Emmanuel Bergasse of the Tacis Energy Efficiency Centre in Tbilisi; Slavtcho Neykov at the Bulgarian State Commission for Energy Regulation; Doina Caloianu and Lulin Radulov of the Black Sea Regional Energy Centre.

Special thanks is given to the following IEA staff: Pierre-Marie Cussaguet and John Paffenbarger, country desk officers respectively for Turkey and Greece, Yukimi Shimura and Sohbet Karbuz for preparing the statistical data, Bertrand Sadin for the preparation of the maps, and Benjamin Parameswaran for the preparatory work.

INTRODUCTION

The IEA, in co-operation with the Energy Charter Secretariat, conducted a study of the energy sectors and policies of Armenia, Azerbaijan, Bulgaria, Georgia and Romania in late 1998 and early 1999. The resulting publication, Black Sea Energy Survey, is an independent review of the major issues facing energy developments in these countries and energy transport in the Black Sea. To round off the regional picture, brief overviews of the IEA Members Greece and Turkey have been added, drawing on the IEA's Energy Policy reviews of these countries. Ukraine and Russia, which have been studied in detail in previous IEA surveys, are not covered by specific chapters in this study.

In preparing this report, missions were undertaken in late 1998 to Armenia, Bulgaria, Georgia and Romania to meet with key energy figures in government and industry, both local and foreign, as well as representatives of multilateral institutions active in the region.

The study team was composed of experts from the IEA Secretariat and from the Energy Charter Secretariat.

Hans Kausch (team leader)
IEA, Head of Non-Member Countries Division for Europe, Middle East and Africa

Erich Unterwurzacher
IEA, Administrator, Non-Member Countries Division

Jean-Christophe Fueg
IEA, Administrator, Non-Member Countries Division

Nina Kouznetsoff
Energy Statistician, IEA

Ian Brown
Phare energy advisor at the Romanian Ministry of Industry and Trade

John Fahy
ERAS Ltd

Sydney Fremantle
Energy Charter Secretariat

Gianni Frescura
OECD Nuclear Energy Agency

Jeff Pierson
Altec

Jacques Royen
OECD Nuclear Energy Agency

Lise Weis
Energy Charter Secretariat

TABLE OF CONTENTS

List of Figures

I. OVERVIEW

This study analyses energy policies and development in the Black Sea region, which lies at the crossroads of major existing and future oil and gas transportation routes.

It features individual chapters on four Black Sea countries: Bulgaria, Romania, Georgia and Turkey. Given the importance of the Trans-Caucasus energy transport corridor, Armenia and Azerbaijan, too, are analysed. The country chapters focus on domestic energy policy and sector developments. A chapter is dedicated to Greece, because of its importance as a gateway for Black Sea energy trade. Country chapters on Russia and Ukraine were beyond the scope of this study. These two countries are analysed here only to the extent they play a role in Black Sea energy trade patterns. The IEA has published earlier energy reviews of these two countries.

The Black Sea shelf and coastal regions, although little explored, are not likely to reveal reserves that will supply any but local markets. The importance of the Black Sea resides in its geographical location, halfway between two major oil and gas supply regions – Russia and the Caspian – and large markets, such as Turkey, Southeast and Central Europe, and the Mediterranean.

A common feature of the Black Sea states is their dependence on Russia for a significant share of their energy needs. Energy supplies to Romania, Bulgaria, Georgia and Armenia still largely follow the old Soviet pattern. Hence these countries' efforts to diversify their supplies. Turkey and Greece, however, have been supplied by Russian gas since 1987 and 1996 respectively, and consider Russian oil and gas merely as one – albeit important – source amongst many.

Intense commercial activity around the Black Sea dates back to Antiquity. Since the end of the Cold War, the Black Sea states have intensified regional co-operation. Beyond oil and gas trade, regional electricity trade in Southeast Europe and Turkey will become increasingly important in the medium term. Electricity trading could resume in the Caucasus states as it existed in the Soviet era, and could be expanded to eastern Turkey and potentially northern Iran. Both Romania and Bulgaria have surplus refining capacity, which, if adequately upgraded, could sell products to the entire Southeast European market.

The countries examined here are very diverse economically and in terms of their energy mixes and markets (*see Graph*). They include two OECD and IEA members – Greece and Turkey – and five transition economies that were either Soviet states – Azerbaijan, Armenia and Georgia – or members of the Soviet bloc – Bulgaria and Romania. All five transition economies suffered severe recessions early in the 1990's and have begun a gradual recovery. All require massive foreign investment to develop their energy production, transport and distribution sectors.

Political stability and economic reform are prerequisites for these countries to compete successfully with other regions of the world for scarce investment dollars. Azerbaijan must attract and retain multinational corporations that will prove up sufficient reserves to justify

Figure 1   Black Sea Countries TPES (1990-97)

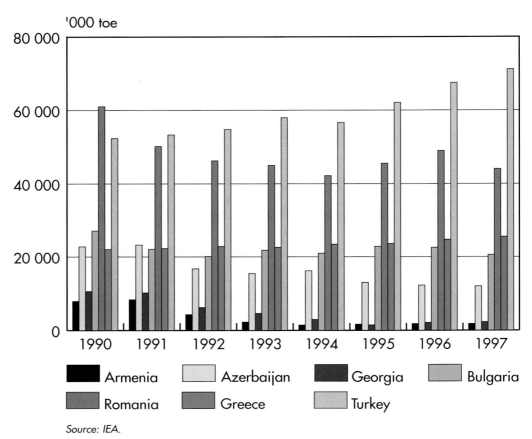

Source: IEA.

large export pipelines. Georgia, Turkey, Bulgaria, Romania and Greece, but also Russia, Ukraine and Iran, are competing to establish themselves as energy transit countries. Several countries, such as Romania, Bulgaria, Georgia and Ukraine, offer potential opportunities in the refining and distribution sector. The gas market is expected to grow substantially in all riparian states.

Regulatory reform has advanced at various paces in the five Transition Economies. EU accession is a powerful motivation for Bulgaria and Romania, whereas Azerbaijan sees little urgency in regulatory reform, given the massive foreign investment into its oil and gas sector so far. The electricity sector is perhaps the one, which has undergone the most reform, although foreign investment has remained relatively low, including in Turkey and Greece.

The energy profiles of the seven countries are very diverse: Bulgaria, Romania and Turkey are trying to reduce their heavy reliance on domestic coal by increasing gas imports. Azerbaijan almost totally relies on oil and gas. Armenia's only domestic "resource" is its nuclear power station, which – like Bulgaria's four older reactors – will need to be closed because of inherent safety issues. Romania – with its Canadian-design plant – and Bulgaria – with two more recent reactors – will continue to rely on nuclear energy. Turkey plans to build a nuclear plant as well. Only Azerbaijan is a net energy exporter. All other countries are net importers, ranging from Romania, which imports 39% of Total Primary Energy Supply, to Georgia (80% of TPES imported) or Greece (92% of TPES imported).

ECONOMIC PERFORMANCE AND OUTLOOK

■ **Armenia**'s economic recovery started in 1994 with robust GDP growth rates (6% expected in 1999), although from extremely low levels. Exports have been increasingly oriented to the EU and US, which buffered the impact of the Russian financial crisis. However, the substantial share of the underground economy (around 40% of GDP) gives rise to concern. Also, Armenia will continue to disqualify itself for regional energy trade routes as long as the Nagorny-Karabakh conflict is not resolved. The government is committed to accelerating economic reform through privatisation of major parts of industry, including the energy sector.

■ **Azerbaijan** has witnessed robust economic growth of more than 5% annually over the past three years, largely driven by foreign investment into the country's oil and gas sector. But the country's resource wealth, which has attracted numerous investors, carries a potential liability. Regulatory reform may not be given due attention by the government and the country could become a single-commodity economy. Internationally, Azerbaijan has moved closer to the US, Turkey and Europe, whilst maintaining relations with its Russian and Iranian neighbours.

■ **Bulgaria** implemented a radical stabilisation and structural reform programme in mid-1997. Rapid privatisation of enterprises, including energy companies, will remain a key element for a sustainable economic recovery. In 1998 the government agreed with the IMF on a three-year privatisation programme. In a landmark sale, the Burgas refinery went to Russia's Lukoil. Negotiations on several energy-related projects are advancing, including $120 million in joint funding by the European Bank for Reconstruction and Development and the World Bank for the country's district heating system, and the sale of the Maritza East lignite and power complex to RWE of Germany. The currency board, introduced in 1997, and the macroeconomic situation remain stable. After GDP receded in 1996-97, it started to grow again in 1998 and is likely to remain at approximately 2% in 2000.

■ Since **Georgia** became independent, political upheaval, separatist conflicts in Abkhazia and South Ossetia and civil war from 1991 to 1993 thwarted substantial economic reform. Between 1990 and 1994, real GDP fell by about 70%. Recovery started in 1995. Growth exceeded 10% in 1996-97, but was reduced to 2.9% in 1998 because of the Russian financial crisis. Growth is estimated at 3% in 1999. In 1998 the government carried out the first major privatisation in the power sector of the Caucasus region by selling the Tbilisi distribution company to AES (US). Georgia has succeeded in establishing itself as a corridor for "early" oil exports from Azerbaijan and Kazakhstan. Chances that a "main" oil pipeline and a gas pipeline will run across the country look good, but continuing uncertainty over Caspian reserves may further delay construction.

■ With its coming into office in 1996, **Romania**'s new liberal government resumed economic reform. However, the reform still lags below initial expectations, in particular with regard to large-scale privatisation of key state enterprises, including the electric utility Conel and the state oil company Petrom. The contraction of the Romanian economy was expected to bottom out in 1999 and GDP to grow moderately in 2000. Overall, Romania's prospects remain weak, as progress in macroeconomic stabilisation is hampered by continued delays in restructuring programmes.

THE ENERGY LANDSCAPE: SOME COMMON THREADS

A common feature of Armenia, Bulgaria, Georgia and Romania is their high dependence on Russian energy imports. Romania and Ukraine are the only riparian states with significant oil and gas production, which is nonetheless insufficient to cover domestic demand. Azerbaijan is the only net oil exporter and recently proved its potential to become a gas exporter. Bulgaria, Romania and Ukraine have larger coal deposits, but all require modernisation and probably downsizing of the industry. Moreover, Romanian and Bulgarian coal is of poor quality. High production costs make large parts of the mining sector uneconomic.

Armenia and Georgia suffered dramatic energy shortages in the early 1990's, as primary energy supplies plummeted by more than 85%! Energy supplies and consumption decreased in Azerbaijan, Bulgaria and Romania too, though not as sharply as in the two Caucasus states that were entangled in wars at that time.

Reform of the energy sector, especially the introduction of cost-based prices for electricity and heat, is still politically sensitive. The absence of cost-based energy prices is often a serious obstacle to foreign investment. Social considerations could hinder government efforts to restructure the energy sector.

As a further common feature, the countries provide transit corridors for oil and gas from Russia and the Caspian region to world markets. Armenia, however, remains a special case, as tensions with Azerbaijan make it difficult for the country to reap the benefits of regional energy trade.

Armenia, Bulgaria, Romania and Ukraine consider nuclear power as an important, if not indispensable, energy source with which to reduce import dependence. With the exception of Romania, the nuclear power plants are Russian-designed VVER reactors, which Western experts consider risky. For Armenia, the reopening of the nuclear power plant in 1995 (after being closed down following a devastating earthquake in 1989) allowed the country to end electricity rationing. But this created yet another energy link to Russia, Armenia's nuclear fuel supplier.

STATE OWNERSHIP AND PRIVATISATION

State ownership of the energy industry is still widespread among Black Sea transition economies, although governments have expressed their intention to divest their interests in the energy sector to varying degrees. The Bulgarian and Romanian governments have begun to privatise the refining sector, and in all countries there is agreement to (partially) privatise electric utilities. On the forefront is Georgia, which privatised almost half of its electricity distribution in the winter of 1998. For Georgia and Armenia, it is important that the new owners improve operational efficiency and that they invest in rehabilitation and new capacity. Azerbaijan intends to privatise the electricity and gas distribution industry by 2001. The largest assets slated for privatisation in the region are Romania's oil company Petrom and electric utility Conel.

Governments regard privatisation as a means to introduce market discipline, improve efficiency, reduce the budget deficit and gain access to modern technology and management practices.

However, major hurdles to attracting large-scale private capital and foreign ownership include electricity tariffs that are below economic costs, poor tariff collection, and economic and political instability. Some governments, like in Romania and Azerbaijan, prefer to restructure and streamline their state assets, hoping to fetch a better price when floating them. Privatisation can also be dangerous if appropriate institutions are not in place to promote greater efficiency rather than opportunistic asset stripping.

Efforts to attract foreign investors in the oil and gas sector are driven by strategic considerations. Bulgaria and Romania depend on Russia for all of their gas imports and Gazprom aims to expand its hold on transit countries and on distribution. It seeks to increase exports to Southeastern Europe, mainly Turkey and Greece, and to safeguard against gas-on-gas competition from the Caspian region. However, both Romania and Bulgaria remain cautious and are unlikely to allow Gazprom to gain control of the domestic gas business. Russian investment has also flowed into these two countries' downstream oil sectors, largely because Russia's Lukoil considers Southeastern Europe as important for the company's strategy. Lukoil also benefited from a lack of interest from Western competitors.

Georgia has gained significant importance as a transit country for both oil and gas. The Baku-Supsa oil pipeline, which started operation in April 1999, allowed the oil companies in Azerbaijan to diversify the exports routes for "early oil". The Northern route from Baku to Novorossiysk, which crosses Chechnya, is likely to have lost its credibility with foreign companies for many years to come. Whether the Chechnya by-pass pipeline currently under construction will prove any more attractive to foreign shippers remains to be seen.

Armenia's strategic interests are different, since political difficulties with its neighbours to the east and west do not allow the country to capitalise on its transit potential. Consequently, it has entered strategic alliances with old energy trading partners. Gazprom became the co-owner of the national gas business. Armenia has been seeking new partners in Iran, with no success so far.

STRUCTURAL REFORM

Governments of the Black Sea countries attach great importance to the restructuring of their energy sectors. It is in the electricity sector that reform efforts show the most promising results, often in response to advice and loan conditions from international finance institutions. Romania, Armenia and Georgia have unbundled their electricity industry and Bulgaria is to follow in 2000. Electricity sector reform in Azerbaijan is still embryonic.

Romania and Bulgaria have introduced competition in the petroleum downstream sector, but have failed to attract major western companies so far. This is mainly due to low domestic demand, which squeezes the business prospects of distributors, and to unfavourable investment conditions. In Georgia and Armenia foreign companies are not yet present in the retail business as domestic transport fuel markets remain underdeveloped.

With the exception of Romania, which has significant resources of its own, the importance of natural gas consumption in all sectors in the Black Sea countries is still low. The collapse of industry and the absence of natural gas in the residential sectors of both Armenia and

Georgia, and an underdeveloped domestic gas market in Bulgaria, limit the interest of the gas industry to transit and – in the medium term – to generate power. Because of limited market prospects and the political sensitivity (i.e. dependence on Russian imports), governments have not yet paid much attention to structural change of the natural gas sector other than establishing strategic alliances with Russia's Gazprom, as it is the case in Georgia, Armenia and Bulgaria.

Setbacks to the Romanian government's effort to reduce coal production in loss-making mines show that the restructuring of the energy sector can be painful. The political force of coal miners has delayed the closure of unprofitable mines, which may – if it is sustained – potentially weaken the restructuring programme for the entire sector and the country's economic stabilisation programme.

REGULATORY AND LEGAL REFORM

All Black Sea countries have expressed a strong commitment to introducing modern regulatory and legal frameworks for energy sector operations, in particular for the electricity and oil sectors. In 1999 the Romanian and Bulgarian parliaments passed legislation to create a modern regulatory framework for energy. Armenia and Georgia have enacted energy laws that include provisions for the establishment of independent regulatory bodies. Romania and Bulgaria have also adopted essential legislation for operations in the petroleum and gas sectors, and have assigned regulatory functions to bodies, which are distinct from ministries. Given the dependence of the region on one single source of gas – which amplifies the sector's strategic importance – reform of the natural gas industry generally lags behind other sectors as governments remain reluctant to open up the industry to foreign investors.

Armenia, Georgia, Bulgaria and Romania have established regulatory offices for electricity and gas that are nominally independent from the government. The regulatory commissions in Georgia and Armenia are tailored on the US regulatory model (both countries were and are advised and supported in their restructuring efforts by USAID). However, these new frameworks still remain largely untested. The new commissions have not yet licensed any new facility. There are also signs that their independence from parliament or government, for example as regards tariff setting and contract negotiations with investors, may be jeopardised if parliaments feel that regulatory acts may potentially have negative social and political impacts.

INTEGRATION OF ELECTRICITY MARKETS

There is potential for the development of regional electricity markets in Southeastern Europe and the Trans-Caucasus.

Recent studies, which were financed by the EU PHARE programme, are encouraging about the prospects of inter-connecting Bulgaria, Romania and Albania with UCTE members[1] in

---

1. UCTE is an association of transmission system operators. Members in the wider Southeastern European region include operators from Italy, Slovenia, Croatia, Greece, FYROM, and the Federal Republic of Yugoslavia. No member has yet been designated for Bosnia Herzegovina.

Southeast Europe. Due to the war in Yugoslavia, the inter-connections of Greece and FYROM with other European UCTE members were broken in 1991. The establishment of a Trans-European Electricity Network (TEN) is a priority of EU policy. The EU envisions setting up a regional electricity market (REM) encompassing Albania, Bosnia Herzegovina, Bulgaria, FYROM, Romania and Greece[1] by 2005. The power sectors of these six countries represent a sizeable market of approximately 150 TWh[2]. Demand is projected to grow to 201.2 TWh in 2010. Peak load of the REM is projected to increase by more than 30% in the period 2000-2010, i.e. to 27.1 GW in 2000 and to 35.6 GW in 2010.

An integrated REM would improve operations between the national power systems beyond the sporadic power exchanges that take place in case of emergency, shortages due to low hydraulicity or late power plant commissioning. Electricity trade would allow coverage of the summer peak load in Greece or winter peaks in the other five countries. Long-term agreements and power trading mechanisms would need to be set up. Investments in capacity expansion could be optimised, system loads would be more balanced, and electricity would be cheaper. According to projections, the utilisation factor of the coal/lignite-fired plants is relatively low, providing opportunities for future exports. There is an overcapacity of oil- and gas-fired plants in the region that could be used to control intermediate loads, while hydropower could secure peak loads. The synchronous interconnection of power networks of UCTE and IPS/UPS[3] countries has so far resulted in investment savings, increased reliability of supply and reduction of transmission losses.

All Southeast European countries have state-dominated power utilities. Liberalisation and market opening is planned or already underway in a number of countries. Those which hope to join the EU will have to open at least 25% of their electricity market to competition and allow for IPPs in order to comply with the EU Directive on Electricity.

The integration of power systems in the Caucasus region faces larger political obstacles than in Southeast Europe. But technically it would be a return to the past, since Armenia, Georgia and Azerbaijan were part of the Trans-Caucasian Interconnected Power System of the Soviet Union. Following the break-up of the Soviet Union and the outbreak of regional conflicts, the three Caucasus states were forced to operate their electricity systems independently. They had to cope with severe supply disruptions that led to rationing. For Armenia and Georgia it is a priority to re-establish reliable domestic supplies. Georgia has a significant untapped hydro-power potential, which could be used for load balancing of regional electricity networks, including those of Turkey and Azerbaijan.

INVESTMENT CLIMATE

Economic, political and legal stability are essential preconditions for investment. Although there have been significant improvements in recent years, investors still perceive a considerable risk in the Caucasus countries and, to a lesser extent, in Bulgaria and Romania. The Black

---

1. For political reasons, the Federal Republic of Yugoslavia is not part of the REM initiative, in spite of its central location in the regional transmission network. Turkey has not been included in the study, but the nascent electricity trade with Bulgaria and Greece is expected to develop.
2. For comparison, this is slightly larger than the Mexican power market, or about 10% smaller than the Spanish or Australian markets.
3. Eastern Europe and FSU.

Sea countries are committed to carrying out corporate reform and privatisation, including in the energy sector. But they have not yet succeeded in attracting substantial foreign investment, except Azerbaijan for its oil and gas sector. Opportunities do exist however, from the upstream sector in Romania to gas transportation in Bulgaria and electricity distribution in Armenia.

The Kosovo crisis has increased Romania's and Bulgaria's need for investment. These two countries have incurred substantial losses because of the war in Yugoslavia and trade sanctions.

A distinction needs to be made between inward-oriented investment for domestic and regional markets and large export-oriented projects in the oil and gas sector. Investors' appetite for inward-oriented projects – which is still small – will depend on the ability of governments to successfully stabilise the economies and to establish regulatory frameworks that meet the needs of modern energy markets.

Large-scale projects to bring Caspian Sea oil and gas to world markets hold many advantages for the Black Sea countries. They will underpin the economic recovery of transition economies in the Black Sea region and diversify supply sources of the region and beyond. As with all large infrastructure projects, and particularly in a region where investment remains risky and project costs uncertain, companies will continue to make decisions on commercial grounds. The risk should be assumed by the private sector, and the role of governments should be limited to setting the legal and regulatory framework that provides for non-discriminatory, stable and transparent rules for investment and energy sector operations.

II. REGIONAL ENERGY TRADE AND TRANSIT

One of the major common features of the Black Sea countries is their potential role in regional energy trade and transit. The enhancement of both regional trade and transit flows is an essential component for economic recovery and energy security.

OIL TRADE AND TRANSPORT

Current Oil Transport

Historically, the main oil transport stream across the Black Sea has been Soviet/Russian sea-borne exports from its two main terminals at Novorossiysk and Tuapse, supplemented by the now Ukrainian port of Odessa. Exports reached a peak of 60 mt (1.2 mb/d) in the late 1980's, before falling to 37.5 mt per annum (750,000 b/d) in the early 1990's, due to declining oil production and bureaucratic and technical export-hampering factors in Russia. After the collapse of the Soviet Union, Russia's oil exporters strove to maximise sea-borne exports via the Black Sea (and via the Baltic Sea) to avoid the constraints and costly tariffs of exporting crude by pipeline through transit countries. The situation, however, has by and large normalised since[1]. (See Map 2: Black Sea Oil Trade Flows)

Current Russian crude and product exports via the Black Sea have risen to almost 55 mt/year (1.1 mb/d), blended with some 3-5% of Kazakh, Azeri and Turkmen crudes.

Novorossiysk has a capacity of 34 mt/annum (680,000 b/d). There are plans to upgrade the port to 42 mt/annum (840,000 b/d). Tuapse can handle 10 mt/annum (200,000 b/d), 60% of which are products. A 5 mt/year expansion is planned at Tuapse. The capacity of Odessa is 10 mt/year (200,000 b/d), including 50% products. Most Kazakh crude, which is exported via Russia and the Black Sea, transits through Odessa.

There are two oil terminals in Georgia: Supsa, which was inaugurated in April 1999, can carry 10 mt/year (200,000 b/d). It is the end point of the 5.75 mt/year (115,000 b/d) "early oil" pipeline, which handles oil produced by the AIOC consortium offshore Azerbaijan. The second Georgian terminal at Batumi is mainly used to export crude produced by the Chevron-led TCO consortium at the Tengiz field in Kazakhstan; its capacity is 3.5 mt/year (70,000 b/d). TCO may increase the capacity of this line to 6.8 mt/year (136,000 b/d).

Current Russian and Caspian oil exports via Black Sea ports total nearly 70 mt/annum (1.4 mb/d). FSU oil exports through the Black Sea have reached peaks of almost 1.7 mb/d, notably in October 1999. Most of these cargoes are shipped via the Turkish Straits. Only a small fraction of these volumes are offloaded in Black Sea ports.

---

1. Russian exporters continue to favour domestic ports for export to avoid third-country transit. Hence plans to build a new terminal near St. Petersburg (Baltic Pipeline System) and further expansion of Novorossiysk, making it no longer necessary to use Odessa for Russian oil exports through the Black Sea.

Figure 2   FSU Oil Exports*

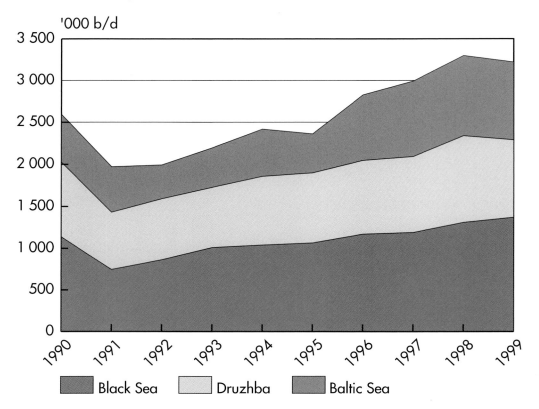

Source: IEA, DOE. 1999 figures are estimated.
*Includes non-Russian FSU exports (Kazakhstan, Azerbaijan, Turkmenistan).

In spite of Turkish alarm over growing traffic through the Turkish Straits and the increased accident risk[1], it is difficult to predict the amount of traffic that would saturate the Turkish Straits. Traffic through the Bosphorus, after a decline in the early 1990's, is now approaching the peak tonnage of the late 1980's (see also Chapter: Oil Transit in the Section on Turkey). Yet oil cargoes have not been the prime cause of the increased traffic across the Straits in recent years. Vessel movements have also increased because of intensified trade in the wake of the break-up of the Soviet Union and increasing traffic on the Danube after the opening of the Main-Danube canal.

Medium-Term Oil Transport (2003-2005)

■ Kazakhstan: Today, Kazakhstan exports most of its crude via the existing pipeline to Samara, whose capacity is being upgraded from 10 mt/annum (200,000 b/d) to 15 mt/annum (300,000 b/d). The crude is blended with West Siberian crudes and ultimately delivered at Russian Black Sea ports or through the Druzhba pipeline. Alternative Kazakh oil export channels, such as TCO's Trans-Caucasus route (max. 3.5 mt/year; 70,000 b/d) or some barge shipments through the Volga-Don canal (max 3.5 mt/year; 70,000 b/d) eventually transit via the Black Sea.

Until 2003-04, additional oil streams out of Kazakhstan can be expected with the commissioning of the CPC pipeline, which will end at the new Yuzhnaya Ozerevka terminal

---

1. Turkish warnings about the risk of tanker accidents have not been in vain. In December 1999, a Russian tanker broke apart in the Sea of Marmara. This is the second major tanker wreckage in the straits, after 1994.

near Novorossiysk. Construction of the system is underway and commissioning is scheduled for mid-2001. Its initial capacity is 28 mt/year (560,000 b/d). During a second phase lasting from 2007 till 2014, the pipeline capacity will be upgraded to 67 mt/year (1.34 mb/d).

The CPC pipeline will carry oil from reserves held today by foreign companies in western Kazakhstan. The most prominent are TCO's Tengiz field (9 billion bbl), which is planned to peak at 67 mt (1.34 mb/d) by 2014, and the Karachaganak field (2.4 billion bbl), which is operated by the KOS consortium (BG, ENI, etc) and will ultimately produce 200,000 b/d of liquids. Combined exports by other smaller foreign operators in western Kazakhstan should not exceed 10 mt/year (200,000 b/d) in the coming five years and will not require new export infrastructure. Kazakh exports are set to rise from a current level of 16.5 mt/year (330,000 b/d) to 30-35 mt/year (600,000-700,000 b/d) by the middle of the next decade. They will be easily channelled through the CPC and Samara lines, the Trans-Caucasus pipe-rail-barge system, through oil swaps with Iran and by barge or train through Russia.

Future oil exports from areas currently being explored by foreign and local companies are obviously more difficult to predict. The most promising acreage lies offshore, where the Shell-operated OKIOC consortium started drilling the Kashagan structure in the summer 1999. Even if Kashagan proves to be a major find, it would not start producing before 2003-04 at the very earliest. A hypothetical 5 billion bbl strike offshore would need some 7-8 years to reach a production plateau of say 50 mt/year (1 mb/d). In other words, a second "post-Tengiz" pipeline will be needed only if massive new reserves will be found, and not before 2006-2010. The routing of such a line – parallel to CPC, across the Caspian to Turkey, or through Iran – is impossible to foretell.

■ Russian oil production, currently running at slightly over 305 mt/annum (6.1 mb/d), seems unlikely to rise substantially over the coming years. Those Russian basins where oil output will increase in the coming decade (Timan-Pechora basin, Pechora Sea, Sakhalin Island), will not export via the Black Sea. One question mark is the Russian "sector" of the Caspian Sea, where Lukoil started exploratory drilling in summer 1999. But reserves which could be found in the "Russian" Caspian, are unlikely to be large enough to warrant additional Black Sea export infrastructure.

So Russian exports through the Black Sea will stabilise at today's levels, or possibly even decrease, if more exports are evacuated through existing or future Baltic Sea terminals, or by pipeline to Europe.

■ Azerbaijan is not likely to export sizeable volumes of its oil via Novorossiysk in the medium-term. The viability of the so-called "Northern Route" for Azeri crude has been jeopardised by hostilities in Chechnya and Dagestan and tariff squabbles between Transneft and Chechnya. Neither Azerbaijan nor foreign companies seem to believe in Russia's ability to make the route safer, although it could transport up to 9 mt/annum (180,000 b/d). But it is also possible that Russia might succeed in establishing a safe pipeline corridor bypassing Chechnya in the future.

Forecasting future oil transports along the Trans-Caucasus corridor – from Baku to the Georgian shore – is more hazardous. The current transport capacity is made up of a 5.75 mt/year (115,000 b/d) pipeline, plus a 3.5 mt/year (70,000 b/d) railway/pipeline system. The AIOC "early oil" pipeline to Supsa could be upgraded to 10 mt/year (200,000 b/d). The pipeline is primarily used by the AIOC consortium, which operates the Guneshli-Cirag-Azeri (GCA) field complex offshore in Azerbaijan, whereas the railway/pipeline infrastructure handles mostly TCO's oil from Tengiz. TCO plans to upgrade the rail/pipeline system to 6.8 mt/year (136,000 b/d).

There has been much discussion about the "Main Export Pipeline" (MEP) for AIOC's Azeri oil. At the OSCE summit in Istanbul on 18 November 1999, Turkey, Azerbaijan and Georgia signed a "declaration" on the construction of the Baku-Ceyhan pipeline. The agreement has been actively championed by the US. The merit of this declaration is that it confers high-level state support for the pipeline and provides a legal foundation for the commercial contracts that are now needed for construction of the pipeline. The publicity given to the signature of the "declaration" contrasts with the reserved reaction of oil companies, who will eventually have to finance the pipeline. Russia and Iran, who are promoting rival pipelines, both expressed disapproval at the Istanbul "declaration".

The next step is for the three signatory states and AIOC to set up an "implementation committee" to develop a financial plan and engineering details and to define the ownership structure of the pipeline. This will lead to the creation of the Main Export Pipeline Company (MEPCO). Some investors are concerned about the Azeri state company SOCAR wanting to hold a controlling stake in MEPCO. The Istanbul declaration calls for construction to start in 2001 and for completion in 2004. AIOC, however, has indicated that a MEP could only become operational in 2007-08 – reflecting its own production targets and progress of other exploration projects in Azerbaijan.

Turkey contracted a preliminary feasibility study in 1997, which put the cost of the 1,730 km, 45 mt/year[1]-capacity pipeline at $2.4 billion. This excludes financial costs. AIOC however, has estimated costs as high as $3.3-3.7 billion. Turkey has agreed to guarantee the $1.4 billion cost of the Turkish leg of the pipeline. Based on a tariff of $2.58/bbl for the whole length of the pipeline, Turkey will earn about $100 million per year in transit fees. The only US financial pledge to Baku-Ceyhan is a $500 million loan guarantee from the OPIC and the American Eximbank. However, US funding hinges on the resolution of the Nagorny-Karabakh conflict, according to an amendment to the foreign appropriations bill voted by the US House of Representatives in July 1999. Laying the pipeline across Armenia would reduce the cost of the pipeline by up to $500 million, according to some calculations.

The Istanbul declaration assumes that Azerbaijan will commit 25 mt/year (500,000 b/d) to the pipeline, while Kazakhstan will commit the remaining 20 mt/year (400,000 b/d). The Azeri commitment is achievable, although it would be some years after the planned pipeline completion date of 2004, since AIOC plans to reach a production level of 500-700,000 b/d only in the second half of the next decade.

The Kazakh commitment, however, is more problematic. The only producer, who could deliver several hundred b/d, is TCO, which will have its own CPC pipeline ready by 2001. Kazakhstan's other producers could muster a combined volume of, say, 250-300,000 b/d. But the wild card is OKIOC's offshore Kashagan structure. If it proves to be a giant discovery, it could require a pipeline the size of Baku-Ceyhan for itself. Furthermore, the infrastructure

---

1.   900,000 b/d.

– pipelines or tankers/ports – to move 400,000 b/d of Kazakh crude across the Caspian to Baku does not exist yet. Consequently, BP Amoco is unlikely to muster sufficient production in Kazakhstan and Turkmenistan for Baku-Ceyhan. The company has set a deadline of October 2000 to find shipping commitments and raise finance for the project.

AIOC's most preferred scenario would have been to postpone a decision of the MEP until more reserves are found by other consortia on the Azeri shelf and possibly offshore Kazakhstan to make a MEP viable. The political situation in Iran might also improve, clearing the way for an evacuation route through Iran, which companies actually prefer, since it is the most cost-effective one. AIOC could upgrade the Baku-Supsa pipeline to 300,000 b/d during this waiting period. Azerbaijan however, is not keen on such a transition solution.

What may have changed AIOC's position on the Baku-Ceyhan pipeline is the Shah-deniz gas discovery, which suddenly made BP Amoco think about future gas exports to Turkey. The opening of the Turkish market for possible future Shah-deniz gas gave Turkey a welcome bargaining chip *vis-a-vis* BP Amoco.

AIOC, which has 4.6 billion bbl of booked reserves at its GCA complex, has indicated that 6 billion bbl of proven reserves are needed to make a MEP feasible. Azerbaijan's proven reserves (besides AIOC's) are about 2.1 billion bbl according to SOCAR's own estimates. So, under current economic conditions, the quasi-totality of proven Azeri reserves would have to be dedicated to a MEP.

By the autumn of 1999, Azerbaijan had signed nineteen production-sharing agreements (PSAs) with foreign companies. With the exception of the AIOC contract and a few minor onshore redevelopment deals, all major offshore contracts are for exploration acreage with no proven oil reserves. Limited rig availability and difficult drilling conditions make it unlikely that new oil reserves will be discovered and developed before 2004-05. Moreover, the recent drilling results of three western consortia, notably BP-Amoco's Shah-deniz, have confirmed that there tends to be more gas on the Azeri shelf than previously assumed.

Consequently, financing and construction of a MEP is unlikely to happen before 2002-03. AIOC, which is currently producing 5.5 mt/year (115,000 b/d), has indicated it may take longer than initially planned to increase production. Phase I (with a production level of 250-300,000 b/d) could be reached by 2003; a plateau of 700-800,000 b/d only by 2007-08. Phase I production could be exported via an upgraded line to Supsa and a number of other "makeshift" routes (railway capacity freed up by TCO, who by 2001-02 could use the CPC line; "Northern" pipeline route to Novorossiysk or barge through Russia; possibly Iran swaps).

The Baku-Ceyhan pipeline, with a projected capacity of 45 mt/year (900,000 b/d) would reduce oil tanker traffic through the Turkish Straits and jeopardise alternative bypass pipeline projects in the Balkans.

Combined Black Sea oil exports are unlikely to exceed 97.5-115 mt/annum (1.95-2.3 b/d) by 2003-05: i.e. 52.5-60 mt/annum (1.05-1.2 mb/d) from Russia, 30-35 mt/annum (600,000-700,000 b/d) from Kazakhstan via Russia and the Caucasus, and 15-20 mt/annum (300,000-400,000 b/d) from Azerbaijan plus modest volumes of Turkmen and Georgian oil. Such volumes, however, are likely to exceed what the Turkish Straits can reasonably handle. Alternative routes will have to be found.

Southeast Europe

Three Black Sea countries – Ukraine, Romania, Bulgaria – have a combined refining capacity of 90 mt/year (1.8 mb/d), of which only one third is used. All three countries want to secure Caspian oil feedstock in order to make full use of their refineries and to re-export products further west into Europe. This would enable them to diversify their supply sources and to replace some products imports. Some of their products could be sold in the wider Black Sea/Balkan region. But these countries will also want to target the Mediterranean and West European markets, once refineries have been modernised so they could technically and financially compete with other European refineries.

The combined oil demand of Black Sea states (except Russia) is expected to grow by between 22.5-35 mt/year (450-700,000 b/d) by 2010.

Romania's ten refineries have a combined effective capacity of 26 mt/year. But primary refining in 1998 amounted to just 12.5 mt. Domestic consumption is expected to rise from 11.5 mt to 14.2 mt by 2010, while domestic oil production is running at 6.3 mt and declining.

Bulgaria became a net product exporter in 1996 due to a fall in domestic consumption. Its Burgas refinery has a capacity of 6.6 mt/year; an additional 1-2 mt/year capacity could become available at two smaller refineries in the future. Domestic consumption is expected to increase from 4.8 mt (1996) to 6.6. mt in 2010.

The following projects – CTPL, SEEL or Bosphorus bypasses – would be competitors of the Baku-Ceyhan pipeline.

The most ambitious projects on the Southeast European oil scene are Romania's Constanta-Trieste Pipeline (CTPL) and ENI's South East European Line (SEEL). Both projects are similar in concept.

The CTPL would run from Constanta through Romania, Hungary and Slovenia to Trieste. There, it would be linked to the Trans-Alpine Line (TAL). A US-financed study found that the line could be commercially feasible. It could be commissioned by late 2002 at an initial cost of $1 billion, with additional upgrades of $200-300 million over the following decade. Peak capacity (attainable in 2012) would be: 47.1 mt/annum (942,000 b/d) from Constanta to the junction with the Adria pipeline in Hungary; 15.7 mt/annum (314,000 b/d) to Lendava (Slovenia); 14.4 mt/annum (288,000 b/d) to Trieste.

The SEEL would follow a similar route, but would also pass through Croatia. Its capacity would be 33 mt/annum (660,000 b/d) from Constanta to Trieste. One sub-variant of SEEL calls for reversing the existing Adria pipeline, which supplies crude from the Croatian terminal at Omisalj to Sisak refinery (Croatia) and the Serbian refineries at Novi Sad and Pancevo.

The CTPL would supply Caspian oil to refineries in eastern and central Europe. Caspian crude has a lower sulphur content than Russian crude, the primary feedstock delivered through the Druzhba system. The CTPL study forecasts that products demand in Hungary, Slovenia, Slovakia and the Czech Republic will grow by 18.8 mt (376,000 b/d) by 2012 and by 21.45 mt (429,000 b/d) by 2022. Caspian crude deliveries to this region could reach 13.9 mt (278,000 b/d) by 2012 and 31.9 mt (638,000 b/d) by 2022. Caspian crude deliveries to Austria and Germany via the TAL pipeline could amount to 14.4 mt (288,000 b/d) by 2012 and 18 mt (360,000 b/d) by 2022. Romanian refineries would receive Caspian crude only at a later stage of pipeline operation.

Two other Balkan pipeline projects – Burgas-Alexandroupolis and Burgas-Vlore – would also bypass the Turkish Straits. The Burgas-Alexandroupolis pipeline with a capacity of 35-75 mt/year (0.7-1.5 mb/d) was actively promoted by Greek, Bulgarian and Russian interests. But in April 1999, perhaps as a sign of flagging support for the project, four Russian companies withdrew from Balkan Oil, the joint venture that is promoting the pipeline.

Longer-Term Oil Transport (2005-2010)

The following factors will influence the longer-term developments:

■ Russian Black Sea exports stabilise at the lower end of a 50-60 mt/annum band (1.0-1.2 mb/d), as domestic production is maintained at between 290-340 mt/annum (5.8–6.8 mb/d) thanks to increased Russian and foreign investment. Growing demand in Russia, Ukraine and Belarus and freeing up of capacity of Baltic and Northeast European pipelines could drain some Russian oil exports away from the Black Sea ports. This could make room for incremental oil exports originating from fields, which will be discovered in Kazakhstan, the Russian part of the Caspian and possibly Azerbaijan in the first decade. Kazakh exports could rise to 45-70 mt/annum (0.9-1.4 mb/d) if fields the size of Tengiz are discovered.

This could result in 95-130 mt/annum (1.9-2.6 mb/d) of combined Russian and Kazakh crude transiting through Novorossiysk, Tuapse, Yuzhnaya Ozerevka and Odessa – assuming that no Azeri oil would transit via Russia.

■ Offshore in Azerbaijan, several consortia are likely to discover new fields in 2001-04 and bring them on stream from 2003 onwards. Currently licensed offshore acreage contains more than 7.5 billion bbl of undiscovered oil equivalent. This increases the likelihood of proving sufficient reserves to commit to a MEP by 2003-04 and commissioning it in the second half of the decade.

Various MEP routes have been mooted. Notwithstanding the support given to the Baku-Ceyhan pipeline in the Istanbul declaration, other routes remain likely:

■ Baku-Ceyhan: This 45 mt/year (900,000 b/d) pipeline carries a higher capital cost than the Baku-Supsa line and is supported by the US and Turkish governments. Tariffs would be $2.58/bbl. It would make construction of a Bosphorus bypass pipeline less likely. But Romania's and Bulgaria's chances of refining some of the oil coming out of Russian ports, particularly if some of these refineries fall under Russian ownership, would remain intact.

Some of the oil moving to Ceyhan would be destined for the Turkish market. Turkey's consumption is set to rise from 27.6 mt (1998) to as much as 44.5 mt by 2010.

■ Baku-Supsa: A new pipeline could eventually transport up to 40 mt/annum (800,000 b/d) to the Georgian Black Sea coast. The advantage of this line is its relatively low construction and operating costs, to which shipping costs must be added. However it would congest the Turkish Straits, if added onto the assumed 1.9-2.6 mb/d being shipped from Russian and Ukrainian Black Sea ports.

So the Baku-Supsa route would help projects aimed at taking the pressure off the Turkish Straits: the 35-75 mt/year (0.7-1.5 mb/d) Burgas-Alexandroupolis pipeline; the Burgas-Vlore line; or any of the two proposed 34 mt/year (680,000 b/d) pipelines from Romania to Trieste.

The Baku-Supsa pipeline would help Georgia to restore and expand its refining sector, since it would involve upgrading the Batumi plant to 2.5 mt/year (50,000 b/d) and possibly building a new 4 mt/year (80,000 b/d) plant at Supsa. Output would not only cover domestic demand, which is expected to increase from 1.5 mt to as much as 4.5 mt, but would also allow products exports to Armenia and Ukraine.

■ Ukraine, in an effort to reduce its dependence on Russian oil, has been trying to capture some Caspian oil, either as feedstock for its own refineries, or for transit via a partly built 667 km line from Odessa to Brody (western Ukraine), at the junction with the Druzhba system. By late 1999, about two-thirds of this pipeline had been laid. Initial capacity of the line will be 14.5 mt/year (290,000 b/d). Ukraine currently imports Kazakh oil via Russia (by pipeline or barge), and Azeri oil could be imported via Georgia and the Black Sea, thereby avoiding Russian territory. Ukraine has started building of a new terminal to handle oil imports at Pivdenny, which will have a capacity of 9 mt/year (180,000 b/d). Commissioning of the Odessa-Brody pipeline and Pivdenny terminal is scheduled for mid-2001. There are also plans to upgrade the capacity of the Odessa terminal from 10 mt/year to 12 mt/year.

Figure 3   Export Capacity Projections for Russian and Caspian Oil through the Black Sea Region

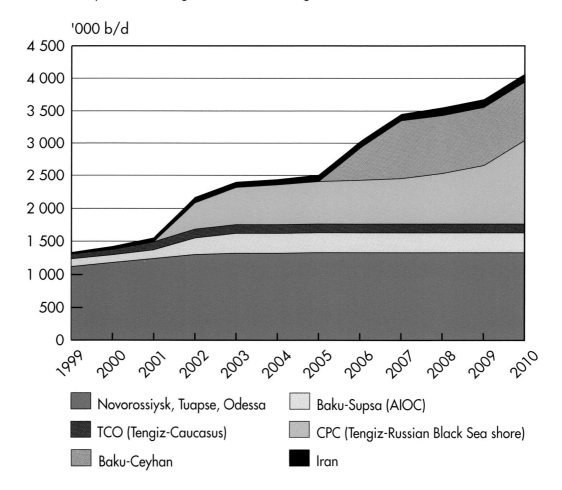

■ Gas imports from Iran via a pipeline from Tabriz to Erzurum. The contract calls for initial volumes of 3 bcm/year, increasing to 10 bcm by 2005. The Iranian section of the line was completed in early 2000, whereas slow construction on the Turkish side could prevent Turkey from taking Iranian gas until September 2001, according to Botas.

There are several large-scale, high-profile pipeline projects, for which financing, technical, rights-of-way and other issues need to be resolved. These are:

■ The "Blue Stream" project promoted by Gazprom and ENI. This would move 16 bcm of Russian gas through a sub-sea pipeline from Dzhubga on the Russian Black Sea coast to Samsun on the Turkish coast. The line would be the world's deepest underwater pipeline. The project is backed by a Gazprom/SNAM gas supply agreement. Some observers are sceptical about the line, arguing that the financing scheme is too highly leveraged, that costs may be exorbitant, and that ENI's dedicated reserves upstream of the line are in Kazakhstan (Karachaganak field). Gazprom however, may object to letting Kazakh gas flow through the line, especially if Kazakh gas will start to compete with future production from Astrakhan, the only proven field in southern Russia with a production potential to match Blue Stream. Gazprom has delayed the development of Astrakhan and ENI's attempts to take part in the field's development have been to no avail so far. For its promoters, however, Blue Stream has the advantage of avoiding any transit country. In November 1999, Turkey complained about Russian gas deliveries falling behind schedule and Ukraine was blamed for siphoning off gas along the line.

In November 1999, "Blue Stream" made some progress. Turkey and Russia ratified a bilateral agreement, which gives the project an institutional foundation. The State Duma voted tax breaks worth $1.5 billion for the project. Gazprom and ENI signed an agreement on the procurement and construction of the pipeline, designating Saipem (Italy) as main contractor for the $1.7 billion project. But full financing of the project has yet to be secured. These latest events have upgraded "Blue Stream" in the eyes of analysts.

■ Another route for moving as much as 8.5 bcm/annum of Russian gas to eastern Turkey is an upgraded and extended pipeline running from southern Russia through Georgia directly to eastern Turkey or possibly via Armenia. But Gazprom does not seem keen on transiting its gas through two countries in the troubled Caucasus region. This would be practically the only project involving Armenia. The country has been overlooked in almost all East-West pipeline initiatives, because of its unresolved conflict with Azerbaijan and strained relations with Turkey. Armenia has seen its gas consumption plummet from a peak of 6.3 bcm/annum in 1989 to approximately 1.5 bcm. Substitution imports through a new line from Iran have failed to materialise.

■ The Trans-Caspian pipeline (TCP) project, which would carry 16 bcm/annum of Turkmen gas (later increasing to 30 bcm/annum) under the Caspian Sea and via Azerbaijan and Georgia into eastern Turkey. The cost of the pipeline is put at $2.5-3.0 billion. Turkmenistan holds gas reserves that could warrant such a project, but the reserves still need to be certified. Shell has studied and rejected an overland variant of this project through northern Iran. The US is promoting the Trans-Caspian project as part of an East-West corridor for Caspian resources bypassing Russia and Iran. Bechtel and General Electric of the US, and Shell formed the PSG consortium to study the project. The project should be seen in the context of companies positioning themselves to evacuate future gas production from Turkmenistan and possibly offshore Iran (in the case of Shell) or to secure future equipment or construction contracts. The project was given full government backing at the December 1999 OSCE summit in Istanbul, when a declaration was signed by Turkey, Azerbaijan, Georgia and Turkmenistan. This elicited angry reactions from Russia and Iran, who raised the issue of the Caspian Sea's status once again.

Azerbaijan has insisted that the TCP would need to accommodate future Azeri gas exports, in particular from Shah-deniz. Azerbaijan has demanded that 50% of TCP capacity be made available for its own gas, whereas Turkmenistan has offered only 20%. Needless to say that Azerbaijan, by being "further down the line", has more bargaining power than Turkmenistan.

The reconciliation between Turkmenistan and Gazprom in late 1999 may change the ground rules once again. Gazprom has choked almost all Turkmen gas transit through its system since the mid-1990's. Turkmenistan was only allowed to export to Ukraine – an insolvent customer for Gazprom. Gazprom finally agreed to buy 20 bcm of Turkmen gas from a cash-strapped Turkmenistan for customers in southern Russia in 2000. This may lead to a revitalisation of Soviet gas trade patterns, whereby some 60 bcm of Turkmen gas were formerly delivered to southern Russia, the Caucasus region and Europe. Turkmenistan, however, wants a fairer share of the end price, which Gazprom charges for Turkmen gas in the end market. Faced with an impending production decline at home, Gazprom may have to resort to Turkmen gas for its southern Russian markets, if it wants to honour and even expand exports to Europe and Turkey. There have been speculations about Gazprom having to pump Turkmen gas through its planned "Blue Stream" pipeline to Turkey.

■ The Trans-Caspian project has been complicated by BP-Amoco's Shah-deniz gas discovery in offshore Azerbaijan in summer 1999. As the second Shah-deniz well was being drilled in the autumn of 1999, operators felt confident about the field containing at least 700 bcm, enough to sustain some 15-20 bcm/annum of Azeri gas exports. Gas could be exported as soon as 2004-2005, since the existing Baku-Batumi gas pipeline could be refurbished at a cost of $230 million for that purpose. An extension pipeline would need to be built from Batumi to eastern Turkey. Construction of a new pipeline would cost some $650 million. The Shah-deniz discovery propelled Azerbaijan from a gas importer to a potential gas-exporter overnight. It may also relegate Turkmenistan to the "waiting line" of Caspian gas-exporting nations.

Other gas-producing nations are vying for the Turkish market: Iraq could potentially supply up to 10 bcm/annum, Egypt between 4 and 12 bcm/annum. If all gas deliveries under signed and tentative contracts are added up, Turkey could receive between 60-80 bcm by 2010. This is certainly more than what the Turkish market will need. Consequently, competition among gas-exporting countries is growing, because latecomers will find it hard to win market share.

Southeast European Markets

Southeastern Europe is another growing market. Romania, Bulgaria, and the Federal Republic of Yugoslavia traditionally have been supplied by Russian gas, and Greece started importing it in 1998. Whilst there is little doubt that Russian gas will continue to be the main source for the region, the southeast European nations have been trying to diversify their gas supplies.

■ Greece has a long-term contract to import 2.4 bcm/annum of Russian gas via a pipeline running through Ukraine, Moldova, Romania and Bulgaria. It is forecast that Russian gas imports could rise to 3.8 bcm by 2005 and 7-8 bcm by 2010. LNG imports (presently at a level of 0.57 bcm/annum from Algeria) are an alternative. A future import route currently under study would be a sub-sea pipeline from Italy to carry Libyan gas imports.

■ Romania is the only southeast European country, whose domestic gas production plays more than a marginal role: current output is at a level of 14.5 bcm/annum, and is expected to decline to 9 bcm by 2010. Foreign investment in exploration could slow the decline. A second pipeline from Khust (Ukraine) to Satu Mare (northern Romania) will allow 4 bcm of Russian gas to be imported from 2000 onwards.

Romanian gas demand is anticipated to grow from 18.5 bcm/annum to 25-26 bcm by 2010. This demand should be met by diverse sources: Russian gas imports should increase slightly, from currently less than 10 bcm/annum to 14 bcm by 2010. Romania also plans to connect itself to the Hungarian – and thus to the European – grid, enabling eventually some 2 bcm/annum to be imported from the North Sea. Over the longer-term, Romania hopes to capture 1-2 bcm/annum of Caspian or Central Asian gas, that would move through Turkey to Europe. LNG imports seem to be unrealistic, because of traffic constraints through the Turkish Straits.

■ Bulgaria relies almost exclusively on Russian gas imports to cover its demand. These imports, currently totalling 3.4 bcm/annum, should increase to meet demand, which will rise to 6.1 bcm in 2010. Longer-term plans call for imports from western Europe via Romania or from the Caspian region via Turkey.

■ Forecasting demand in the former Yugoslavia is difficult. The Federal Republic of Yugoslavia produces some 0.67 bcm of gas and normally imports 2.1 bcm of Russian gas via Hungary. The Yugoslav gas grid does not extend to southern Serbia nor Kosovo. Domestic production is not likely to increase, whereas demand will ultimately grow, albeit at a pace which is difficult to predict. Gas imports from Russia could be increased, while alternative imports through the European grid or eventually through a Caspian-Turkey-SE Europe system are possible.

Similar considerations about Russian supplies and possible future imports from western Europe and/or the Caspian region apply to Bosnia-Herzegovina, FYR of Macedonia (FYROM) and Croatia. Bosnia-Herzegovina's current consumption of some 0.5 bcm is covered exclusively by Russian gas. Croatia produced 1.57 bcm in 1998, has some production potential offshore, and imported slightly over 1.1 bcm from Russia. FYR of Macedonia (FYROM) has been supplied by Russian gas transiting through Bulgaria since 1997.

■ Albania meets its small annual demand of less than 0.03 bcm exclusively from domestic production, which is declining. The economic situation in Albania will need to stabilise and a clearly identified gas market will need to emerge before gas import pipeline projects can be seriously considered. It has been estimated that Albanian gas demand could rise to 1 bcm/year if the country would build a projected 300MW gas-fired combined-cycle power plant. The gas could come from Russia (via Bosnia-Herzegovina, FYR of Macedonia (FYROM) or Greece). More remote sources could be North Africa (via Italy and/or Greece) or the Caspian (via Turkey and Southeastern Europe).

Ukraine

Ukraine has a gas consumption of 72 bcm/annum, only 25% of which is covered by domestic production (18.1 bcm in 1998). Production is expected to decline to 12-15 bcm by the year 2010, as offshore exploration is unlikely to yield reserves sufficient to offset the natural depletion of mature onshore fields. Three-quarters of demand are covered by gas imports from Russia (typically 45 bcm/annum) and Turkmen gas transiting through Russia (typically 12.5 bcm/annum). Gas deliveries, however, are periodically interrupted or reduced due to payment problems.

Consumption could be reduced in the medium-term to 64 bcm through greater energy efficiency, and even more in the longer-term. The geographic location of Ukraine and its interconnection with the Russian network make non-FSU gas supplies not viable. So, Ukraine has not been seeking to diversify its gas imports as it has for oil.

Summing up

The Black Sea region will continue to depend heavily on Russian or Caspian gas imports. Considerable gas demand growth is expected in all Black Sea riparian states. Russia faces the fiercest competition from non-FSU gas suppliers in the Turkish market, and to a lesser extent in Greece. In the medium-term, Romania and Bulgaria may find alternative gas supplies from the North Sea, whereas Azerbaijan may challenge Russian gas in Georgia. But none of these alternative gas suppliers will erode the dominance of Russian gas in Black Sea markets.

III. AZERBAIJAN[1]

AZERBAIJAN AT A GLANCE

Population	7.91 million (1998)
Area	86,600 km²
Capital	Baku, 1.726 million inhabitants
President	Heydar Aliev (next election 2003)
Currency	US$ = 4359 manat (November 1999)

Azerbaijan's economy relies heavily on oil and gas. Foreign direct investment, two-thirds of which went into the oil and gas sector in 1998, has been the main driver for GDP growth in recent years. More than 98% of TPES is oil and gas. The dramatic drop in GDP in the early 1990's, caused by the break-up of Soviet trade patterns and the Nagorny-Karabakh conflict, was reversed in late 1996. TPES was more than halved between 1990 and 1996, largely because gas imports from Turkmenistan were halted. This contributed to economic decline. Power plants had to be converted from gas to heavy fuel. Output from the Baku refineries dropped 40%. As gas imports shrank, Azerbaijan changed from a net energy importer to an exporter. Since independence, the government has used oil as an instrument for economic and foreign policy: the economic goal was to attract foreign investors, which the government successfully did by signing two dozen production-sharing and joint venture agreements (representing some $2.5 billion in sunk and committed investment). The foreign policy goal was to steer the country closer to the West without rebuffing its two mighty neighbours – Russia and Iran. Oil has served the Azeri diplomacy, when "early oil" pipelines routes were chosen partly to balance geopolitical interests in the region, or, when foreign oil consortia were formed not only based on the technical and financial know-how, but also on the sensitivities of the companies' home governments. Because of its success in the oil and – more recently – in the gas sector, the government has not regarded institutional reform as a priority. De-regulation and privatisation of energy companies could afford to drag on, since foreign investors have been primarily interested in the country's oil and gas export potential. This underscores the risk of mineral wealth leading the country towards a single-commodity economy. Azerbaijan is poised to become a major oil and gas export and transit country. In late 1999, Azerbaijan was exporting some 158,000 b/d (55% of total production) – including 110,000 b/d by the AIOC consortium via Georgia. Furthermore, some 120,000 b/d of Kazakh oil were transiting via Azerbaijan to Georgia. Today, the only proven reserves capable of boosting Azeri production and exports are AIOC's. The consortium's production targets are 250,000 b/d in 2003 and a peak of 700,000 b/d later in the decade, for which additional pipeline capacity is needed. AIOC's 4.6 billion bbl of reserves, however, do not justify construction of a "main oil" pipeline, such as the Baku-Ceyhan line. AIOC may find it hard to garner enough reserves from Kazakh and Turkmen producers to feed a Baku-Ceyhan line. More likely, Azerbaijan will have to wait for more reserves to be discovered on its shelf by some of the dozen foreign consortia, who have signed exploration contracts. The recent Shah Deniz discovery – with more gas discoveries expected – has propelled Azerbaijan amongst potential gas exporters, primarily for the Turkish market, where it could have a competitive edge over additional Russian gas and certainly over Turkmen gas.

---

1.   This section draws on IEA's *Caspian Oil and Gas* (1998).

ECONOMIC AND POLITICAL OVERVIEW

Recent Economic Developments

Azerbaijan's economy went into a recession in the years that followed independence in 1991. Real GDP declined by about 60% between 1991 and 1995. A three-year war with Armenia over the enclave of Nagorny-Karabakh, resulting in Azerbaijan losing 20% of its territory, accelerated the economic downtrend. A reform programme was launched in early 1995 and Azerbaijan has achieved sustained financial stability. The sharp decline in output of the early 1990's was reversed in the second half of 1996. The upward trend was confirmed throughout 1997 and 1998 with official GDP growth reaching 5.8% and 8.1% respectively. GDP growth slowed down in the first half of 1999, largely because massive foreign investment to bring oil-related infrastructure and services to international standards is levelling off. Overall GDP growth for 1999 is estimated at 6%. Increasing oil export revenues in 2000 should maintain GDP growth at 6% or more.

The Azeri economy is now among the strongest in the former Soviet Union, not least due to significant influx of foreign capital. Inflation, which was about 1,700% in 1994 was close to zero in 1998 and is expected to be negative in 1999. The main reasons of success were foreign investment (mainly into the oil and gas sector), the contraction of government spending, tight monetary policy and increasing state oil revenues.

The government has been struggling to keep the budget deficit within 3% of GDP to comply with IMF conditions. It has done so by slashing spending, rather than improving tax collection from large state companies. Cash-strapped state oil company SOCAR is a prominent tax culprit.

Azerbaijan is aware of its geopolitical vulnerability and has steered a course of balanced and accommodating relations with its powerful neighbours. President Aliyev is attuned to Russia's desire to maintain influence in the Caspian region, but has counterbalanced Russian and Iranian pressures by strengthening co-operation with Turkey, which has close ethnical ties with the Azeri people, and the United States. Iran, meanwhile, is home to 20 million Azeris – more than three times the population of Azerbaijan. Azerbaijan has also increased co-operation with Central Asian states across the Caspian and Georgia, which is a vital corridor for the country's westbound exports.

Oil and gas lie at the heart of Azerbaijan's foreign policy and economic development. SOCAR, which is closely controlled by President Aliev himself, has been carefully looking at the "nationality" of the oil companies it has been negotiating with. SOCAR knew that signing contracts with US, West European, and later Turkish, Russian, Iranian, Japanese or Saudi companies would bring Azerbaijan political support from the home governments of the companies. Foreign direct investment (FDI) was kick-started in September 1994 with the signing of the first oil Production Sharing Agreement (PSA) between the BP Amoco-led AIOC consortium and SOCAR. Since then, 18 more PSAs have been signed. FDI increased from $22 million in 1994 to an estimated $1.2 billion in 1999. Total per capita FDI for 1999 is estimated at $164, the highest in the FSU.

Most FDI has been directed at the oil sector, but the share of non-oil investment is gradually increasing. In 1998, 33% of the foreign investment went into the non-oil sector, up from 15% in 1994. Overall, foreign investment accounted for 27% of the country's GDP in 1998. Although the oil sector remains the driving force behind economic growth, there were signs of growth in 1998 in other sectors, such as services and industry.

Azerbaijan's medium-term prospects are potentially excellent if the Caucasus region can be stabilised and the country can fully capitalise on its rich hydrocarbon resources. A possible risk is the country's ill-preparedness for the post-Aliev era. Of greatest concern for Azerbaijan is a settlement of the Nagorny-Karabakh conflict with Armenia. Some 800,000 people have been displaced within Azerbaijan, partly contributing to the 19% unemployment rate and the large share of the population that lives below the poverty line. OSCE and direct US efforts to reconcile Azerbaijan and Armenia have made little progress since the cease-fire in 1994.

There is still a great uncertainty about the ultimate oil and gas resources offshore Azerbaijan. Economic development will largely hinge on oil and gas revenues. The government will need to prevent the country from becoming a single-commodity economy. According to IMF projections, the share of oil in total exports is expected to increase from $825 million or 37% in 1997 to $5.27 billion or 75% in 2005. Furthermore, secure access to international oil and gas markets, if possible through diverse export routes, is a pre-condition for the Azeri petroleum industry to prosper. Co-operation among producers, transit countries and consumers in the region will foster stability and reduce the investment risk.

Privatisation and Foreign Investment

According to the EBRD, the private sector accounts for an estimated 45% of GDP and 50% of employment, mainly in services, construction, trade and agriculture. Significant progress has been made in the privatisation of small public enterprises. About 13,000 small enterprises have been sold through cash auctions, while more than 800 medium enterprises (about 25% of total) have been privatised through voucher auctions starting in 1997.

The Azerbaijani Government did not have to put in place many incentives for foreign investors, who were lured to Baku by the country's large hydrocarbon potential. The 1992 Law "On the Protection of Foreign Investments" generally provides foreign investment with the same legal regime as local investors. In January 1997, a presidential decree abolished most tax privileges previously granted to foreign investors. The decree, however, had no retroactive effect on PSAs that had been ratified by parliament. PSA terms have become tougher on foreign companies with time[1]. Contracts signed with foreign oil firms by late 1999 could represent over $40 billion in new capital to be invested in Azerbaijan over 25 to 30 years, provided all exploration contracts lead to commercial oil and gas discoveries.

Overall, foreign companies have bought controlling interests in about 30 privatised companies, none of which has a major significance on a national scale. Under the current privatisation programme, the government envisages the privatisation of 70% of all state assets by mid-2000. In addition, the government is planning to privatise 50 large-scale enterprises, for which strategic investors are being sought.

Plans to part-privatise gas distribution company Azerigaz and state oil company SOCAR, starting in the third quarter of 1999 and ending in mid-2000, have not materialised yet. The main reason for the delays in the privatisation of SOCAR is that the company would not fetch an acceptable price in its present state. SOCAR has debts (taxes, unpaid wages,

---

1. The AIOC consortium paid a signature bonus of US$300 million for the 4.6 billion bbl of proven reserves at the GCA field complex – a ratio of US$0.65 per barrel of proven oil. AIOC benefited from Azerbaijan's readiness to compromise on financial terms in return for signing a landmark contract with a powerful foreign group. The financial terms of the AIOC PSA were openly criticised by Azeri opposition forces as a sell-out of the nation's mineral wealth. More recent PSAs provide for signature bonuses of US$10 million for no proven hydrocarbons whatsoever. Moreover, SOCAR's equity in the contracts has gradually increased from 10% (in AIOC) to 50% or more in recent contracts.

investment share into joint ventures), its onshore production costs are prohibitive[1], and its workforce will need to be downsized at least 30%. In May 1999, Arthur Andersen was hired to audit the SOCAR accounts and Miller & Lents to certify SOCAR's reserves in view of a privatisation. Rising oil prices have certainly embellished SOCAR's financial performance in 1999. In 2000, SOCAR will receive first "profit oil" revenues from the AIOC contract[2].

The government also plans to privatise the electricity and gas distribution entities through public tendering by 2001, which may be followed by a sell-off of power plants. If offers are unsatisfactory, the government plans to transfer the assets of the distribution entities to the municipalities. The government plans to maintain state ownership of gas transit and storage.

Main Economic Indicators

	Unit	1997	1998	1999*
GDP growth	%	5.8	6.7	5.0
GDP	US$ million	10,964	11,698	n.a.
GDP per capita	US$ per person	1,386	1,479	n.a.
Industrial gross output	%	0.2	2.2	n.a.
Unemployment rate	%	19.3	n.a.	n.a.
Consumer Price (end year)	%	0.3	− 7.6	2.6
Foreign Direct Investment	US	1093	1077	1300
FDI per capita	US$ per person	140	137	164

Source: EBRD, CEPII.
* Projections.

THE ENERGY SECTOR

Energy Overview

Azerbaijan's TPES has been halved in the 1990's, from 23.3 mtoe in 1991 to just under 12 mtoe in 1997. The country changed from a net energy importer in 1990 (when 10% of TPES were imported) to a net exporter (energy exports were equivalent to 17% of TPES in 1997). Oil overtook gas as the number-one fuel in 1993 as a result of falling energy consumption and the elimination of gas imports in 1996: Oil accounted for 58% of TPES in 1997 (vs. 40% for gas), whereas gas covered 62% of TPES in 1990, followed by oil with only 37%. Other fuels are marginal in the country's energy balance (less than 2% in 1997).

Azerbaijan was an important refining centre and oil and gas transit country in Soviet times. More than 30% of the feedstock for the Baku refineries were "imported" from Russia and Kazakhstan in 1990. At the same time, Baku "exported" almost 35% of its domestic crude production to Russian refineries. Oil product "exports" back to Russia were considerable too (equivalent to about 15% of TPES in 1990). Oil trade rapidly declined after the break-up of the USSR: Crude oil imports dropped from 3.8 mt in 1990 to zero in 1996, before slowly resuming in 1997. Most of the imported crude is re-exported. Oil product exports decreased from 3.2 mt in 1990 to 2.1 mt in 1993, and have stabilised at this level since. Crude exports fell from 4.2 mt in 1990 to zero in 1995, before resuming in 1997. Gas transit volumes (from Russia mainly to Armenia and Georgia) collapsed from 4.3 mtoe in 1990 to zero in 1994.

---

1. Up to US$19/bbl in some fields!
2. Under PSA terms, profit oil is paid once the foreign investors have recovered a pre-determined amount of their initial investment. At US$20/barrel, SOCAR can expect some US$100 million in 2000.

Main Energy Indicators

		1995	**1996**	**1997**
TPES	mtoe	12,999	12,240	11,987
Net Exports	mtoe	1,726	2,147	2,041
Net Oil Exports	mtoe	2,196	2,209	2,115
Net Gas Exports	mtoe	− 430	0	0
Electricity Production	GWh	17,044	17,088	16,800
TPES/GDP	toe per thousand 90US$ PPP	1.72	1.60	1.52
TPES/Population	toe per capita	1.73	1.62	1.58
CO_2 Emission from Fuel Comb.	mt of CO_2	34.62	32.66	32.09
CO_2/TPES	t CO_2 per toe	2.66	2.67	2.68
CO_2/GDP	t CO_2 per 1990 US$ PPP	4.59	4.28	4.08
CO_2/Population	t CO_2 per capita	4.61	4.32	4.22

Source: IEA.

Figure 5   Azerbaijan TPES and Net Energy Imports

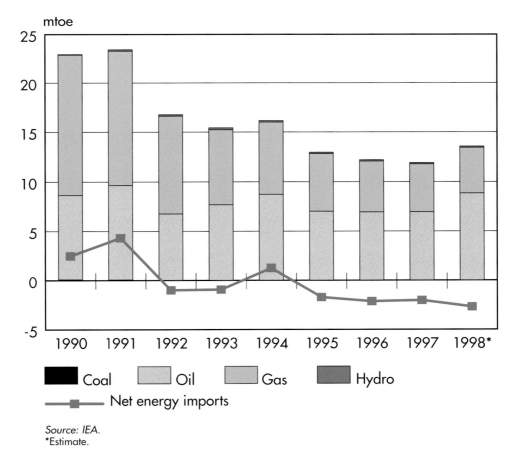

Source: IEA.
*Estimate.

In 1997, the refining sector consumed 75% of primary energy supplies. Oil- and gas-fired CHP plants used the equivalent of 26% of TPES[1]. The largest final consumers were the commercial-residential sector (45% of final consumption), followed by industry (39%) and transport (15%).

Energy Sector Structure

Azerbaijan does not have a co-ordinating body for energy issues. Policy is made by the President's office and the state-owned companies that operate in the various energy sub-sectors.

The state oil company **SOCAR** (Azerbaycan Respublikasi Dövlet Neft Sirketi) was created in 1992 by combining the onshore upstream operations of Azneft and the offshore activities of KhezerDenizNeft, successor organisations to the former Soviet Ministry of Oil and Gas operating in Azerbaijan. SOCAR negotiates contracts with foreign investors on behalf of the government. SOCAR is closely controlled by President Heydar Aliev, whose son Ilham is a Vice-President of SOCAR. The re-structuring of SOCAR, based on the organisation of Statoil and approved by the World Bank, was to be completed by end-1999, but has been lagging. SOCAR's licensing and commercial functions are to be separated. The re-structuring is to streamline the company in view of privatising it. Non-oil company functions are likely to be spun off (see also Chapter on Privatisation above).

Azerigaz is responsible for the transportation, storage and sales of natural gas (while SOCAR handles production and processing). It was formed in 1992 with the merger of the national gas transmission company and the natural gas distribution branch of the State Fuel Committee. Azerigaz was corporatised in May 1997 and its shares were transferred to the State Property Committee for sale at a later date. The government plans to privatise the gas distribution companies. Gas storage and transportation/transit pipelines will not be privatised.

Azenergo (Azerenerji) is responsible for electricity production, transmission and distribution, as well as for industrial steam and hot water production from CHP plants. Similar to the gas industry, the government intends to privatise the distribution companies, possibly in 2000 already. Privatisation of power plants are not *a priori* excluded, but investors have not shown much interest so far. In November 1999, President Aliev decreed that the Baku city electric grid will be privatised. No schedule has yet been published.

The government announced in 1997 that it wanted to set up a Ministry of Fuel and Energy. The functions of the new ministry were to include energy policy, preparing legislation, setting tariffs and ensuring the state's energy security. It is not clear how much the ministry would interfere in the oil and gas sector. Although the separation of SOCAR's policy making and licensing role from its commercial functions has been mooted, the new ministry might concentrate on electricity and the domestic gas market. In any case, most important policy decisions affecting the oil and gas industry will probably continue to be made by the President's office.

The Status of the Caspian Sea

The Caspian Sea status, although still not resolved, is not discouraging foreign oil companies from investing into offshore projects. Azerbaijan – like Kazakhstan and Turkmenistan – have proven reserves or large resources on their shelves. These countries advocate splitting the Caspian Sea into national sectors. Only Russia and Iran, who have no or little proven

---

1. Some of the fuel used by power plants is heavy fuel oil, which has been refined at Baku. Hence, the refining and power sectors' shares of TPES exceeding 100%.

offshore reserves off their coasts, are proponents of a "condominium" to manage the sea's resources, because they would gain a significant share in proven reserves[1].

Azerbaijan has mitigated Russian and Iranian claims on its sector by letting Russian (Lukoil, CFC) and Iranian (OIEC) companies take up interests in offshore PSAs. Baku's only territorial disputes so far has been with Turkmenistan over the proven Kapaz field (Serdar in Turkmen nomenclature), which was discovered by SOCAR's predecessor midway between the Azeri and Turkmen coasts. The two countries have decided to find a mutually acceptable solution for the field, which has not attracted serious interest from foreign companies so far[2]. No hydrocarbons have been found so far in those zones, where Azeri offshore claims conflict with those of Russia or Iran. Azerbaijan has been wise to award the Yalama exploration tract, which borders the Russian claim, to Lukoil (Russia). Disputes may arise over the southern shelf, where Iran is understood to have granted rights to PEDCO, an affiliate of state company NIOC, over structures that may overlap into BP Amoco's Alov block.

Energy Prices and Tariffs

Energy prices remain regulated at all levels. With the exception of utilities for households, energy prices have been raised gradually toward international levels.

Quantitative foreign trade restrictions have been eliminated and most tariffs reduced. The export registration system has also been simplified. For strategic exports, including oil, a tax is levied on 70% of the difference between the higher world market price and the domestic price, although this tax does not appear to be applicable to most projects with foreign investment.

Energy Legislation

Due to a lack of specific petroleum and investment legislation, most PSAs were negotiated on an ad-hoc basis with foreign companies and conferred the status of law by parliamentary vote. The government intends to develop petroleum legislation to standardise some terms of licences, but has made it clear that existing PSAs would not be negatively affected by subsequent changes in the law.

In February 1999 the Energy Law came into effect. It covers the objectives of the state energy policy and its exclusive ownership of all energy resources, control of exploration, development of oil fields, and the construction and maintenance of transport systems. In 1998, the Parliament adopted a new gas law, which regulates the production, transportation, storage and marketing of natural gas.

The Law on the Protection of Foreign Investments allows enterprises with foreign investments to exercise any type of activity not prohibited by law and includes a number of safeguards for foreign investors. The Law enables foreign legal and natural persons to invest in Azerbaijan, e.g. through ownership of enterprises. Article 40 of the Law on the Protection of Foreign Investment allows foreign investors to acquire exploration and development rights.

The government advertises opportunities for new concessions and invites tender applications. In principle, all oil and gas fields at depths of at least 120 metres and enhanced oil recovery (EOR) projects at producing fields are open for application. Official tenders have not been successful so far. All signed PSAs are the result of out-of-tender negotiations.

---

1. Russia and Iran, in spite of their condominium rhetoric, have not refrained from licensing exploration rights, which often overlap into the waters claimed by neighbouring states.
2. Turkmenistan granted Mobil preliminary rights to Kapaz/Serdar field in 1998, but Mobil refused to pursue the project as long as jurisdiction over the field was not clarified.

According to the Law on the Protection of Foreign Investment, the area covered by a PSA is considered a "free economic zone", with a specific tax and customs regime defined by a decree of the Cabinet of Ministers.

THE OIL SECTOR

Oil Reserves

According to SOCAR, Azerbaijan's oil reserves total some 17.5 billion barrels (2.4 billion tonnes). The figure plausibly refers to oil in-place, and not recoverable reserves. A more precise reserves audit of proven reserves reads as follows:

Azerbaijan: Proven Oil Reserves

	Billion barrels	Million tonnes
SOCAR onshore fields	1.130	155
SOCAR offshore fields	0.985	135
AIOC	4.600	630
Total	6.715	920

Source: AIOC and SOCAR reported by IHS Energy.

A 1996 US Government report estimates proven oil reserves at 3.6 billion barrels (493 mt), with some 27 billion barrels (3,690 mt) additional reserves classified as possible. Over 83% of oil reserves are offshore. Future discoveries are expected in the little explored parts of the Azeri sector of the Caspian Sea, i.e. south of the so-called Apsheron Sill and along the northern shelf. Both zones have been covered by extensive seismic surveys, but have been little drilled so far. Remaining onshore prospects are by far less promising than the offshore.

Oil Production

Azerbaijan has a long oil history. Production began in the 1860's and gradually built up to a level of some 40 mt/year (800,000 b/d) in the early 1940's. The Soviet Government voluntarily sabotaged the oil fields of Azerbaijan to prevent them from falling into the hands of the advancing Axis forces. Azerbaijan has never reached the pre-war output levels again, because many wells had been irreparably damaged. According to projections, Azeri production will reach production levels that are comparable to pre-war levels only after 2005.

As from the 1950's, declining onshore output was compensated by the development of new offshore fields. This brought the country back to an intermediate production peak of 440,000 b/d in 1967. From then on, production declined again (except for a small recovery in the late 1970's) until 1997 (9.022 mt, 180,400 b/d). In 1998, output was rekindled to 11.539 mt (230,780 b/d) by the coming on stream of AIOC's GCA field complex. 1999 production is expected to reach 14.5 mt (290,000 b/d).

Cumulative production by the end of 1999 will be 1.382 billion tonnes (10 billion bbl).

The bulk of production stems from offshore fields (110,000 b/d from AIOC plus 150,000 b/d from SOCAR fields). Onshore fields yield about 31,000 b/d. SOCAR operates about two-thirds of onshore production, five joint ventures with foreign companies the remaining third.

SOCAR operates approximately 7,210 wells at 67 oil fields (5,725 onshore wells in 42 onshore fields and 1,395 wells in 25 offshore fields). SOCAR has been directing the lion's share of

Figure 6   Azerbaijan Oil Production

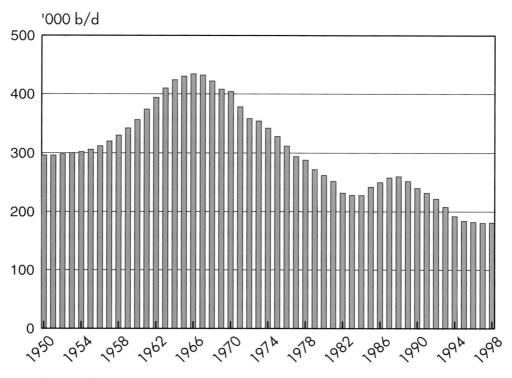

Source: IHS Energy.

its scarce E&P funds to rehabilitation of wells and field facilities – including ramshackle offshore platforms and piers, some of which have been in operation for decades longer than what they were designed for. The old onshore fields are characterised by low productivity and high water-cuts in wells. The typical onshore well produces 10 b/d with a water-cut of 92%, while the typical SOCAR offshore well produces 100 b/d, with a water cut of 46%[1]. SOCAR's offshore fields are in water depths of less than 200 metres. Almost 80% of SOCAR's offshore oil production comes from the shallow-water part of Guneshli field (the deeper-water section of this field is operated by AIOC).

AIOC brought the Guneshli deepwater field on stream in November 1997. It is the only foreign-operated offshore production in the country. Production rapidly built up to 110,000 b/d and has stabilised at this level because of limited processing and transport capacities. AIOC hopes to reach a production level of 250,000 b/d by 2003. AIOC's production cost in May 1999 was $2.11/bbl, but the consortium was planning to reduce it to $1.50/bbl.

Oil Production Projections

A 1997 SOCAR study predicts that oil production will increase more than three-fold from currently 14.5 mt/year (290,000 b/d) to 46.9 mt (938,000 b/d) in 2010. Foreign operators will account for almost 70% (31.9 mt) of this volume.

In the meantime, AIOC has adopted a slower pace for developing its fields, whilst CIPCO and NAOC have failed to find new reserves. This does not jeopardise Azerbaijan's potential

1.   By comparison, in late 1999 AIOC was producing 110,000 b/d – about 38% of countrywide output – from merely ten wells.

for ultimately approaching a production level of 1 million b/d, but that production target is likely to be reached after 2010.

SOCAR has not made any long-term projections of domestic oil consumption. According to the study, SOCAR will produce some 15 mt (300,000 b/d) on its own by 2010. This is almost 4 mt more than primary oil consumption before the economic decline in 1991 and should therefore amply cover growing future demand.

Figure 7   Azerbaijan Projected Oil Production

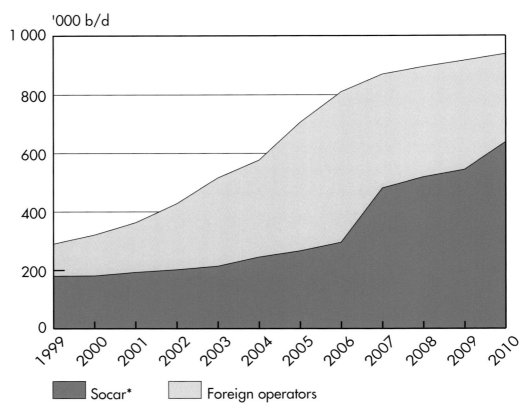

Source: SOCAR.
*Note: Figures for 1999 and 2000 have been adjusted in light of actual figures. SOCAR figures include operated and non-operated production (i.e. SOCAR equity in PSA's and JV's). This explains the steep increase in SOCAR production after 2006, when SOCAR expects production to start from exploration tracts, in which it holds stakes of up to 50% (as opposed to its minor 10% stake in AIOC).

Recent Drilling Results

Because of budget constraints, SOCAR has drilled very few exploratory wells in the 1990's. The only noteworthy drilling result was the sub-commercial offshore Naxcevan gas-condensate discovery.

Foreign consortia have been obliged to spread out in time their exploratory drilling plans, because of the lack of drilling rigs[1]. Only three consortia – apart from AIOC which has drilled

---

1. By late 1999, there were only two semi-submersible rigs available for foreign operators in Azerbaijan. Both have been upgraded to western standards by the western companies, who have formed so-called "rig clubs" to share the rigs. The "Dada Gorgud" was refurbished at a cost of US$40 million, and the "Istiglal" at a cost of US$250 million. Two additional rigs are being refurbished/built by foreign operators and will become available as from late 2000. By comparison, more than 50 rigs are active in the North Sea and up to 20 rigs offshore West Africa.

appraisal or development wells – have drilled offshore exploratory wells so far. The main lesson is that the Azeri deep-water zone is more gas-prone than initially assumed by western geologists. Two consortia terminated their contracts after disappointing drilling results:

- In February 1999 the CIPCO consortium (which included Pennzenergy, Lukoil and ENI) was wound up after having drilled three unsuccessful exploration wells on the Karabakh structure (two wells struck small amounts of gas, the third struck some oil and condensate, but not enough for CIPCO to decide on development). CIPCO had spent some $180 million on the project.

- In April 1999 the NAOC consortium (Amoco, Unocal, Delta, Itochu) decided to relinquish the offshore Ashrafi/Dan Ulduzu block (near CIPCO's Karabakh block) after having drilled three unsuccessful wells.

- The third consortium engaged in offshore exploration so far is led by BP Amoco and has had more luck than CIPCO and NAOC. In summer 1999, the group struck gas at the Shah Deniz prospect. By late 1999, the consortium was appraising the size of what may be a world-class gas field. It was confident that Shah Deniz holds at least 700 bcm of gas reserves, thereby more than doubling Azerbaijan's current reserves. Shah Deniz has considerably changed the Caspian oil and gas picture (see Introductory Chapter on Regional Oil and Gas Trade and Chapter 4 on Gas below).

Oil Prices

Although most prices in Azerbaijan have been liberalised, those for utilities and petroleum are still regulated. Domestic crude oil prices have been gradually raised toward world market prices minus transport costs. Domestic oil product prices before VAT, road tax and excise taxes, are comparable with international oil product prices.

Oil Refining

Total refining capacity in Azerbaijan is 22 mt/year (440,000 b/d), more than twice the country's oil production in 1999. Of the three refineries, the two main ones are in the Baku area, and the third in Sumgait. All are state-owned.

In 1997, Azerbaijan refined 9 mt (180,000 b/d), almost tantamount to the country's crude production[1]. This is almost 25% less than in 1990, when refinery input totalled 11.8 mt (236,000 b/d). Under the Soviet regime, Azerbaijan "imported" almost 4 mt/year of crude from other Soviet republics to be refined at Baku. The imported Kazakh crude is largely low-quality Buzachi grade, with a high sulphur and metals content. The main Azeri refineries were designed to run on higher quality domestic crude. Most imports have had to be refined at the more sophisticated Azernefteyag refinery[2].

1998 statistics indicate 8.3 mt of refinery output, including 3.9 mt of heavy fuel oil which was sold to state-owned utility Azenergo to produce electricity. Almost all dual-fired Azeri power plants, which can switch from gas to fuel oil, have done so to cope with decreasing gas imports. Other 1998 oil product output included 2.4 mt of fuel oil, 0.695 mt of kerosene and 0.63 of gasoline.

---

1. Some 300,000 t of crude were exported unrefined, while 260,000 tons of Turkmen and Kazakh crude were imported to be refined in Baku.
2. SOCAR was to announce a tender to upgrade the Azernefteyag refinery in November 1999. The US$500 million upgrade will allow the plant to produce 500,000 t/year (10,000 b/d) of high-quality products.

The pioneering small joint ventures involving foreign oil companies in onshore projects have been refining practically all their crude at Baku and exporting products. But with AIOC starting producing and exporting crude as from late 1997, the share of refined crude vs total domestic production has and will further decrease.

Foreign Investment

Joint Ventures and Production-Sharing Agreements

The production-sharing and joint venture contracts signed so far in Azerbaijan are listed in the table below. Early contracts for the redevelopment of old onshore fields were modelled on joint venture terms. Since the signing of the AIOC deal in 1994, the production-sharing agreement (PSA), which is favoured by foreign companies, has become the standard contract type (see Map 4: Azerbaijan – Production-Sharing and Joint Venture Contracts).

Most contracts cover scarcely explored offshore tracts, where SOCAR conducted seismic work and drilled anywhere between zero and two wells prior to signature. It should be stressed that all offshore tracts except AIOC's are pure exploration acreage with no proven hydrocarbon reserves. The figures – typically several hundred million barrels of oil (equivalent) – that have been associated with these tracts, are hypothetical. The typical contract calls for the foreign party(ies) to pay SOCAR a so-called signature bonus ranging from \$10 to 32 million upon signature. The foreign parties are committed to run a seismic survey and drill from two to four wells during an exploration period of three to five years. During this period, the foreign parties will pay SOCAR a rental fee (typically \$2000/year/km^2 of contract area). SOCAR, with a typical non-paying equity of 50%, is "carried through" the exploration phase by the foreign partners, i.e. SOCAR's share of costs in exploration is paid by the foreign partners. Expenditures during the exploration phase amount to anywhere between \$50 and 150 million. If commercial hydrocarbons are found, the contract will be extended into a 20- or 25-year development phase. The foreign companies will pay SOCAR further bonuses at various project milestones and recover their initial exploration and development costs through a share of future production (so-called "cost oil"). After initial costs are recovered, "profit oil" production is shared according to equity holdings in the project and foreign companies will be subject to a profit tax. The huge investment figures, typically several billion \$, that have been publicised at the signature of contracts, pertain to field development costs that will be incurred only in case a future discovery is developed.

Azerbaijan: Production Sharing Agreements (November 1999)

Name	Partners	Block	Comments
AIOC (Azerbaijan International Operating Company) signed September 1994; ratified December 1994	**BP Amoco** (34.1%), Lukoil (10%), Socar (10%), Unocal (10%), Statoil (8.6%), Exxon (8%), TPAO (6.8%), Pennzenergy (4.8%), Itochu (4.%), Ramco (2.1%), Delta (1.6%)	Oil reserves: 4.6 billion barrels at Azeri, Chirag, and Guneshli deepwater fields	First production in November 1997, currently producing 110,000 b/d. Exporting through Baku-Supsa pipeline. Total development cost may reach $11 billion. Peak production planned at 850,000 b/d.
CIPCO (Caspian International Petroleum Company) signed November 1995; ratified February 1996; terminated February 1999	LukAgip (50%), Pennzenergy (30%), Lukoil (7.5%), Socar (7.5%), ENI (5%)	Karabakh structure, no commercial reserves	Three exploratory wells found non-commercial oil and gas reserves. Spent $180 million.
Shah Deniz Signed June 4, 1996; ratified October 1996	**BP Amoco** (25.5%), Statoil (25.5%), Lukoil (10%), Elf (10%), Socar (10%), OIEC (10%), TPAO (9%)	Gas reserves of Shah Deniz estimated at 700 Tcm.	Commitment: 3 wells (est. $350 million). Found major gas field at Shah Deniz in summer 1999. Drilling second well at Shah Deniz in late 1999. Development costs estimated at $4.5 billon, if development is decided.
NAOC (North Absheron Operating Company) signed Dec 1996; ratified Feb 1997; terminated April 1999	BP Amoco (30%), Unocal (25.5%), Itochu (20%), Socar (20%), Delta (4.5%)	Dan Ulduzu/Ashrafi structures, no commercial reserves	Failed to find commercial oil reserves after 3 exploration wells
Lenkoran-Talysh Deniz signed Jan 1997; effective June 1997	**Elf** (40%), Socar (25%), OIEC (10%), TotalFina (15%), Wintershall (10%)	Potential 700 mbbl in Lenkoran-Talysh Deniz block	$10 million signature bonus. Committed 2 wells by 2002. Seismic surveys in 1997-98. First well planned in late 2000.
Yalama Signed July 1997; ratified November 1997	Lukoil (60%); Socar (40%)	Potential 365 mbbl in offshore Yalama block	Ran seismic survey. Drilling of first well delayed since early 1999. Arco withdrew from contract in mid-1999.
Absheron signed Aug 1997; ratified November 1997	**Chevron** (30%), Socar (50%), Totalfina (20%)	Potential 850 mbbl oil and 400 Tcm gas in offshore Absheron block	$10 million signature bonus. Commitment: 2 wells by 2000, optional 2 wells by 2002. First well planned in 2000. Seismic survey in 1998.
Oguz Signed Aug 1997; ratified November 1997	**Mobil** (50%), Socar (50%)	Potential 730 mbbl in offshore Oguz block	$10 million signature bonus. Seismic planned in 2000. First well planned in late 2000.
Nakhichevan Signed Aug 1997; ratified November 1997	**Exxon** (50%), Socar (50%)	Potential 650 mbbl oil and 400 tcm gas in Nakhicevan offshore block	$10 million signature bonus. Seismic survey in 1998. Commitment: 2 wells by 2001 (first well planned in early 2000), optional third wells by 2003
Kurdasi-Araz-Kurgan Deniz Signed July 7 1998; ratified July 1998	**ENI** (25%), Socar (50%), Mitsui (15%), TPAO (5%), Repsol (5%)	Potential 700 mbbl in offshore Kurdasi block	Signature bonus: $32 million. Committed 2 wells by 2001, plus 2 optional wells by 2003. First well planned in early 2000, second well in 2001.
Gobustan Signed June 1998; ratified November 1998	**Commonwealth Oil & Gas** (40%), Socar (20%)	Potential 365 mbbl oil in onshore SW Gobustan block	Seismic survey planned.
Inam Signed July 1998; ratified December 1998	**BP Amoco** (25%), Socar (50%), LASMO (12.5%), CFC (12.5%)	Potential 1.4 Bbbl in offshore Inam block	Signature bonus: $32 million. Commitment: 2 wells by 2001, plus 2 optional wells by 2003. First well planned in 2000. Exploration costs till 2001 estimated at $80 million.

Azerbaijan: Production Sharing Agreements (November 1999) *(continued)*

Name	Partners	Block	Comments
Abikh (Alov-Araz-Sharg) Signed July 1998; ratified December 1998	**BP Amoco** (15%), Socar (40%), Statoil (15%), TPAO (10%), Alberta Energy (5%), Exxon 15%	Potential 3.7 Bbbl in offshore block	$100 million signature bonus. Seismic planned in 2000. Committed 3 wells by 2001 (ab $150 million).
Muradhanli-Jafarli-Zardab Signed July 1998; ratified November 1998	**Ramco** (50%), Socar (50%)	Max 650 mbbl in-place oil in onshore Muradhanli field	Ramco took over field operations with a production level of 800 b/d from Socar in fall 1999. First foreign-drilled well planned in 2000. $20 million initial investment by Ramco.
SOL (Salyan Oil) Signed December 1998	**Frontera** (30%), Socar (50%), Amerada Hess/Delta (20%)	Redevelopment of Kyursangi-Karabagly onshore fields	Seismic survey planned in 2000. Initial work programme includes well workovers.
JAOC (Japan-Azerbaijan Oil Company); Signed December 1998; ratified June 1999	Japex (22.5%), Socar (50%), Inpex (12.5%), Teikoku (7.5%), Itochu (7.5%)	Atasgyah-Mugan Deniz-Yanan Tava offshore block, no reserves; potential: 0.5 billion barrels	Seismic planned in late 1999.
North Karadag	**BMB** (50%), Socar (50%)	North Karadag onshore blocks	Ran seismic survey and drilled one well. Small production (180 b/d) from North Karadag field.
Padar, signed April 1999	**Moncrief** (80%), Socar (4%), ISR (16%)	Padar onshore block	
Lerik, signed April 1999	**Mobil** (30%), Socar (50%), unallocated (20%)	Lerik offshore block	
Zafar-Mashal, signed April 1999	**Exxon** (30%), Socar (50%), unallocated (20%)	Zafar-Mashal offshore block	
Ansad joint venture	**Attila Dogan** (31.8%), Land & General (17.2%), Socar (51%)	Redevelopment of four small onshore fields	Producing about 850 b/d.
Azgermoil joint venture	**Grünewald** (50%), Socar (50%)	Redevelopment of onshore Ramany field	Currently producing about 1,000 b/d.
Azerpetoil joint venture	**Pet Oil** (50%), Socar (50%)	Development of four small onshore fields	Currently producing about 2,750 b/d.
Shirvan Oil joint venture	**Whitehall** (51%), Socar (49%)	Redevelopment of onshore Kurovdag field	Shirvan took over operations from Socar in 1998. Producing about 4,300 b/d.

Note:
Shaded row indicates terminated contract.

US companies: Exxon, Mobil (merger with Exxon pending), Amoco and Arco (prior to merger with BP) (Arco owns 46% of Lukarco), Unocal, Pennzenergy, Chevron, Frontera, Amerada Hess, Moncrief.
UK companies: BP Amoco, LASMO, Ramco, Whitehall.
French companies: Totalfina, Elf (acquisition by Totalfina pending).
Russian companies: Lukoil, CFC.
Japanese companies: Itochu, Mitsui, Japex, Inpex, Teikoku.
Other countries: ENI (Italy), Statoil (Norway), Wintershall, Grünewald (Germany), TPAO, Attila Dogan, BMB, Pet Oil (Turkey), IEOC (Iran), Delta (Saudi Arabia), Commonwealth, Alberta Energy (Canada), Repsol (Spain), Land & General (Malaysia)

Source: IHS Energy.

AIOC

The Azerbaijan International Operating Company (AIOC) is the largest foreign investment project in Azerbaijan. It is also the only offshore consortium producing oil in the country, since all others are still at the exploration stage. AIOC's largest shareholder and operator is BP Amoco, which holds slightly over 34% of the project since BP and Amoco merged.

Production began in late 1997 and was initially exported via the "Northern route" pipeline to Russia's Black Sea port of Novorossiysk. AIOC's "Western route" pipeline to Supsa (Georgia) was opened in April 1999. Since then, all AIOC oil has been pumped to Supsa, leaving the northern route to SOCAR[1].

As of late 1999, AIOC was capping production at 110,000 b/d because of processing and export capacity limitations. The consortium drilled ten wells in the deep-water section of the Guneshli field and installed a platform. The field is also producing associated gas (some 80 million ft^3/day), which is marketed domestically by SOCAR. Before bringing the field on stream, AIOC drilled four appraisal wells to refine the reserves estimates for the Guneshli-Chirag-Azeri field. One well discovered a new gas pool. AIOC reports 4.6 billion bbl of oil[2], plus sizeable gas reserves (the gas reserves belong to SOCAR). Production is scheduled to rise to 250,000 b/d by 2003 (Phase I) and will ultimately peak at 700,000 b/d between 2005 and 2010. Production costs were $2.11/barrel in May 1999, which is lower than costs of many North Sea producers. By mid-1999, AIOC had invested some $1.8 billion in the project. Low oil prices in late 1998/early 1999 compelled AIOC to reduce its 1999 budget 25% to $238 million and to defer some work. Total project cost will be $10-12 billion.

Other Negotiations

Some major companies have pulled out of Azerbaijan before finalising a contract. CIPCO's and NAOC's misfortunes dampened the euphoria of the mid-1990's, that compared Baku to another Kuwait. In spite of some exploration setbacks and difficult evacuation of oil to world markets, Azerbaijan remains attractive for many companies. Azerbaijan needs to prove more oil reserves to justify the construction of a major oil pipeline. The Shah Deniz gas discovery has made Azerbaijan appear as a potential gas exporter, corroborating the predictions of many Azeri geologists about gas exploration plays in the deeper parts of the shelf. Chances for large future oil discoveries remain intact, especially in the near-shore southern Caspian, where Elf's Lenkoran block and JAOC's Atashgyah block are located.

Oil Distribution and Consumption

One-third of Azerbaijan's petrol stations have been privatised. All stations were previously run by the State Fuels Committee, which was abolished in 1994. Lukoil has built three filling stations in Baku and plans to construct three others. Products are transported by rail or road within Azerbaijan. There are no significant product pipelines.

Domestic consumption of oil products in 1997 was 5.33 mt, down from an estimated 8.3 mt in 1990. In 1997, 66% of Azeri oil product consumption was by the power sector (heavy fuel oil). The transport sector accounted for 19% and the residential-commercial sector for 11% of oil products consumption.

---

1. The "Northern route" has been out of operation since the summer of 1999, because of Chechen rebel incursions into Dagestan and Russia's war in Chechnya.
2. In November 1999, AIOC revised its reserves upwards to 4.9 billion bbl.

Oil Transportation and Trade

For the following paragraphs see Map 5: Trans-Caucasus Oil and Gas Pipelines

Export Trends

Azerbaijan has traditionally refined most of its own crude and some crude imported from its neighbours, and has exported products (plus some crude). Throughout the 1990's, Azerbaijan remained a net oil (crude and products) exporter, exporting a net 2.1-2.2 mt/year (24% of domestic output) in 1995-97. With AIOC starting exports in 1998, Azerbaijan's exports will rise in the future, albeit parallel to production since all foreign-produced crude is earmarked for exports.

Prior to the break-up of the Soviet Union, Azerbaijan was a significant "exporter" of refined products, especially to Georgia, Armenia and Ukraine. Total product exports in 1990 were 3.25 mt, of which about 1 mt was diesel and 1.4 mt heavy fuel oil. By 1994, oil product exports had dropped to 1.88 mt, still accounting for about 75% of hard currency earnings. About 1 mt went to Iran.

Oil product exports bounced back to 2.15 mt in 1997. With the increased domestic demand for heavy fuel oil as a substitute for gas in power generation, most product exports were diesel. About one-third of this volume was transported via the Georgian Black Sea ports of Batumi and Poti. The rest went via rail, road or across the Caspian Sea by tanker. For example, Russia's Lukoil shipped some 0.5 mt of products by tanker from Baku to the Russian Caspian port of Makhachkala. 1997 revenues from products exports amounted to $2.62 million.

"Early Oil"

The major Azerbaijani oil export pipeline projects are co-ordinated by AIOC. In October 1995, AIOC adopted a phased approach for evacuating its oil. "Early oil" (pre-peak production) was to be exported through two routes: the "northern route", which meant using the existing pipeline to Russia's Black Sea port of Novorossiysk, and the "western route" to the Georgian Black Sea port of Supsa, which had to be largely re-built and was inaugurated in April 1999. Once "early oil" pipelines were available, AIOC had some respite to study, finance and build a "main oil" pipeline to accommodate peak production from its fields.

The northern route, owned by Russia's Transneft, was opened in December 1997. An important issue for this pipeline has been the division of responsibilities and transit revenues between Russia's Transneft and the local Chechen oil company, through whose territory the pipeline passes. The northern route has a capacity of up to 9 mt/year (180,000 b/d). The line soon proved to be unreliable, with up to 25% downtimes due to technical problems, sabotage and squabbles between Transneft and the Chechen authorities. AIOC stopped using this line as soon as the pipeline through Georgia became available in April 1999, leaving the "northern route" to SOCAR's exclusive use. In summer 1999, the Chechen incursions into Dagestan and the war in Chechnya closed the pipeline altogether. Transneft has tried to re-assure AIOC about security concerns in Chechnya and has vowed to build a bypass around the rebellious republic. As of late 1999, in spite of much ado, Transneft had laid only 7 km of a total 150 km of pipeline.

The 920-km "western route" from Baku to the Georgian Black Sea port of Supsa was completed in February 1999 and the first tanker was loaded in April. It originally was to incorporate existing stretches of pipeline, but in the end most of the existing pipeline had to be replaced, leading to significant cost over-runs for AIOC. The pipeline to Supsa has an initial capacity of 5.75 mt/year (115,000 b/d). Installation of additional pump stations could allow AIOC to ship more than 300,000 b/d, i.e. more than the Phase I level AIOC plans to reach by 2003. The new terminal at Supsa includes four storage tanks with a capacity of 250,000 barrels each. It has an annual capacity for 10 mt (200,000 b/d).

The Georgian International Oil Corporation (GIOC) receives a tariff from AIOC that is equal to $0.17/bbl, adjusted quarterly by the US GDP deflator. The overall tariff on the Baku-Supsa line is $3.10 per tonne ($0.42/bbl), compared to $15.67 per tonne ($2.1/bbl) to Novorossiysk.

"Main Oil" Pipeline See Chapter about Regional Energy Trade and Transit port and the Baku-Ceyhan pipeline in particular.

In July 1997 AIOC announced that it had narrowed the possible "main oil" pipeline routes to three: expanded versions of the two routes used for early oil (to Novorossiysk and to Supsa), plus a third route to the Turkish Mediterranean port of Ceyhan. A possible pipeline through Iran was never considered an official option, although some oil companies privately prefer it as the most cost-effective one.

AIOC would like to delay further the decision on a main export route, since development of its offshore fields is lagging behind initial schedule. AIOC has repeated that its proven reserves do not warrant construction of a pipeline from Baku to Ceyhan. By deferring a decision, AIOC may find some partners with yet-to-be-discovered oil reserves to spread the risk associated with the pipeline. The more AIOC postpones a decision, the more it faces impatient governments in Azerbaijan, Turkey and United States, all of which favour the Ceyhan route for various political, security and environmental reasons.

The Shah Deniz gas discovery in summer 1999, which is operated by BP Amoco who are also the largest shareholder in AIOC, has given Turkey some leverage against AIOC. Turkey may have extolled some compromising from BP Amoco in return for the opening of the Turkish gas market.

The Ceyhan route is important to Azerbaijan, Turkey and the US because they see it: 1) strengthening the independence of the Caspian states by reducing their dependence on Russia or Iran for exports; 2) creating mutually beneficial economic bonds between the nations of the region; and 3) helping alleviate environmental concerns about increased oil tanker traffic through the Turkish Straits.

The Ceyhan route's biggest drawback is that it needs larger volumes than available today to make it economically viable. AIOC has calculated that a throughput of 1.2-1.6 mb/d is needed to make the pipeline economical. AIOC's fields are not expected to reach their peak production of 700-800,000 b/d until around 2010. BP Amoco has pledged it would seek additional oil volumes from foreign companies operating in the Caspian region. But by far the only producer that could commit the required volumes is TCO, which develops the Tengiz field in Kazakhstan and is building its own CPC pipeline.

AIOC estimates the Ceyhan pipeline price tag would be $3.7 billion, while the Turkish government has claimed the project could be completed for as little as $2.4 billion. The

Turkish government has pledged to cover costs in excess of $2.4 billion. However, there are important differences in the technical specifications and routes between the two estimates. This compares to about $2.5 billion for a main oil pipeline to Novorossiysk, and $1.8 billion to the Georgian Black Sea port of Supsa. The latter is the preferred route of many companies in the AIOC consortium, either as a final main route, or as the first stage to an eventual main line to Ceyhan.

The Azeri government will take the price of the route into consideration because AIOC will be able to recoup its construction costs. This will impact on the timing of Azeri government revenues. According to AIOC, choosing a main oil pipeline to Ceyhan over one to Supsa could "cost" the Azeri government some $500 million per year in revenue foregone.

NATURAL GAS SECTOR

Gas Reserves and Production

In early 1999, SOCAR estimated the country's proven gas reserves are about 800 bcm, while most outside estimates were in the range of 300 bcm. A 1997 US Government report estimated recoverable gas reserves at around 300 bcm, with another 1,000 bcm classified as possible[1]. The discovery of the Shah Deniz field by a BP Amoco-led consortium in summer 1999 should at least double the country's reserves. By late 1999, the consortium was confident that Shah Deniz contains some 700 bcm of gas, thereby lifting the country's overall reserves to between 1,000 and 1,500 bcm. The Shah Deniz figures are still preliminary as the consortium was drilling its second well. Full field appraisal may reveal yet larger reserves.

Cumulative gas production as per end-1999 was 453 bcm, of which 130 bcm were produced onshore.

The three offshore fields being developed by the AIOC consortium alone are estimated to contain 70.8 bcm of natural gas[2], while the Nakhichevan and Kapaz fields, once fully appraised, may contain an additional 280 bcm. Onshore reserves appear nearly depleted.

The main upstream gas producer is SOCAR. Most of Azerbaijan's gas production is associated with offshore oil production. Azerbaijan has been trying to attract foreign investors into projects to harness associated gas. The most prominent such projects were the Neft Daslary and shallow-water Guneshli fields, where western-made equipment was installed in 1995 to harness up to 1 bcm/year of gas that were previously flared. According to most contracts signed with international investors, associated gas belongs to SOCAR.

Gas production in Azerbaijan reached a high of 14 bcm in 1985, before starting a steep decline to 6.7 bcm by 1993. Since then, the decline has slowed down. 1998, when production bottomed at 5.58 bcm, marked a turning point. 1999 production is expected to reach 6.1 bcm, largely due to rising production by AIOC.

In early 1999, SOCAR predicted that gas production would triple by 2010 to 16.5 bcm, including 3.6 bcm by foreign operators. This forecast needs to be re-visited in light of the

---

1. Report to Congress on Caspian Region Energy Development, 1997.
2. AIOC gas production averages about 0.6 bcm/year. The gas is delivered to SOCAR.

Figure 8   Azerbaijan Gas Production

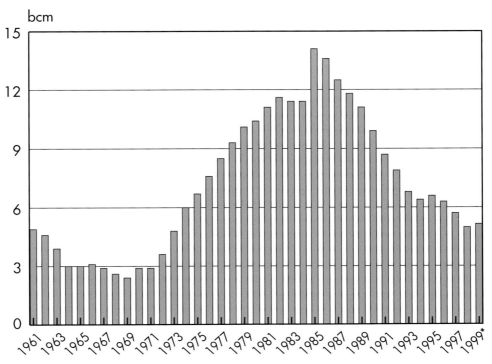

Source: IHS Energy.
*Estimate.

Shah Deniz discovery, which could potentially produce up to 24 bcm/year. A more recent SOCAR study foresees that gas production will rise to 20 bcm by 2017 under a low-case scenario and to 40 bcm under a high-case scenario. Both scenarios assume that Shah Deniz will start producing in 2005. Domestic gas demand is set to rise from approximately 5 Bcm to 15-17 bcm by 2017, i.e. roughly equal to 1990 consumption of 15.8 bcm. The gas export potential would be anywhere between 3 and 23 bcm, depending on production growth.

Sources with the Shah Deniz consortium believe that the field could be brought on stream by 2005 and could export 15 bcm to Turkey (with some gas sales to Georgia) within a few years from production start-up. Early calculations show that the field could be developed at

Azeri natural gas production, trade and consumption (bcm)

	1990	**1991**	**1992**	**1993**	**1994**	**1995**	**1996**
Produced*	9.925	8.681	7.873	6.805	6.378	6.643	6.305
Delivered*	8.779	7.694	6.969	5.998	5.353	5.677	5.301
Imported (gross)	13.113	14.165	5.264	2.972	2.502	0.594	0.24
Exported/transited	5.424	5.995	0.951	0.448	0.0	0.0	0.0
Consumed	12.190	10.956	11.235	8.881	8.880	7.237	6.239

* The definition of production apparently includes gas flared and gas vented, while delivery includes only gas delivered to the transmission/distribution
  system, whether processed or not.
Source: Azerigaz.

a cost of only $1/boe. In 2000, industry observers will be anxiously watching Chevron's first well at the nearby Absheron prospect, which is geologically very similar to Shah Deniz.

Currently, the largest gas producer is the offshore Bahar field, which accounted for more than half the country's gas production in 1991. Since the mid-1980's, however, production at Bahar and most other large fields has declined. Only production from Guneshli has remained relatively constant. SOCAR's lack of funds has delayed re-development of Bahar and the shallow portion of Guneshli fields, which could supply an incremental 6 bcm/year.

In the early 1990's, natural gas accounted for more than 62% of primary energy supply, making Azerbaijan one of the most gas-intensive economies in the world. At that time, Azerbaijan "imported" 75% of its gas from other Soviet Republics (Russia, Turkmenistan). The share of gas in the Azerbaijani energy balance decreased to 40% by 1997, mainly because of decreasing gas imports from Turkmenistan (import levels have become insignificant as from 1995).

Meeting internal gas demand, mainly for power generation and industry needs, has been a priority for the government for many years. Gas exports and transit and electricity exports (from gas-fired plants) are longer-term governmental objectives. The recent Shah Deniz discovery should make these goals easier to reach.

Gas Transmission and Distribution

State-owned Azerigaz is responsible for transportation, transit, storage and distribution of natural gas. The company was formed in 1992 with the merger of the national gas transmission company and the natural gas distribution branch of the State Fuel Committee. Azerigaz's charter forbids it to engage in gas production, which remains the prerogative of SOCAR. In May 1997, Azerigaz was corporatised as a condition for a World Bank loan for the rehabilitation of the country's gas industry (*see below*). Its shares were transferred to the State Property Committee to be sold at a later date. (See Map 5: Trans-Caucasus Oil and Gas Pipelines)

Azerigaz's high-pressure gas transmission system has a total length of about 4,500 km, with pipes up to 1,200 mm in diameter, and a total annual throughput capacity of 30 bcm. It includes the following lines with connections to neighbouring countries (See Map 5: Trans-Caucasus Oil and Gas Pipelines):

- **Mozdok (Russia) – Kazi Magomed**: Total length 700 km, of which 240 km in Azerbaijan. Annual throughput capacity is 13 bcm. The line was built for "importing" gas to Azerbaijan from Russia and Turkmenistan.

- **Bind – Bland (Iran) – Astara – Kazi Magomed (Igat-1)**: Total length 1,147.5 km, of which 296.5 km in Azerbaijan. Annual throughput capacity is about 10 bcm. It was built in 1971 for a triangular gas trade agreement, whereby Iran delivered gas to the southern Soviet Union and the USSR equivalent amounts of gas to Europe. The line has been mothballed since 1993.

- **Kazi Magomed – Kazakh (2 lines)**: This dual-line system (length 378 km) has a capacity for 10 bcm and 13 bcm respectively. At Kazakh, the system branches off into two lines: one (120 km long, 10 bcm/annum capacity) continues into Georgia. This is the line, which is currently being examined by the Shah Deniz consortium for a possible upgrade for future gas exports. The second branch pipeline (38 km in Azerbaijan, 7 bcm capacity) leads into

Armenia. Both pipelines were used in Soviet times to deliver Russian or Turkmen gas to Georgia and Armenia via Azerbaijan. The pipeline to Armenia has been closed since 1992.

■ **Yevlakh – Nakhichevan (via Armenia)**: Total length of this pipeline that connects Azerbaijan proper to the Azeri province of Nakhichevan, which lies on the other side of Armenia, is 350 km, of which 290 km is on Azeri territory. Capacity is 4.5 bcm.

Seven compressor stations are currently in operation in Azerbaijan, and 150 distribution stations. Two underground storage facilities in depleted gas fields at Kalmas and Karadag have a capacity of about 3 bcm. According to Azerigaz, these could be expanded to 10 bcm at relatively low cost. The sites do not contain gas processing or dehydration facilities to separate large amounts of water and liquid hydrocarbons absorbed by the gas during storage. Expansion and reconstruction of the storage facilities is reportedly underway.

Azerigaz has 12 regional distribution companies, which deliver gas to over 1 million customers via some 31,000 km of medium – and low-pressure distribution lines[1]. This high degree of gasification has been achieved despite some 50% of the population living in rural areas. At the end of 1997, however, due to ongoing gas shortages, only about one third of the network was being supplied, mainly in the Baku region.

In many areas there are parallel gas distribution systems, a low-pressure network for households, and a medium-pressure one for industries. According to the World Bank, operational efficiency could be improved by eliminating the low-pressure system in such areas.

According to Azerigaz, 8% of the transported gas was lost in the gas distribution system in 1997, down from 15% a few years earlier. It is estimated that up to two-thirds was due to non-technical losses such as theft and metre tampering. It is not clear if the fact that only one-third of the system has been operating has massively reduced the losses. According to outside experts, the transmission and distribution system as a whole is highly dilapidated. Poor measurement devices and lacking modern control and communication systems impede efficiency.

Another important problem contributing to loss is insufficient cathodic protection of pipelines, which are often in a corrosive environment. Many pipelines appear to have been built in unsuitable areas, for example under buildings and close to main roads and rail crossings.

Total investment needs for rehabilitating the gas transportation system are estimated by Azerbaijan at around $150 million. The World Bank is to make available $20.2 million in the first stage of a $100 million gas industry rehabilitation programme. Priority investments identified under this programme include corrosion inhibition for pipelines, the purchase and installation of gas metres for large customers, and corporatisation of the LPG distribution system.

The EC, under its TACIS programme, has provided €2.7 million to Azerigaz for improving accounting systems related to customer services and for rehabilitating and expanding the two gas storage facilities.

---

1. According to a 1997 Azerigaz brochure, the company serves "65 towns and district centres, 43 small towns, about 2000 villages, 800 industries and over 13,000 communal properties and social services", including 1.2 million families.

LPG

In addition to distribution by pipeline, Azerigaz is responsible for bottling and distributing LPG. LPG is produced at four plants: the Novo-Bakinskiy refinery (annual LPG capacity of 90,000 t), the Karadag processing plant (30,000 t), the Azerigaz NGL processing plant (1,100 t), and the Sumgait rubber factory, which produces propane and butane as by-products. Some LPG is also imported from Russia.

LPG is dispatched to five bottling plants by rail, and to three others by truck. It is then distributed in bottled form to distribution points and to end-users by road. According to Azerigaz, LPG operations are profitable, due in part to stricter payment procedures than those for piped gas.

LPG demand is expected to increase in the future, since the delivery system for piped gas may have to be cut back in an effort to rationalise distribution. The government is considering separating LPG operations from Azerigaz and soliciting foreign investment for improving and enlarging LPG operations.

Gas Consumption

Azerbaijan traditionally has met most of its non-transport energy needs with gas. Total gas supplied was more than halved in the 1990's, from 15.8 bcm in 1990 to 5.3 bcm in 1997. The main cause for this decline were decreasing gas imports from Turkmenistan and ensuing restrictions on consumption imposed by the Azeri government. In 1990, almost 44% of Azerbaijan's primary gas consumption was imported. Gas imports practically stopped in 1995. Gas-saving measures included switching Azerbaijan's dual-fired power generating units from gas to fuel oil and restricting gas use by industry. Industrial use dropped by around 25% between 1993 and 1995.

Non-payments – both in the industrial and in the residential sectors – continue to cripple the gas industry. The government has used cheap oil and gas as compensation for not paying salaries in the past.

Azeri natural gas consumption (bcm)

	1990	1991	1992	1993	1994	1995	1996
Total*	12.190	10.956	11.235	8.881	8.880	7.237	6.239
of which Azenergo	5.474	4.423	1.621	0.817	0.936	1.182	1.440
of which households	2.700	3.100	2.850	3.085	2.686	2.487	1.685
of which industry and other	4.016	3.433	6.764	4.979	5.258	3.568	3.114

Source: Azerigaz.

According to Azerigaz statistics, 1990 gas consumption was about 12.2 bcm, of which approximately 5.5 bcm was used for electricity and heat generation, and 4.0 bcm consumed by industry. By 1996, total gas consumption had dropped to 6.2 bcm, of which around 3.1 bcm was consumed by industry, with only 1.4 bcm used for electricity and heat generation[1]. SOCAR uses approximately 1 bcm annually for its own operations. Household consumption dropped from 3.1 bcm in 1993 to 2.5 bcm in 1995 due to supply restrictions. Azeri households use gas for cooking, water and space heating.

---

1. In 1997, about 30% of electricity generation was by gas during the summer, and 70% by mazut. During the winter, all electricity and heat was generated by mazut in order to deliver more gas to households for heating.

As of 1993, only half of industrial gas consumers were equipped with metres, while there were no metres for individual households. Lack of metres makes it difficult to control flows, and to develop a pricing and incentive policy based on amounts consumed. Most residential consumers are currently charged according to a formula based on household floor space, number of persons, and assumed consumption rates of various appliances.

A programme to install household gas metres in Baku began in 1994. By the end of 1997, some 39,000 metres had been installed out of approximately 450,000 households in the capital. The priority has been to install metres in households that both heat and cook with gas. The Cabinet of Ministers has ordered gas metres to be installed in 535,000 households by 2008, out of approximately 1.2 million total households in the country. This is to include metering of almost all households in the metropolitan areas of Baku, Ali Bayramli and Sumgait. According to Azerigaz, pre-paid metres will be tested on a number of private small businesses.

Gas Pricing

Gas prices are controlled by the government. In 1996, SOCAR sold gas to Azerigaz for the equivalent of $10.80/1,000 m^3, while the nominal price of imported Turkmen was $80/1,000 m^3 [1]. Industrial consumers paid Azerigaz $53.30/1,000 m^3, communal users paid $23.60, and the residential sector only $2.80 (raised from approximately $1.40 in June 1996).

In its negotiations for a gas rehabilitation loan from the World Bank in 1996 and 1997, the government agreed to review its gas pricing system, taking into account its investment goals and the need of potential foreign investors to make an adequate return on capital. In November 1998, SOCAR gas prices were increased to 55,000 manat/1,000 m^3 ($12.6/1,000 m^3), which covers approximately 80% of production costs [2].

Gas Trade and Transit

Between the mid-1970's and mid-1980's Azerbaijan produced a small gas surplus (around 2 bcm), which it exported to neighbouring Soviet republics. In the late 1980's and prior to 1992, Azerbaijan imported 13-14 bcm per year, of which 5-6 bcm were re-exported to Armenia and Georgia. Gas re-exports to Armenia ceased in 1992 at the outbreak of the Nagorny-Karabakh conflict. Azerbaijan practically stopped importing gas as from 1995.

In the 1970's, Iranian gas was sent to Azerbaijan and the other Soviet Caucasus republics through the Iranian Gas Trunkline (Igat). Igat was built in 1971 to supply gas to the Soviet Union as part of a triangular arrangement under which Russia could sell gas to Europe on behalf of Iran. Annual throughput capacity was 10 bcm, although actual volumes were reportedly never as large as planned, and ended at the Iranian revolution in 1979.

In 1992 Azerbaijan began importing gas from Turkmenistan, which subsequently remained its main supplier until the first quarter 1995. Deliveries were often disrupted because of tariff disputes between Turkmenistan and Gazprom (Turkmen gas must traverse Uzbekistan, Kazakhstan and Russia in order to reach Azerbaijan). Moreover, Azerbaijan's inability to finance its gas imports proved an even greater problem.

The World Bank has estimated that Azerbaijan could potentially earn transit fees of $5-8 million per bcm crossing its territory. Assuming gas re-exports to Georgia and Armenia

---

1. The World Bank calculated that the effective price may have been closer to US$43/1,000 m^3, since much of the Azeri payment is in barter. Figuring in the 15% losses in the Azeri transmission network makes the wholesale prices from SOCAR and Turkmenistan around US$12.40 and US$49.50 per 1,000 m^3, respectively.
2. SOCAR reported average gas production costs of 67,700 manat/1,000 m^3 in September 1999.

would resume at a level of 6 bcm/year, yearly transit fees could total some $30-48 million. With the construction of a proposed Trans-Caspian pipeline, transit of some 20 bcm/year of Turkmen gas could conceivably represent some $100-160 million in annual transit revenues.

Ukraine signed an agreement with Iran in 1992 to import Iranian gas via Azerbaijan. However, discussions have stalled over Ukraine's incapacity to pay. Reportedly, there also have been difficulties gaining transit rights for the gas in Russia.

The recent Shah Deniz gas discovery could propel Azerbaijan into the role of a regional gas exporter. Reserves estimates as of late 1999 could warrant exports of 15 bcm/year at an initial stage. Early findings of an expert group, which was set up after the discovery, is that the existing gas pipeline to Georgia could be upgraded and a new pipeline link laid from South-West Georgia to Hopa on the Turkish Black Sea coast. Azerbaijan could export 3-4 bcm/annum to Turkey within four years at an infrastructure cost of $150 million. Capacity of the system could be further upgraded to 10-15 bcm/annum as early as 2007.

ELECTRICITY

Electricity Industry Overview

Until the break-up of the Soviet Union, the electric grids of the Caucasus republics were integrated. After independence, the government created **Azenergo (Azerenerji)**, a state-owned electricity utility responsible for production, transmission, trade and distribution, as well as for industrial steam and hot water production from combined heat and power plants (CHP) for industrial and residential consumers.

Traditionally, 90% of the installed capacity has been fired by natural gas. After the disintegration of the Soviet Union and the break-up of traditional trade flows, gas-fired electricity generation almost came to a halt in 1993-94. Oil – mainly high-sulphur heavy fuel oil imported from Russia – became the main source for electricity generation. Since 1996, heavy fuel oil imports have been replaced by domestically produced oil.

Electricity Generation

Both oil and gas play an important role in electricity generation in Azerbaijan. Total electricity generating capacity is about 5.1 GW, of which 3.6 GW (70%) is accounted for by the country's nine thermal plants. Azerbaijan's nine hydro-electric plants account for 820 MW of capacity, and its CHPs for 616 MW.

In fact, only 3.8 GW of the total 5.1 GW installed capacity is available due to chronic lack of maintenance of the ageing plants. About 2 GW installed capacity have been in operation for more than 30 years and need to be retired in the medium term. By and large, the equipment at the plants is obsolescent, resulting in high fuel consumption, low thermal efficiency and a high level of emissions[1]. Production losses account for some 85% of output. Azerbaijan continues to suffer from sporadic shortages of electricity, as inadequate collection continues to delay modernisation of the majority of the power stations and networks.

---

1. Average annual SO_2 (type 2 as index in SO_2) emissions per plant amount to 3,310 t.

■ The Law authorises the Regulatory Commission to define quotas for production, import and export of electricity. This could be seen as a potential intervention in the power market, which could be a disincentive to investors in generation or distribution.

■ The Law provides for court appeals against decisions or regulations by the Regulatory Commission (except tariff decisions). This could potentially devoid the Commission of its powers.

■ The Law states that electricity imports are subject to a maximum tariff, established by the Regulatory Commission.

An Oil and Gas Law has been drafted by the Government in early 1999 and is being reviewed by parliament. Adoption of the law is scheduled for mid-2000.

THE OIL SECTOR

Exploration

Armenia has no domestic oil production and refining industry, and depends entirely on imports to meet its petroleum product needs. The country has not been explored systematically. The some 200 exploratory wells drilled over the past 50 years failed to discover any commercial hydrocarbon deposits. Estimates of the country's oil potential vary between 60 and 100 mt, but these figures are highly speculative.

Early in 1995, the Ministry of Energy organised an international bidding round offering the whole country for exploration under production sharing terms. The country was divided into five blocks of around 5,000 km². In 1997, Armenian-American Exploration company (AAEC), a joint venture involving Rand-Paulson Exploration (US), signed a production sharing agreement for acreage covering roughly the western half of the country. AAEC has shot some seismic and drilled its first well, which was dry. Operations have been halted, although AAEC is committed to drilling two additional wells. Hemco (US) has been rumoured to be negotiating for the yet unlicensed part of the country.

Oil Distribution

The petroleum industry in Armenia is under the joint control of the Ministry of Energy and the Ministry of Trade and Industry. Petroleum imports, storage and distribution are under the control of **Armoilproduct**, which is under the Ministry of Industry and Trade. Armoilproduct has 18 major storage facilities with a capacity of 800,000 t, which have also been used by district heating companies. Total storage capacity in Armenia is 1.2 mt for refined products. Armoilproduct does not have a monopoly over imports and is competing with a number of small private importers. Competition between Armoilproduct and private importers is biased by the fact that only Armoilproduct has access to storage capacity. Private importers can only sell directly from rail tankers to consumers, according to pre-arranged contracts. The oil industry was one of the first segments of the energy sector that was privatised. Today, all gasoline stations are private.

Access to storage allows Armoilproduct to sell when demand (and prices) are highest. Official statistics indicate that in 1998, about 450,000 t of oil products were imported. However, actual imports were probably much higher, because unofficial trade is not accounted for.

Mazut imports for the thermal power stations are handled by Armturtrade, which is under the Ministry of Energy.

Oil Consumption

In 1998, oil consumption in Armenia amounted to 3.91 mt, compared with 4.39 mt in 1991. During the years in-between, consumption slumped, but not as low as 0.155 mt suggested by official statistics, which do not record smuggling and consumption by the shadow economy.

In the early 1990's, about one-third of total oil consumption was mazut for thermal power stations. The rest was used primarily in the transport sector. As from 1992, oil imports were massively impaired due to the Azeri blockade. As a result, mazut combustion at electricity plants dwindled from an early 1990's level of 1.3 mt to 0.1 mt or less as from 1994. The current transport route through Georgia makes the use of oil in power generation economically unattractive if compared to natural gas. Mazut accounts for only 5% of fuel consumption in the power sector, but it remains important as a back-up fuel. Storage capacity for mazut at the country's three thermal power plants amounts to 350,000 t (of which 220,000 t are at Hrazdan TPP). Actual mazut reserves are, however, only a small fraction of the capacity.

In 1993, petroleum product prices were liberalised and the price of mazut soared. By 1997, prices had risen over 2,800% above 1992 prices. In 1998, the price of mazut in Armenia was with about $110-120/t comparable to the European OECD average of $122/t. This is partly explained by the high shipping costs; the transport costs from Novorossiysk to Yerevan are estimated at $55/t. By comparison, the transportation cost for mazut from Baku to Yerevan via Georgia would be only about $25/t. The price for gasoline is about 35 cents per litre.

Oil Trade and Transit

Armenia has no import pipelines for crude oil or oil products, and no product pipelines for domestic distribution. All imports are by rail, although a small amount of gasoline and diesel fuel are transported by tanker truck. There are two main rail lines – from Georgia and from Azerbaijan. A connection also exists with Turkey, but the different rail gauges between Armenia and Turkey require transhipment. In the past, most Armenian imports of petroleum products were from refineries in Baku (Azerbaijan) and Grozny (Chechnya, Russia). The dissolution of the Soviet Union and Nagorny-Karabakh disrupted Armenia's traditional oil supply routes. The trade embargo with Azerbaijan and the war in Chechnya closed supplies from both refineries.

As a result, Armenia was forced to switch to supplies from Russia. Refined products are transported by ship from Novorossiysk to Georgian Black Sea ports, from where they are loaded onto rail tankers for shipment to Armenia. In addition to supplies of refined products from Russia, Armenian importers buy Russian crude oil, which is refined at Batumi refinery in Georgia. But importers are making less use of this option, because of the inefficiency of the Batumi refinery. There are indications that, in spite of the Azerbaijani embargo, some Azeri mazut is supplied to Armenia via Georgian intermediaries. Some gasoline and gasoil are imported from Iran.

At the beginning of the Azerbaijani oil embargo, the Armenian Government studied the feasibility of constructing a refinery in Yerevan. The main objective of the refinery, which was planned to have a capacity of 1 mt/year, was to produce mazut for power production. A pilot refinery was constructed in Armenia at a polyvinyl-acetate plant. The pilot refinery produces about 50,000 tonnes of gasoil and heavy fuel oil annually. The gasoil is being used mainly in the chemical industry for further processing.

COAL

Armenia's coal resources were too small to catch serious attention of Soviet planners prior to independence. Pressed by the energy crisis of the early 1990's, the government resumed coal exploration and small-scale coal mining in 1992.

Armenia's initial development phase focuses on three lignite deposits – **Idjevan**, **Djadjur** and **Nor Arevik**. There are several coal test sites at **Germanis**, **Antaramut** and **Shamut**. Total proven reserves are very small – some 3-5 mt. There was some limited coal exploration at Idjevan already in Soviet times. Proven reserves at Idjevan are 500-750,000 t. The lignite, which is produced from the Idjevan open-cast mine, has a low calorific value (2,700 Kcal/Kg) and is found in a narrow and sharply dipping seam. Production is very low – less than 150 t/day. The Djadjur mine near Gumri and the Nor Arevik mine also produce small quantities of coal on a pilot production basis. Djadjur holds 500,000 t of reserves.

Industrial mining is uneconomic because of the geographic spread and geological conditions of the reserves. Current production is used for residential heating in the immediate area of the mines.

In the mid-1980's Armenia imported 300-400,000 t of coal per year from the Donbass basin in Ukraine. Coal imports peaked in 1988-89 at 550,000 t/year, used primarily for domestic heating. Since then coal imports have fallen to negligible levels of less than 5,000 t/year. High transportation cost would make imports prohibitive. Furthermore, Armenia's power plants have not coal-burning units. Therefore coal will remain a marginal fuel in Armenia.

Responsibility for the coal industry is divided between the Ministry of Environment and Mineral Resources and the Ministry of Energy. The former is responsible for coal exploration and pilot exploitation, the latter for mining, through the State Solid Fuel Enterprise. However, this remains theoretical, since no mine has yet entered commercial production. The State Solid Fuel Enterprise handles coal imports. Coal is sold through 12 depots (there are 22 coal depots, but only 12 are currently functioning). Consumers are required to pay for transportation, loading and unloading.

ELECTRICITY[1]

Structure of the Electricity Industry

During the Soviet area, the Armenian power system was part of the Trans-Caucasus Interconnected Power System (IPS), which encompassed Georgia, Azerbaijan and Armenia. Thus, Armenia's system was basically designed as a baseload system, with peaking supplies coming from hydro stations in Georgia. In addition, thermal plants were designed to run on Azerbaijani oil and Iranian and eventually Russian or Turkmen gas. The break-up of the Soviet Union forced the Armenian electricity system, which had been planned and built as part of an interconnected system, to operate as an island.

In the Soviet era, **Armenergo**, the vertically integrated electric utility, reported to the Ministry of Power and Electrification in Moscow. After independence, Armenergo was transferred to

1. This section draws on information obtained from numerous reports prepares by Hagler Bailly that have been funded by USAID and the World Bank.

the Armenian Ministry of Energy. Since 1995, Armenia's power sector has undergone some re-organisation under the impetus of international aid agencies, including the World Bank, the European Bank of Reconstruction and Development (EBRD), and bilateral aid agencies, in particular USAID.

In March 1995, Armenergo was unbundled into distinct generation and distribution enterprises, with transmission and dispatch remaining within the remit of Armenergo. In December 1995, the **Hrazdan** thermal power plant and the **Sevan-Hrazdan** hydro-power cascade were separated from Armenergo. In mid-1997, the system was completely unbundled. Six separate generation companies were created: three thermal power plants, two hydro-electric generation companies, and the nuclear power plant. Several micro/small hydro-power plants were not included in these six generation companies. In the latest restructuring, a separate transmission company – ArmTrans – was set up, whilst dispatch remained under Armenergo. The distribution sector was consolidated, initially into 11, and later into 4 companies.

At present, there are six generating companies, one transmission company, one dispatcher and four distribution companies. As dispatcher, Armenergo remains responsible for the financial settlement and clearing of the electricity system.

Armenia: Consolidated Distribution Companies

	Population	**Customers**
North	943,000	189,070
Centre	820,000	193,140
South	510,000	120,760
Yerevan	1,200,000	276,000

The electricity sector was under the control of the Ministry of Energy until September 1998, when Government Decree 555 placed it under the joint authority of the Ministry of Energy, the Ministry of Finance and the Ministry of Privatisation.

The Energy Law of June 1997 has certain safeguards against the concentration in the energy industry. As part of the anti-monopoly legislation, it stipulates that any shareholder that owns 35% or more of an electric facility is not allowed to own shares in any other energy company without permission from the Regulatory Commission. Furthermore, the law defines the basic principles for tariffs, which should be based on costs and should have attained cost-recovering levels by July 1999.

The Regulatory Commission sets maximum rates for electricity, including large industries. It also sets prices for the different generating plants and Armenergo's selling price to the distributors, thereby effectively controlling the entire financial flow in the electricity industry. The Commission is elaborating the legal framework for the wholesale electricity market. The market rules were to be decided in 1999, e.g. whether direct sales to end-user or through a pool. Armenergo would prefer to operate as a "single buyer". At present, however, the scope for competition is limited as generating capacity is limited to one nuclear power station (33% of production), two thermal stations (40%) and two hydro-power cascades.

Privatisation

Since independence, the Government has prepared the framework for privatisation with the passage of key legislation, such as the Privatisation Law, the Foreign Investment Law, the Energy Law, the establishment of an independent regulator, and the corporatisation and unbundling of the electricity industry.

The early privatisation process did not include the energy sector. With the exception of small hydro-power plants (SHPPs), the electricity industry is still largely state-owned. Between 1994 and 1998 the Government privatised 25 SHPPs representing about 85 MW of installed capacity. Three of these small plants have been sold to foreign investors.

Privatisation of major parts of the electricity industry has started, with the planned sale of the four distribution companies. The deadline for bids was 7 December 1999, and winners are to be announced in February 2000. The long-term goal is to sell-off between 51% and 70% of the electric sector companies to investors before 2001. The sales of the main generation facilities and transmission company are likely to follow after the privatisation of the distributors is completed. The Government is devising a strategy with EBRD for the sale of the generators. The dispatcher and Medzamor nuclear power plant (NPP) are excluded from the privatisation plan.

The government has drawn up a list of potential hydro-electric plants with a total capacity of 102 MW that are available to private investors. Negotiations for some of the sites have begun with US-based HYE-DRO Power. A dozen small hydro-plants with capacities ranging from less than 1 MW to 7.5 MW have been privatised. Only two of these were sold to foreigners, i.e. a group of French citizens.

In the second quarter 1999, the government opened a tender for the sale of four distribution companies, starting with Yerevan distribution company. The deadline for bids was 12 November 1999.

Investors will face problems such as poor payment discipline, low tariffs, poor financial information and a regulatory regime whose independence is uncertain. The announcement by the Regulatory Commission in November 1999 that electricity tariffs would remain unchanged at 25 Dram/kWh until 2001 was another discouragement for investors. Officially, the current tariff is described as "enough for the energy sector to operate without massive state subsidies". Experts argue that these tariffs barely cover costs and prevent investment. The minimum tariff for the industry to operate and develop efficiently has been calculated at 30 Dram/kWh. A loan agreement with the World Bank obliges Armenia to free electricity tariffs. The Regulatory Commission instructed the electricity companies to cut costs in 2000 – amongst other measures, by reducing the workforce by 7000 – so as to improve their financial performance in view of privatisation. Furthermore, electricity production is targeted to increase 4-5% in 2000.

The privatisation of the hydro and thermal plants requires some problems to be resolved beforehand:

■ Excess generation capacity (in the absence of large export markets) and dispatch constraints;

■ Lack of clarity on the availability and regulation of water resources for hydro-power plants;

■ Uncertainty on the future market rules ("single buyer" or pool);

■ Risks of non-payment by the transmission company (Armenergo) for generation purchases;

■ The risk of default of fuel supply and power purchase agreements.

The Government does not count on significant revenues from the privatisation, given the low asset value, large liabilities and investment risk. Instead, the Government will give more importance to investment commitment by investors. It has been estimated that Armenia's electricity sector needs about $2 billion over the next decade.

Electricity Generation

Armenia has a small, but relatively diverse mix of generating capacity. The major facilities include two large thermal combined heat and power plants (TPPs), two major hydro-power cascades, a nuclear power plant (NPP) and a number of small hydro-power plants.

The total nameplate capacity of the Armenian electricity system is about 3.2 GW, excluding Unit 1 at Medzamor NPP which is unlikely to restart operation. The available generating capacity is far less than the installed capacity, because of lack of maintenance and fuel shortages. At present about 2.2 GW are available, which is still a remarkable improvement compared to the crisis in the early 1990's, when just 1 GW was available.

The Medzamor NPP was shut down in March 1989 in the aftermath of the 1988 earthquake. The NPP is a Soviet-built VVER-440/230 model, which was commissioned in the late 1970's (see chapter 7 on Nuclear Power below). Unit 2 at Medzamor NPP was re-commissioned in 1995, which helped Armenia overcome the energy crisis and gain some degree of energy independence. Given the importance of Medzamor for power supply and independence, there are doubts about closing the plant by 2004 as demanded by international organisations. Total decommissioning costs are estimated at $4 billion, which is beyond the country's financial capacity. A new Tacis project will investigate the decommissioning aspects.

The thermal power plants are designed to run on natural gas or heavy fuel oil (HFO). HFO is used only when gas supplies are interrupted. The installed capacity of thermal power stations is about 1.8 GW, about 55% of capacity. The smallest plant, Vanadzor, is at out of operation. The two larger plants – Hrazdan (1110 MW) and Yerevan (550 MW) – are designed as combined heat and power plants. They supply steam for industry and district heating.

The construction of a fifth unit at Hrazdan (300 MW) has been suspended due to the lack of funds and mismanagement. In 1993, EBRD earmarked a $57 million loan for the unit. The Government is seeking an investor willing to put up $110 million for the completion. EBRD has agreed to another loan, but the Ministry of Finance refused to give a sovereign guarantee. It is uncertain if Unit 5 will ever be completed, although the unit would facilitate the closure of Medzamor NPP by 2004.

Steam and heat production have sharply decreased in the past years, mainly because of the collapse of industrial production. Only 50 MW CHP units are operating at Yerevan and Hrazdan. In the crisis years, district heating broke down because of fuel shortages and the population switched to other fuels – mainly fire wood, kerosene and electricity. Temperatures in residences fell as low as -5°C in the winters. Although the availability of fuel has improved, the district heating network has not yet been restored (with the exception of Yerevan). District heating is unlikely to regain the level it had before the crisis, given the economic advantages of other fuels, the high rehabilitation costs and climatic conditions that make large district heating systems economical less attractive.

As a resource-poor country, hydro-power production has a strategic importance for Armenia. Total capacity of hydro-power is 988 MW and production is concentrated in two large cascades,

Sevan-Hrazdan (550 MW) and **Vorotan** (400 MW). Although Sevan-Hrazdan has a higher capacity than Vorotan, it produces less because of its ageing equipment and the depletion of Lake Sevan. The third large hydro-power system – **Pambak-Dzoraget-Debed** – is relatively undeveloped. In addition, there are several small hydro-power plants with an annual generation of 120 to 130 GWh.

Lake Sevan, which feeds the Sevan-Hrazdan cascade, plays an important role in the Armenian electricity system. Between 1992 and 1994, when the country was relying solely on hydro-power, the forced operation of the cascade lowered the water level of Lake Sevan to ecologically dangerous levels. Sevan-Hrazdan is now running at about half its capacity (about 490 GWh/year), to allow replenishment of the lake. Sevan-Hrazdan will continue to operate at reduced levels until 2007.

Armenia Power Plants

	Units × MW	Year of Commissioning	Generation GWh	
			1996	**1997**
Thermal				
Hrazdan	1110		1561	2273
	2 × 50	1966-67		
	2 × 100	1969		
	3 × 200	1971-74		
	1 × 210	1974		
Yerevan	550		754	758
	5 × 50	1963-65		
	2 × 150	1966-68		
Vanadzor	94	1964-76	2	0
Nuclear				
Medzamor Unit 2	440	1980/95	2	1618
Medzamor Unit 1	440	1976	out of service	
Hydro				
Sevan-Hrazdan Cascade	532			
Sevan	34	1949		
Aterbekian	79	1959		
Argeli	211	1953		
Arzni	67	1956		
Kanaker	96	1936		
Yerevan 1	n.a.	1961		
Yerevan 2	5	1956		
Vorotan Cascade	400	n.a.		
Spandarian	75	1984		
Shamb	168	1977		
Tatev	157	1970		
Sub-total large hydro-power	*n.a.*	*–*	*889*	*760*
Small HPPs	56	1913-54	86	86
Total Capacity	**3182**		**5617**	**5495**

In 1994 the Ministry of Energy elaborated a least-cost plan for the power sector with support from EBRD. The plan was updated in 1996 to take account of the re-opening of the Medzamor NPP. The plan covers the period 1996 to 2010.

The plan envisages the rehabilitation of the large hydro-power stations, the development of new hydro-power facilities with a capacity of 230-250 MW, the construction of SHPPs with a total capacity of 75 MW and the construction of a pumped storage plant. For thermal power plants the investment programme includes the commissioning of a new 300 MW unit at Hrazdan TPP and the refurbishment of Yerevan TPP by using combined-cycle gas turbines (CCGT).

The study also analyses the option of building a new 500 MW nuclear unit, which would replace Medzamor Unit 2, which is scheduled to close in 2004. The scheme would make construction of a CCGT at Yerevan TPP superfluous. The nuclear option, with an estimated cost of $2.11 billion, is hardly affordable by the local industry. The construction of a new NPP would increase the share of expenditures of the electricity sector vs. GDP to 14% (in the case of CCGT to 11%).

The scenario without new nuclear capacity assumes the installation of 3 new CCGT units with a capacity of 176 MW each – two at Yerevan TPP in 2005 and one at Hrazdan TPP in 2008. These turbines would replace obsolete units and will also produce heat for industrial and residential purposes. Cost of this scenario is $1.45 billion.

The following projects are ongoing:

- Emergency repair of the generation and transmission system, approved by the World Bank in 1994 amounted to $14.5 million. The programme includes maintenance of two 200 MW units at Hrazdan TPP, one 150 MW unit at Yerevan TPP, one 100 MW and one 44 MW plant on the Sevan Hrazdan hydro-power cascade, and one 170 MW plant at the Vorotan HP hydro-power cascade.

- Completion of unit 5 at Hrazdan TPP: In 1993, total project costs were estimated at $83 million, of which $57 million were to be financed by EBRD. The project has not been completed although most of the allocated funds have already been spent. Numerous technical and logistical difficulties led to hefty cost overruns. The re-assessment of the project status and cost by independent consultants identified further investment needs of $110 million in order to complete the project. The Government and EBRD are contemplating privatisation of the project. The future of the project remains uncertain, especially since the plant is based on now outdated Russian technology.

- KfW (Germany) finances a $13.9 million rehabilitation of generators and other electrical equipment at Kanaker HPP. The agreement was signed in 1997.

- The World Bank plans to finance a $100 million rehabilitation of the transmission and distribution systems and enhancing metering. The latter component will improve the metering of electricity flows between the generation, transmission and distribution companies. The project would also finance fuel supply (natural gas). The project includes the privatisation of the Yerevan distribution company. The first phase of the project – a $21 million IDA loan – was approved by the World Bank Board in March 1999.

■ There are also plans to construct a new $235 million, 400 MW CCGT plant in Yerevan and a fluidised-bed combustion plant at Hrazdan which would use local coal. Although the latter project would reduce Armenia's import dependence, its economic justification remains doubtful. Armenia has not yet established any coal-mining infrastructure.

■ A Dutch co-operation project on the assessment of the country's wind power potential has started.

Hydro-power is Armenia's only significant indigenous energy resource. Its potential is estimated to be 21.8 TWh a year – 18.6 TWh from large and medium rivers and 3.2 TWh from small rivers. The hydro-power potential, which can be technically harnessed, is about 7 to 9 TWh, of which about 1.5 TWh is exploited (20%). The economically available potential is estimated at 6 TWh.

Electricity Production and Consumption, Outlook

Between 1990 and 1994 electricity generation dropped from 10.3 TWh to 5.6 TWh. Thermal production slumped by 5.8 TWh[1] during that period. Whereas in 1988 thermal power contributed 85% of total supplies, this share fell to 38% by 1994. Nuclear and thermal power production had increased their respective shares back to 27% and 50% of total production by 1997. During the economic embargo hydro-power provided about two thirds of total production, but between 1994 and 1997 hydro-power production declined from 3.5 TWh to 1.4 TWh.

Armenia: Electricity Production by Fuel (GWh)

	1990	**1991**	**1992**	**1993**	**1994**	**1995**	**1996**	**1997**
Oil	8807	5300	3900	546	636	425	127	127
Natural Gas	0	2670	2060	1456	1508	2913	2191	2905
Hydro	1550	1546	3044	4293	3514	1919	1572	1600
Nuclear	0	0	0	0	0	304	2324	1389
Total	10362	9516	9004	6295	5658	5561	6214	6021

The maximum peak demand fell from 2.275 GW in 1988 to 1.260 GW in 1997, which is substantially below the available capacity of 2,2 MW. The Government reckons that the peak of the late 1980's will not be reached before 2010. Given the significant reserve margins, in particular for thermal power stations, Armenia could bolster its currently marginal electricity exports to neighbouring countries.

Electricity consumption in industry dropped from 4.6 TWh in 1988 to less than 600 GWh in 1993, while consumption in the service sector and in agriculture decreased only moderately. As a result of the breakdown of the district heating system and natural gas supply, residential electricity demand grew between 1988 and 1992, but declined in 1993 and 1994 due to rationing. In 1997 electricity demand in the residential sector decreased because of the utilities' efforts to improve collections. In the region of Ararat, for example, electricity consumption dropped about 50% after an efficient metering, billing and collection system was introduced. In 1997, households consumed about 2.1 TWh (49% of total consumption), whereas the share of industry was only 17%.

The Government published short-term electricity supply and demand projections in Decree No. 555 in 1998. Electricity production is expected to increase from 6.3 TWh in 1998 to

1. Hagler Bailly, The Armenian Fuel Sector: Recommendations for Reform, September 1998.

6.7 TWh by 2001 (2.2% annual growth). Electricity consumption should increase from 4.7 TWh to 5.3 TWh (3.3% annual growth). These projections assume a reduction of the distribution losses by 2 percentage points to 9% of electricity production net of own use.

Long-term demand projections assume that electricity demand will increase parallel to GDP by about 6% a year between 1998 and 2010. Electricity consumption would increase from 4.7 TWh in 1998 to about 9.5 TWh by 2010.

Armenia: Electricity Supply and Demand Projections (GWh)

	1990	1992	1994	1996	1998	2000	2005	2010
Net Generation	6592	6469	4479	5583	5919	6573	9361	11822
Import	1700	700	0	0	10	80	130	180
Export	800	400	0	0	300	550	800	1050
Final Consumption	6667	5782	3640	4560	4718	5100	7400	9500

Source: Ministry of Energy.

Electricity Network and Interconnections, Trade and Transit

The Armenian transmission system was designed as part of the Soviet Trans-Caucasus Interconnected System, but has been operating independently since 1991. International connections are the following:

Destination	Power line	Status
Georgia	220 kV (200 MW)	Operational – temporarily out of order as several km of wire were stolen in October 1999.
Iran	220 kV (150 MW)	Completed in 1997, operates synchronously at 50 MW.
Azerbaijan	330 kV (400 MW) + 110 kV (50 MW)	Interrupted because of Nagorny-Karabakh conflict
Azerbaijan (Nagorny-Karabakh)	110 kV	Operational
Turkey	220 kV (250 MW)	Completed in 1987, only used for trials prior to Nagorny-Karabakh conflict
Azerbaijan (Nakhichevan)	2 × 220 kV (500 MW)	Out of service

Armenia has 1300 km of 220 kV lines and 3200 km of 110 kV lines. During the energy crisis, Armenergo operated its 110 kV lines primarily as a radial network, which allowed better control of electricity rationing. This decreased the system's stability. The re-opening of the Medzamor nuclear plant in 1995 forced the utility to operate parts of the 110 kV lines as a meshed network to achieve the frequency stability required for the operation of the nuclear plant. Nevertheless, network stabilisation is still a concern for the safe operation of Medzamor (See Map 6: Trans-Caucasus Power System).

The low voltage distribution lines have a length of about 40,000 km, with about 9,000 transformers supplying over 780,000 end-users. The Armenian distribution system operates at 35, 10, 6 and 0.4 kV levels. Most of the consumption is metered. However the meters are generally not suited for a more flexible end-user price schedule that allows for time-of-day tariffication.

Until 1991, Armenia exported about 4 TWh to Azerbaijan and Georgia. Exports to Azerbaijan were halted at the outbreak of the Karabakh conflict. Armenia currently exports some electricity to Georgia and indirectly (via Georgia) to Turkey. It also engages in seasonal electricity swaps with Iran. Furthermore, Armenian electricity is delivered to Nagorny-Karabakh and the so-called Lachin corridor[1].

The Government emphasises the importance of re-integrating Armenia into a regional energy market. Various interconnections and spare transmission capacity would allow Armenia to become again a net exporter. Since Medzamor went on-line again, Armenia could export up to 300 MW during summer. Exports would also allow Medzamor to run more efficiently until it is decommissioned. After completion of Unit 5 at Sevan-Hrazdan, up to 500 MW could be exported.

Electricity Prices

The electricity sector reform has enhanced the financial performance of the sector, but the sector remains financially weak. Tariffs need to be adjusted and payment discipline enforced for utilities to operate soundly and invest in overdue modernisation. Decree 555 allows the Ministry of Finance, the Ministry of Energy and the Ministry of Privatisation to distribute sales revenues among generation, transmission and distribution companies. In the past the generators received only a small percentage of their sales in cash, as revenues paid to distributors did not make their way up the payment chain to the generators.

The Energy Law entrusts tariff-setting powers to the Regulatory Commission (for details, see above Chapter 2.2. Energy Policy and Legislation). Electricity tariffs are uniform across the country and differentiated according to the voltage level and consumer groups. They range from 15 Dram/kWh for residential consumers of less than 100 kWh per month consumption to 20 Dram/kWh for medium-sized industries. Although rates have increased more for households than for industry since August 1997, household tariffs are generally still lower than for industry. This indicates that cross-subsidies between consumer groups still exist.

The Regulatory Commission also sets maximum prices for generators. These prices range from 1.4 Dram/kWh for the Vorotan HPP to 16.3 Dram/kWh of the Yerevan TPP. The average price of Armenenergo sales to the distribution companies is 15.3 Dram/kWh.

Armenia: Electricity Tariffs, Dram/kWh (September 1998)

Selling price of: – Vorotan HPP	1.37
– Sevan-Hrazdan HPP	4.21
– Small HPPs	13.00
– Hrazdan TPP	15.48
– Yerevan TPP	16.26
– Medzamor NPP	12.37
– Armenenergo to distribution companies	15.34
Sales at 35 kV level and higher	16.00
Sales at 6 and 10 kV levels	20.00
Sales to 0.4 kV customers: – up to 100 kWh a month	15.00
– between 100 and 250 kWh a month	22.00
– for each kWh above 250 kWh and other 0.4 kV customers	25.00

Source: Resolution No. 6 of the Energy Regulatory Commission.

1. Territory between the enclave and Armenia, which is occupied by Armenian forces.

The collection ratios have increased for households and the commercial sector to 90% or higher, also because of a substantially improved service level (continuous electricity supply). However, they remain low (50 to 75%) in the public sector, for example for state companies, water utilities, industries, budgetary institutions and agriculture (irrigation). Overall collections increased from merely 35% in 1994 to 70% in 1998. The financial performance of the electricity sector is eroded by large non-technical losses, which were about 17% of production in 1998. As a result of insufficient collection, Armenergo is unable to fully pay generators; e.g. the privatised small hydro-power plants have been paid only 25% on average.

NUCLEAR POWER

Structure of Nuclear Utility

Armenia is highly dependent on nuclear energy. The contribution of Medzamor Unit 2 to total Armenian electricity production is in the order of 33% (37% in 1996, 26% in 1997).

The first unit of **Medzamor** NPP (35 km west of the capital Yerevan) was connected to the grid in 1976, the second unit in December 1979. The units are two pressurised light water reactors of Soviet VVER 440/230 design. The plant was shut down in March 1989 in the aftermath of the 1988 earthquake. In 1995, Unit 2 was re-commissioned after a period of power shortage. Several safety enhancement programmes have been launched with the objective to operate the unit until alternative power sources are available. Unit 1 was partly "cannibalised" to re-commission Unit 2, which will make it difficult, if not impossible to restart Unit 1.

The Armenian Nuclear Regulatory Authority (ANRA) was established on 16 November 1993, as an independent governmental body. The Head of ANRA reports directly to the Prime Minister. ANRA is organised in compliance with international recommendations. International organisations have conducted several inspections and an international advisory committee is available to ANRA. The main tasks of ANRA are:

- To initiate nuclear safety legislation;

- To develop, approve and put into action norms and regulations in the field of atomic energy use;

- To implement with the purpose of safety provision licensing activities in the field of atomic energy use;

- To conduct inspections connected with implementation of authorisations;

- To ensure that Armenia complies with its international commitments in the field of nuclear safety.

The law on "The safe utilisation of nuclear energy for peaceful purposes" was prepared by ANRA and approved by the International Legal Group in February 1997. It passed parliament in October 1998. It defines the legal basis and principles of the management and regulation of the process of nuclear energy utilisation and is intended for the protection of public health, life, property, and the environment. Armenia has signed and ratified the Convention on Nuclear Safety.

Operation of Medzamor NPP

The nuclear power plant is state-owned by law. The operating organisation reports to the Ministry of Energy under the Department of Atomic Energy. Training in nuclear operation is offered at the University of Technology of Yerevan. For the two blocks approximately 2000 staff were employed up until 1989. Since only one unit is in operation, staff has been reduced. Management is 100% Armenian. The fuel and many spares come from Russia. There have been difficulties with less-than-optimal fuel batches, requiring the plant to re-fuel earlier than planned. Framatome has installed a dry storage facility for FF40 m.

Twenty-three events were reported to ANRA from the re-start of Unit 2 in 1995 until November 1998. Two incidents were rated level 2 and four level 1 on the international INES scale. The two highest rated events occurred during 1998. Reports of the events are made available to the international community via IAEA/NEA Incident Reporting System, IRS. An international mission to enhance event analysis was carried out by IAEA in 1998.

The operation of Medzamor-2 is connected to certain conditions. EBRD granted a loan for Unit 5 of the Hrazdan thermal plant with the aim that it would contribute to replacing Medzamor-2. The initial time frame for completing Hrazdan-5 (and de-commissioning Medzamor-2) was 2004. But work at Hrazdan has been delayed and the unit is not likely to be completed by that date. Furthermore, Armenian officials regard 2004 for the closure of Medzamor-2 as premature given the safety upgrades that have been made, and advocate extending the unit's life until 2010-14.

Nuclear Safety Aspects

The VVER-440/230 type was developed in the Soviet Union between 1956 and 1970. The heat from the primary circuit is removed in six coolant loops using horizontal steam generators, which is probably the most specific feature of all VVERs. The secondary side of steam generators contains large water volumes covering the heat transfer tubes, which are horizontally placed between the hot and cold collectors. The steam generators can be isolated by main gate valves (MGV) located in both the hot and cold legs. The MGVs isolate the primary coolant pumps as well, however the connecting tubes of the pressuriser and emergency core cooling injection are not isolated. The MGVs allows the operators to take one or more of the six loops out of service in case of emergency. The accident localisation system, which serves as a reactor confinement, was designed to handle only one 100 mm pipe rupture. If a large loss of coolant accident happens, this system vents directly to the environment through safety flaps, which open at 0.2-0.5 bar overpressure. The confinement has small volume, poor leak-tightness and poor hydrogen mitigation. The VVER-440/230 has no emergency core-cooling systems and auxiliary feedwater systems similar to those required in Western plants. The plant instrumentation and control, safety systems, fire-protection systems, quality of materials, construction, operating procedures and personnel training are below western standards. The VVER-440 core has low power density, which is a positive feature regarding severe accident progression.

The Medzamor plant safety has been upgraded with help from the Armenian budget, a Russian loan, the US DOE, Tacis and France. The list of safety measures for Unit 2 is long. Some are fulfilled and some in progress, whilst others are still under discussion. Only some achievements are listed here:

■ Elaboration and approval of list of Design Basis Accidents, DBA and beyond DBA for Unit 2;

■ Analysis of all DBA and beyond DBA on the basis of modern techniques;

■ Implementation of measures connected with reactor vessel integrity;

■ Implementation of additional interlocks and reactor protections on coolant level steam generator and pressuriser;

■ Installation of additional valves on the high-pressure injection pipeline to the primary circuit;

■ Establishment of steam/gas mixture removal from SG headers in emergency situations;

■ Seismological investigation of the site, buildings and equipment, verification of the site seismicity;

■ Reinforcement of buildings, the non-hermetic part of the reactor, electrical racks and cabinets, service water pumping station etc.;

■ Installation of new type of batteries;

■ Investigation to identify which of existing equipment should be replaced (cables and equipment);

■ Dismounting of pipeline with a diameter 200 mm of hot water injection to pressuriser;

■ Loading of reactor with reduced neutron flow to the reactor vessel.

The following measures are in progress or mooted:

■ Establishment of a two channel system for essential service water supply;

■ Replacement of non seismic resistant relays in the emergency and technological protection systems;

■ Measures to enhance the plant security;

■ Elaboration of design for the spent fuel storage and its implementation.

■ General operational safety and on site assistance;

■ Training programs for plant personnel;

■ Primary circuit integrity verification;

■ Multifunctional simulator;

■ Improvements to fire protection system;

■ Leak detection system between primary and secondary loops;

■ Replacements of valves;

■ Confinement tightness improvement;

■ Spare components from Greifwald NPP (former East Germany).

V. GEORGIA

GEORGIA AT A GLANCE

Population	5.28 million (1998)
Area	69,700 km²
Capital	Tbilisi
President	Eduard Shevardnadze (next election in April 2000)
Currency	$ = 2.06 Lari (100 Tetri) (November 1999)

Georgia is recovering from a collapse of the (official) economy due to civil strife and secessionist wars in Abkhazia and South Ossetia in the first half of the 1990's. Recorded TPES dwindled some 85% from 10.6 mtoe in 1990 to 1.4 mtoe in 1995, before slow growth resumed again. Georgia has so far been successful in establishing itself as an important transit corridor for Azeri and Kazakh "early" oil to western markets. This harbingers well for the country to funnel future large exports of Caspian oil and possibly gas to the West. Chances of Russian overland gas exports to Turkey crossing Georgia look more remote. The Soviet legacy and years of turmoil have taken their toll on the country's power sector. The share of thermal electricity output, which accounted for almost 45% of total power in the early 1990's, dwindled to 15%, because of the country's incapacity to pay for Russian gas imports and inadequate plant maintenance. Hydro-power, however, has declined "only" 20%, but represents the country's unique major domestic energy source for the future. With proper investment, generation capacity could be rehabilitated to 5 GW and another 1.7 GW of new capacity could be built, which would amply cover future domestic demand and support peak loads in neighbouring countries. The sale of Telasi distribution company, which supplies Tbilisi (about 40% of the national market), to AES (US) is a test case for the country's transition to a market-based economy. AES's first year of experience at Telasi has been positive enough for the company to bid for three generation companies.

POLITICAL AND ECONOMIC OVERVIEW

Recent Economic Developments

Georgia became independent in April 1991 and was quickly entangled in civil war between 1992 and 1994, following the overthrow of the first democratically elected head of state Gamsakhurdia. In addition, Georgia was divided by separatist struggles in Abkhazia (north-west Georgia) and South-Ossetia (north-central Georgia). Sporadic hostilities continue in these regions, most recently in March 1998 in Abkhazia. Unlike Abkhazia, the third major autonomous region, Adjaria (south-western Georgia and bordering Turkey), has had no separatist aspirations so far. The growing antagonism between the Adjar leader Abashidze, now President Shevardnadze's main political opponent, has strained the relations between Adjaria and Tbilisi.

Eduard Shevardnadze, the former Minister of Foreign Affairs of the Soviet Union, returned to his native country in March 1992. He won the presidential election in November 1995.

Political stability has increased since the cease-fire with Abkhazia in 1994. Under President Shevardnadze's leadership, the government has restored law and order in most parts of the country. Georgia has kept good relations with all its neighbours, including Russia, and has developed close economic ties with Turkey and Azerbaijan.

Growing political stability helped the country to overcome the economic crisis, which has plagued Georgia since 1990. Georgia suffered not only from the collapse of the Soviet economic system leading to higher prices for basic commodities, including energy, but also from the disruption of traditional trade routes. The war in Abkhazia cut trade links with Russia and what energy supplies got through were prohibitively expensive. Around one-half of the country's economic activity went underground and the tax base shrank from over 40% to less than 10% of GDP.

In 1997, economic output grew by 11%, the highest rate in the CIS. Because of the Russian financial crisis, GDP growth slowed down in 1998 (4%), is expected to reach 3-4% in 1999, and rebound to 6% in 2000. Dry weather in 1998 also sharply reduced agricultural output and electricity production. Private sector participation in production grew substantially, from 20% in 1994 to 65% in 1997. Annual inflation reached a maximum of more than 10,000% in 1994, but declined to about 40% in 1996, and to just 7.3 in 1997, mainly due to strict monetary policy. Inflation is expected to reach 19% in 1999, before dropping back to a single-digit figure in 2000.

Georgia's trade deficit has widened, because of the Russian crisis and the rise in economic activity, leading to an increase in imports of consumer and capital goods, mainly associated with the rehabilitation of the "early oil" pipeline from Baku to Supsa at the Black Sea. Russia remains Georgia's main trading partner, accounting for about 14% of its total trade. Trade and transit are a major driver of economic recovery in Georgia. The country lies at the heart of the **Traceca** transport corridor, an EU funded project designed to revitalise the ancient "silk road" trade route[1].

Georgia still faces major challenges. Infrastructure, after years of deterioration and war damage, poses a serious obstacle to economic development. Also, the shadow economy and bribery

Main Economic Indicators

	Unit	1997	1998	1999*
GDP growth	%	11.0	4.0	3.0
GDP	$ million	7730.0	8425.0	
GDP per capita	$ per person	1498.1	1649.1	
Industrial gross output	%	8.1	–2.8	
Unemployment rate	%	7.8	10.6	
Consumer Price (annual average)	%	7.0	3.7	20.0
Foreign Direct Investment	US	189.0	219.0	116.0
FDI per capita	$ per person	36.6	47.8	22.9

Source: EBRD, CEPII, EIU.   * Preliminary estimates.

---

1.   The Traceca project (**TRA**nsport **C**orridor **E**urope-**C**aucasus-**A**sia) was launched in 1993 to create a Europe-Caucasus-Asia transport corridor. Twenty-seven nations signed in September 1998 the "Baku Declaration" with the aim to implement the Great Silk Road programme, giving Caucasian and Central Asian nations access to existing Trans-European and Asian transport networks.

need to be reduced and tax collection enhanced. Low state revenues are threatening the sustainability of macroeconomic stabilisation. The country has one of the lowest ratios of tax to gross domestic product on any non-oil producing country in the world, indicating an exceptionally large shadow economy. The problem has been recognised by the government and reforms in tax and customs administration in the last three years have already tripled tax revenues (as a percentage of GDP).

Privatisation and Restructuring

Georgia began to restructure the industrial sector in 1995. By June 1996, small-scale privatisation involving nearly 10,000 firms mainly in trade and retail sectors, was officially completed. Early in 1997, about half of the medium-sized and large companies earmarked for privatisation had been sold, mostly through management and employee buy-outs and voucher auctions.

In May 1997, a new law was introduced to speed up the privatisation process to encourage direct sales rather than auctions. In August 1997, the President abolished a decree suspending the privatisation of "strategic" enterprises – a group of about 50 enterprises mostly in heavy industry. These are now being privatised on a case-by-case basis. Some were sold at a zero price and others through tender and auctions, such as the country's largest iron and steel plant in January 1998. By April 1998, some 880 medium- and large-scale enterprises had been privatised.

The Government has announced that it will concentrate on the privatisation of energy, telecommunication and the transport sectors. Privatisation of the energy sector took off in October 1998 with the sale of Telasi, the largest electricity distribution company in Tbilisi, to US company AES. Other distribution companies and power stations are now up for sale (see above Chapter on the Electricity Law).

Georgia is actively encouraging foreign investment, which has been gradually rising since the civil strife stopped in 1996. Preliminary estimates for 1998 put FDI figures at $244 million. About a third of the foreign investment was directed at the rehabilitation of the Baku-Supsa oil pipeline. Most FDI came from the US, the UK, Russia, Azerbaijan and Norway.

THE ENERGY SECTOR

Energy Overview

The economic collapse and civil war severely disturbed the country's energy infrastructure. The interruption of traditional trade links with Russia that supplied most of the country's oil and gas needs and the incapacity to pay for energy imports resulted in a severe energy crisis, in particular in the electricity sector.

Georgia is poorly endowed with energy resources, making it overwhelmingly dependent on imports. In 1997, the country imported 80% of its energy needs (TPES), mostly as oil products and gas. There are some oil fields in western and eastern Georgia, but known oil reserves are only 12 mt. Some oil could be discovered on the yet undrilled narrow Black Sea shelf. There is little natural gas production, making Georgia dependent on imports from Russia (imports from Turkmenistan stopped in 1997). But even under optimistic assumptions concerning hydrocarbons exploration, Georgia will remain dependent on its neighbours for most of its oil and gas needs.

Main Energy Indicators

		1995	**1996**	**1997**
TPES	mtoe	1.469	2.112	2.295
Net imports	mtoe	0.904	1.466	1.665
Net oil imports	mtoe	0.104	0.805	0.883
Net gas imports	mtoe	0.729	0.631	0.765
Electricity production	GWh	6,900	7,226	7,172
TPES/GDP	toe per thousand 90$ PPP	0.26	0.34	0.33
TPES/Population	toe per capita	0.27	0.39	0.42
CO_2 Emission from Fuel Comb.	mt of CO_2	2.30	4.20	4.59
CO_2/TPES	t CO_2 per toe	1.56	1.99	2.00
CO_2/GDP	t CO_2 per 1990 $ PPP	0.41	0.68	0.67
CO_2/Population	t CO_2 per capita	0.42	0.78	0.85

Source: IEA.

Hydro-power is the country's main domestic energy source, accounting for 23% of TPES or 75% of domestic energy production in 1997. Hydro-power plants need extensive rehabilitation. The Georgian government has kept control over the country's largest hydro-power plant at Inguri, but has to share Inguri's capacity with the Abkhazian secessionist power, who controls the transmission lines from the plant. The rehabilitation of existing hydro-power stations, the construction of new facilities and securing fuel supplies for thermal power stations is essential for the country to overcome the still difficult economic situation. Georgia has enough hydro-power potential to become a net exporter of electricity in the medium term.

Figure 11   Georgia Energy Balance (1997)

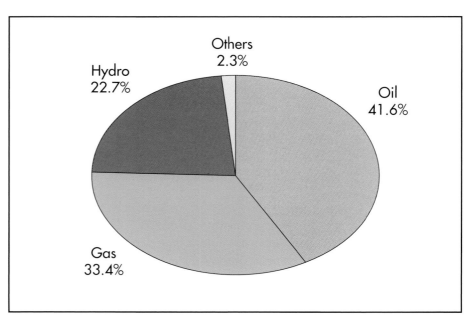

Source: IEA.

Figure 12   Georgia TPES (1990-97)

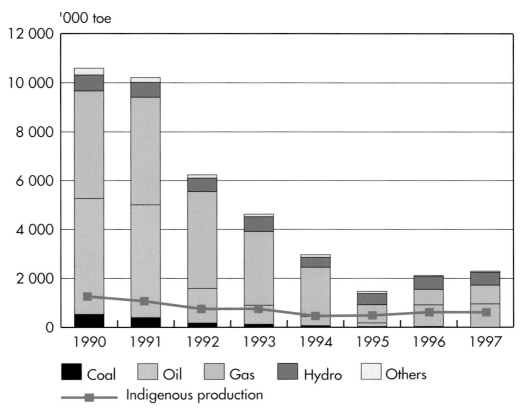

Source: IEA.

Georgia has coal reserves of around 450 mt. Peak coal production was 3.5 mt in 1956, but has since dropped to less than 30,000 tons. Low quality and largely uneconomic coal is mined in ten underground mines in Tkibuli, Tkvarcheli (under Abkhazian control) and Akhaltsikhe near the Turkish border. The last open-cast mine was closed in 1998.

Energy supply has dramatically declined in the 1990's: TPES slumped from 10.59 mtoe in 1990 to 1.47 mt in 1995, before recovering to 2.3 mt in 1997. Electricity output declined 40% from 11.5 TWh in 1992 to 6.8 TWh in 1994, and rebounded to 7.1 TWh in 1997. According to projections by the Georgian Energy Research Institute, energy consumption will not reach its 1990 level before 2005.

Georgia is important to world energy markets because of its location as an oil and gas transit corridor between the resource-rich Caspian region and western markets. With the start of the first deliveries of oil through the Baku-Supsa pipeline in late spring 1999, Georgia will collect approximately $8-10 million a year of transit fees.

Energy Policy and Legislation

Primary responsibility for energy policy lies with the **Ministry of Fuel and Energy** (MOFE), although some conflicts and lack of co-operation appear to exist concerning responsibility for energy policy with the Ministry of Economy. The Ministry of Economy is responsible for the regulation of gas pricing and for the collection of energy indicators and balances. In addition, the Ministry of Economy imposes an informal control (which is not set out in the Electricity Law) on the electricity pricing proposals made by the National Electricity Regulatory Commission. The Council in the President's Office (President's Council) also plays an important decision-making role, circumventing several layers of bureaucracy in state run companies.

Electricity Law

The Electricity Law of July 1997 established the National Electricity Regulatory Commission (NERC) and separated policy-making (the responsibility of MOFE) from regulation, operation, and ownership. The Law established NERC as an independent body, "not subordinated in any way ... to any other governmental or private agency or institution". NERC (which follows the US Public Utility Commission model) has three members who are appointed by the President for six-year terms, with a two term maximum time limit. The Law also sets out MOFE's policy-making prerogatives with regard to the electricity sector. The main functions of the ministry are:

- Elaborating electricity programmes based on short, medium, and long-term strategies, and priorities, and co-ordinating their implementation;

- Promoting inward investment into the electricity sector;

- Promoting the restructuring and privatisation of State enterprises in the sector;

- Co-ordinate the preparation and implementation of programmes to improve efficiency in generation, transmission, and consumption of electricity;

- Promote environmental protection;

- Promote the establishment of transit and import/export relationships;

- Develop state strategies for electricity supply in crisis situations.

The Law specifically states that "The Ministry of Fuel and Energy shall relinquish ownership, regulatory, and operational rights in the electricity sector". MOFE, however, is responsible for the granting of permits regarding the siting of generation facilities and transmission facilities.

NERC has the following rights and responsibilities:

- To set the rules and requirements for generation, transmission, dispatch, and distribution licences;

- To grant, modify, or revoke generation, transmission, dispatch, and distribution licenses;

- To set wholesale and retail tariffs for electricity generation, transmission, dispatch distribution, and consumption;

- To arbitrate in disputes between Licensees in generation, transmission, dispatch, and distribution; and between Licensees and consumers;

- To monitor the compliance with the conditions of Licenses, and to impose sanctions for non-compliance where necessary.

NERC is financed through license fees. The Commission has issued interim 2-year licenses for 90% of the utilities (accounting for 98% of total capacity). NERC is preparing indefinite licenses for transmission, dispatch and distribution, and for the planned remaining plant lifetime for generation.

The Electricity Law spells out the tariff-setting principles to be used by NERC. One principle is that tariffs should allow for a return on invested capital sufficiently attractive for investment into rehabilitation and further development of the sector. Another provision prohibits cross-subsidisation from one category of consumers to another. Cross-subsidies have existed from industrial to residential consumers, although the June 1999 recent price increase to 9 Tetri/kWh (about 4.5 UScents) for all consumers has reduced this cross-subsidy. NERC planned to increase end-user prices to full cost recovery and to remove cross-subsidy between consumer classes by the end of 1999.

Oil & Gas Law

In April 1999 Parliament passed a new Oil and Gas Law, which governs exploration, production, transportation, and marketing of oil and gas and also formalises the responsibilities of domestic and foreign industry participants. The law became effective in May 1999. It covers licensing and provides the legal basis for production-sharing agreements (PSA's). Existing agreements will be grandfathered, unless both parties choose to re-structure the project under the new legislation. In September 1999, the tax regime for foreign oil & gas investors was eased: corporate profit tax was reduced from 10% to 4% and equipment imports were exempted from VAT.

The Oil and Gas Law establishes a State Agency for the Regulation of Oil and Gas Resources, which will organise acreage tenders, negotiate on behalf of the government and administer the state share in oil and gas production. At present, exploration and production licences are issued by the Ministry of Fuel and Energy (MOFE), but agreements must also be agreed with the Ministry of Finance, the Ministry of Environment and Natural Resources, and the Ministry of Economy.

A law on the planning, construction, and use of pipelines is being drafted in connection with the development of a Trans-Caucasus corridor, linking the Caspian Region with the Black Sea. At present the regulatory responsibility for pipelines rests with the Georgia International Oil Corporation (GIOC), which was set up by a Presidential Order. GIOC fulfils both a commercial and a regulatory function. The Government wants GIOC to become a purely commercial company (the government considers privatising 20-35% of GIOC) and to split off the regulatory functions. GIOC is working with USAID to develop legislation on eminent domain, double taxation avoidance treaties, environmental impact assessment, and environmental liabilities, all of which are missing in the Georgian legislation.

Oversight of the gas industry is the responsibility of MOFE, but the remit of NERC was extended in 1999 to cover natural gas production, transit and distribution. End-user gas prices for captive consumers are currently set by the Ministry of Economy in consultation with MOFE.

Draft Energy Policy

A formal energy policy is being drafted. The principal goals of the long-term energy strategy are as follows:

■ Development of competition, with the establishment of open markets for oil, gas, and electricity; creation of a stable investment climate; support of transit flows and liberalisation of international energy trade;

■ Improved taxation and price setting mechanisms, regulation, and improved energy forecasting and energy planning. This should be within the context of the goals of improved energy efficiency, the development of renewable energy sources, and the improvement of environmental protection;

■ Improvement of the legal and regulatory framework for the energy sector, based on the principle of transparency of the operation of the legal and regulatory system.

The energy policy lists the chief priorities for the short and medium term as:

■ Completing re-structuring and privatisation;

■ Improving energy regulation;

■ Improving tariff collection and market-based pricing;

■ Improving energy forecasting and energy planning;

■ Establishing a legislative and regulatory framework for the reformed energy sector.

By sector, the short-to-medium-term actions foreseen in the energy policy are:

Electricity	• Rehabilitation and modernisation of existing hydropower plants, Gardabani thermal plant, Tbilisi and Rustavi CHP plants, and increasing production capacity up to 18-20 TWh (i.e. about 2.5 times electricity generated in 1997); • Increasing efficiency and reliability of the Georgian power system through integration with the power systems of neighbouring countries; • Elaboration of a master plan for the development of the power sector; • Start of construction of a power plant using Tkibuli coal; • Construction of wind turbines.
Oil & gas production, oil refining and transportation	• Promote oil and gas exploration and production to attain production levels increasing of up to 0.7-1.0 mt/year of oil and 0.5-0.6 bcm/year. The oil production target looks ambitious, compared to the 0.13 mt of oil produced in 1997. • Development of the oil and oil-product transportation system (including transit); • Modernisation of oil refining capacity to a capacity of 6-7 mt/year (vs. some 5.1 mt/year at present); • Provision of a strategic state oil product reserve.
Natural Gas	• Rehabilitation and modernisation of infrastructure (including the development of metering system) to increase annual gas supplies to domestic consumers up to 5 bcm; • Improvement of reliability and economic efficiency of natural gas supply by optimal use of transit pipelines; • Design and construction of natural gas storage.
Coal	• Rehabilitation and modernisation of the Georgian coal mining industry to raise production to a level of 0.7-0.8 mt/year; this level is comparable to the one of the early 1990's. Given the low quality of the coal and geological conditions, there are doubts whether domestic coal can be profitably mined. • Creation of a strategic (state) coal reserve.
Heat supply[1]	• Development of district heating based on natural gas base; • Using Georgian coal for heating and cooking in areas not supplied through the natural gas grid; • Use of geothermal energy and development of solar power and heat pumps.
Energy efficiency[2]	• Design and implementation of an energy efficiency improvement programme for energy-intensive industry; • Design and implementation of programmes to improve the energy efficiency of existing buildings.

1. The district heating system is largely obsolete and damaged. The high repair costs and the relatively mild Georgian climate make it doubtful to justify the reconstruction of the large-scale, Soviet-type district heating system.

2. A draft energy efficiency law and strategy was prepared and funded by the EU Tacis programme in 1997-99, but the MOFE failed to follow up on it. A new energy efficiency law is now being drafted with assistance from USAID. The current economic conditions in the country, notably the structure of energy tariffs and bill collection, are not propitious for fostering energy efficiency. The Energy Efficiency Centre, which was funded by Tacis in 1998, is targeting niche projects with major consumers.

Energy Projections

Official energy projections are shown in the table below. They postulate that overall energy consumption will more than double in the coming fifteen years or increase by a factor 1.5 above the level of 1990. This assumption is debatable, insofar as it may not sufficiently take into consideration the country's potential for improving energy efficiency. The forecast minimises energy imports by banking on a 20-fold increase of oil production and 10-fold increase of gas production, which are both unlikely to occur within the forecast period. Hydro-power is set to rise 1.6 times above 1997 levels. The coal production target for 2015 is merely 0.348 mt, less than half the objective quoted in the draft energy strategy. The economic viability of massive increases in coal mining is questioned.

But even under this (over-)optimistic forecast, which underscores efforts to boost domestic energy production, massive increases in energy imports are inevitable: oil imports are set to increase 1.2 times and gas imports almost six-fold!

Georgia: Energy Supply and Demand Projections

	'000 toe	1993	1995	1997	2000	2005	2010	2015
Oil	Production	43	44	138	721	2060	2266	2575
	Net Imports	2594	2278	2952	3914	3090	3399	3605
	Consumption	2637	2322	3090	4635	5150	5665	6180
Coal	Production	34	18	2	41	205	287	348
	Net Imports	144	20	0	0	0	0	0
	Consumption	178	38	2	41	205	287	348
Natural Gas	Production	40	0	0	240	400	480	560
	Net Imports	2934	728	758	2320	3200	4000	4400
	Consumption	2974	728	758	2560	3600	4480	4960
Hydro-power	Production	1773	1652	1638	1773	2122	2470	2686
	Consumption	1773	1652	1638	1773	2122	2470	2686
Other	Consumption	800	1300	1300	850	900	1000	1100
Total	**Production**	1890	1714	1778	2775	4787	5503	6169
	Net Imports	5672	3026	3710	6234	6290	7399	8005
	Consumption	8362	6040	6788	9859	11977	13902	15274

Source: Georgian Energy Research Institute.

Tacis has produced a more moderate forecast:

	1990	1997	2010		Change 2010/1997 (ref. case, %)
			High case	Reference case	
TPES (mtoe)	12	3.2	9.5	7	+118%
Final energy consumption (mtoe)	8.5	2.3	6.5	5	+117%
Electricity supply (TWh)	14	7.5	12	10	+ 33%
Electricity demand (TWh)*	10.5	4.4	7	6	+ 36%

* Losses not included.
Source: Ministry of Economy, Black Sea Energy Centre review, Tacis EEC.

Investment Framework

Georgia has made significant progress in improving the conditions for foreign investors. Although foreign investment in Georgia is still modest, investors are showing increasing interest because of gains in security and stability. Georgia is encouraging direct foreign investment through its privatisation process, new projects, joint ventures and greenfield opportunities.

The Government has adopted key legislation to create a stable and predictable legal and institutional system. In general, laws do not discriminate between foreign and local investors. Industrial land can be purchased or leased up to 99 years. Unlimited foreign ownership in most sectors is allowed, but there are some limits applying to infrastructure, including gas and oil pipelines and power transmission.

The Law on Promotion and Guarantees of Investments and the Law on Entrepreneurship (both passed in November 1996) are the most important legal acts applying to foreign investments.

The Law on Promotion and Guarantee of Investments (Law on Investments) creates the legal basis for domestic and foreign investments and guarantees their protection. It allows unlimited repatriation of capital and profits and places no limitation on holding foreign currency bank accounts. Parliament may, however, prohibit foreign investment into some sectors.

The Foreign Investment Law bans the expropriation of investments, except for cases involving natural disasters, force majeure and epidemic emergency. In any case of expropriation, the government must offer due compensation. Furthermore, all investors are guaranteed equal treatment. Foreign investors are afforded privileges, such as: full profit repatriation and free hard-currency conversion; the right to refer to ICSID arbitration or to any international arbitration agency established in accordance with arbitration rules of UNCITRAL if the dispute is not considered at ICSID.

In June 1997 the Georgian Tax Code was adopted. The corporate tax in Georgia is 20% for all types of businesses. The withholding tax for dividends and interests is 10%. In addition, there is a company property tax of 1% of the value of the company's property. VAT is applied to transactions with goods and services at a rate of 20%. Certain goods including fuels are liable to excise tax. Transit, re-export and export of goods are exempt from VAT and excise tax. Corporations are also subject to a 27% social security contribution, a 1% unemployment contribution, and a 3% health protection contribution.

The Georgian Law on Bankruptcy Proceeding came into force of 1 January 1997. According to the law, a legal or physical person can be declared bankrupt by court upon submission of an application by the insolvent person or any of its creditors. The law does not grant any priority rights for local creditors over foreign creditors, the State or any other entities.

An Anti-monopoly Policy Department was established in 1992 and a new Law on Monopolistic Activity and Competition was enacted in 1996. Consumer and anti-trust laws were also passed in 1996. Through the adoption of these laws, the legislative basis for competitive markets was established, also eliminating existing government restrictions on competition in some markets.

The 1997 Law on Privatisation of State Property replaced all previous legislation on privatisation and establishes the legal, economic, organisational and social basis for privatisation of the state property, except for land and state household asset. The list of companies to be privatised is to be approved by the Ministry of State Property Management in conjunction with the Ministry of Economy and with corresponding ministries and agencies. Among others, certain economic activities of relevance to the energy sector are excluded from privatisation: these include mineral and water resources, state emergency stocks, state reserves, electricity transmission and dispatching services, and main gas pipelines.

State property may be sold through auction, tender, lease with the purchase right and direct sale. No preference is given to Georgian citizens as such but employees or pensioners. Company-registered unemployed receive for free up to 10% of registered capital, but not exceeding 100 times the minimum salary fixed in Georgia.

THE OIL SECTOR

Oil and Gas Policy

The main aim of Georgian energy policy is the development of oil and gas transit. This aspiration is linked with the other central tenets of Georgian policy, such as diversification and security of supply, finance for oil and gas purchases, and the development and rehabilitation of oil, gas and power infrastructure.

The legislative programme includes laws regulating the planning, construction and use of transit pipelines and production. First drafts were presented to the Georgian parliament in 1998. The government has already established the **Georgian International Oil Company (GIOC)** and **Saktransgas** to manage international oil and gas transit issues. The proposed legislation on transit pipelines is expected to clarify the roles of these companies, the regulatory regime and tariff issues. GIOC was set up to promote Georgia as a gateway for oil exports from the Caspian region. In addition, the company plans to become involved in upstream projects.

The state-company **Saknavtobi** is responsible for oil and gas upstream activities. It represents the state interest in any joint upstream project with foreign companies.

The existing pipeline infrastructure is owned by **Saknavtprodukti**, which is a state-owned company responsible for oil product storage and transportation. In addition, Saknavtprodukti concludes agreements for imports of refined petroleum products.

The Oil and Gas Law, which came into effect in May 1999, deals with licensing and exploration and production agreements. Until now contracts have been negotiated on a case-by-case basis by the President's Council. The new law should lead to more formalised procedures and greater clarity in terms of departmental responsibilities. The favoured type of contract are Production-Sharing Agreements (PSAs). Contracts, which were signed prior to the promulgation of the law, will not be negatively affected. Most of these contracts, have been or are being converted into PSAs.

Oil and Gas Exploration and Production

Oil and gas developments in Georgia have long been influenced by activity in and around Azerbaijan, using Georgia as the main transit country to access markets. At the end of the 19th century, up to 20% of the world's oil production flowed to world markets through the Georgian Black Sea port of Batumi.

E&P activity in Georgia commenced in 1930, with production increasing up until the early 1980's, when it peaked at over 3 mt/year. However, production has been below 0.2 mt/year since 1985, with no new oil fields coming on stream since. Production has been at a level of 130,000 t over the past few years. 1999 output is expected to be as low as 70,000 t.

Saknavtobi estimates ultimate oil resources at 580 mt (4.2 billion bbl), including 200 mt (1.4 billion bbl) offshore. These are highly inflated figures, in view of the country's exploration maturity and cumulative oil production to-date (26.5 mt, i.e. only 4.6% of expected ultimate resources). More realistically, remaining proven commercial reserves have been reported at 12 mt. Gas reserves are officially pegged at 98 bcm – also an unlikely figure if compared to cumulative gas production of 0.4 bcm.

Prior to the collapse of the Soviet Union, E&P funding came from the Ministry of Geology and of Oil in Moscow. When this source dried up, domestic E&P activity came to a halt between 1991 and 1994. The government invited foreign companies to explore, but the response has not been enthusiastic given the country's limited exploration potential.

By now, practically all prospective parts of the country, both on- and offshore, are covered by licences or are under negotiation. No major oil company has ventured into Georgia[1]. International E&P players are small start-up companies from the UK (JKX, Ramco), US (Frontera), Canada (CanArgo), Switzerland (National Petroleum), as well as Hellenic Petroleum of Greece. In the years following independence, the larger part of exploration and development work was gradually taken over by foreign operators, as Saknavtobi's funds were drying up. At present, the largest fields (Ninotsminda, Samgori, Mirzaani) and some 95% of production are in foreign hands. Saknavtobi operates only the small Teleti field on its own. The major foreign projects are listed below:

Foreign company	Project
CanArgo (Canada)	58% interest in the Ninotsminda field, currently producing some 1,135 b/d (50% of country total). Drilled few wells. Also holds licence for the Nazvrevi block, where XCL (US) and CNPC (China) are farming in. Plans to build small power plant fuelled by associated gas from the field.
Frontera (US)	Holds licence to the Mirzaani and Taribani fields. Production is 220 b/d. Carried out seismic exploration. Monument (UK) farming into the block. Drilling is planned.
National Petroleum (NPC, Switzerland)	50% interest in the Iorisveli joint venture, which operates the Samgori field, which is producing some 700-850 b/d*.
Ramco (UK)	Signed for 50% in Kakheti exploration block in 1997, carried out seismic work. Drilling is planned.
JKX (UK)	Acquired three licences in 1993; relinquished one licence, is seeking partners for retained onshore Kartli and offshore Black Sea block.
Hellenic Petroleum (Greece)	Negotiating PSA for two small fields (Norio and Satskhenisi)

* National Petroleum has been threatened to lose its rights, because it failed to reach production targets that were set three years ago, possibly banking on illusionary estimates of the country's hydrocarbon potential.

1. Arco has considered farming into an offshore licence and Total has studied an offshore project, but no contract has yet been signed.

Georgia: Annual Oil Production

Year	1991	1992	1993	1994	1995	1996	1997	1998	1999
Production (tonnes)	181,000	92,000	88,000	67,000	42,300	128,000	141,000	119,000	*80,000

Source: IHS Energy Group.
* 1999 figure is preliminary.

Refining

Georgia has one large refinery at Batumi on the Black Sea coast with a capacity of 5 mt/year (100,000 b/d). The plant was first built in 1920. In the 1990s, it never operated at more that 50% of design capacity and stopped production in 1995 as a result of lack of feedstock and the severe decline in Georgian consumption of oil products. Mitsui (Japan) expressed interest in May 1999 to invest $250 million for an upgrade. A similar project was discussed in 1996/7 with Marubeni (Japan), but never came to fruition.

There is a mini-refinery at Sartichala (with a 2000 b/d capacity), close to Tbilisi. It was built by a joint venture of McOil (US) and Saknavtobi, and was completed in June 1998. In October 1998, CanArgo obtained a 24% share in the joint-venture.

Itochu (Japan) proposed to build a new refinery at Supsa, at the Black Sea end of the recently construction oil transit pipeline. The most likely initial design would be for a relatively simple refinery concentrated on production of lubricants for the Turkish, Georgian and Armenian markets. Cracking capacity could be added at a later date. Capacity of the facility would initially be 40,000 to 60,000 b/d, gradually increasing to 300,000 b/d.

Frontera is considering to construct a small refinery (10,000 b/d capacity) close to the fields it operates. It would primarily be used to fuel the Gardabani thermal power plant.

Oil Transit Infrastructure

Georgia has already completed the first part of its ambitious plans for transit of oil and diversification of supplies, with the construction of the **Baku-Supsa oil pipeline**. The pipeline transports "early oil" (pre-peak production) from the GCA field complex operated by the AIOC consortium offshore Azerbaijan. First oil was pumped in January 1999, and the first tanker sailed in May 1999 (See Map 5: Trans-Caucasus Oil and Gas Pipelines).

Initial line capacity is 5.75 mt/year (115,000 b/d), but could be increased to about 10 mt/year (200,000 b/d) with additional pumping stations. It was constructed under a partnership between the GIOC and AIOC. The pipeline runs 814 km from Baku to Supsa (444 km in Azerbaijan and 370 km in Georgia). The original cost of the project was estimated at $315 million, but escalated to $590 million, when more sections of a mothballed old pipeline had to be replaced rather than repaired. There are four 40,000 tonne storage units at Supsa.

Georgia also serves as transit corridor for Kazakh oil, which is produced by the Chevron-led TCO consortium at Tengiz. Crude is transported by barge across the Caspian Sea to Dubendi (near Baku), and then moved by a combination of railcars and pipeline to Supsa. In 1998, about 2.2 mt of Kazakh oil transited through Georgia. The target for 1999 was 4 mt. Transit fees in 1999 for Kazakh oil to Batumi were 2.63 $/bbl (for the Georgian segment 0.685 $/bbl).

Chevron plans to increase the capacity of the Baku-Batumi route by initially 2 mt/year by rehabilitating and reversing a 232 km product pipeline running from Batumi to Khashuri.

Currently, Chevron exports some 2.5 mt/year through Azerbaijan and Georgia by a complex combination of rail and pipeline. This pipeline was damaged by the hostilities in the early 1990's. The project also calls for laying 500 km of new pipeline from Ali-Bairamli in Azerbaijan to Khashuri. The TCO consortium will have exclusive access to this new system, whose capacity could progressively be stepped up to 10 mt/year. The port facilities at Poti are being expanded to more than double the current capacity of 5 mt/year in anticipation of the increased deliveries from the pipeline.

Georgia prides itself in having succeeded in channelling considerable quantities of Caspian oil through its territory. The war in Chechnya has disqualified the so-called "northern route" running from Baku to the Russian port of Novorossiysk in the eyes of foreign companies. But Georgia also wants to see the so-called "main oil" pipeline pass through its territory. This line will transport peak production from AIOC's field, as well as likely other Caspian producers. A decision on the routing of this pipeline has been postponed many times, partly because of geopolitical sensitivities, but largely pending the discovery of sufficient proven reserves to justify such a project. No matter what the final the pipeline route will be – Baku-Ceyhan or Baku-Supsa – Georgia is well-poised to see large flows of Caspian oil crossing its borders (See Chapter on Regional Energy Trade and Transit for more details).

Also, gas from recent discoveries offshore Azerbaijan (and possibly Turkmenistan) is likely to be evacuated to world markets via Georgia.

Georgian Oil Transit Forecasts

Million tonnes	Baku-Supsa	Rail/TCO	Total
1999	3	3	6
2000	8	5	13
2001	15	7	22
2004	20	8	28
2012	20	10	30

Source: AIOC, ERAS Estimates.

Oil Consumption

Statistically recorded Georgian oil products consumption collapsed from 4.6 mt in 1990 to merely 141,000 tons in 1995, before mounting again to 0.9 mt in 1997. Consumption in 1998 was quoted as 1.3 mt. Consumption decreased across all sectors, including power generation, refining and transport. Given the significant amount of unaccounted imports, official consumption statistics may underestimate actual Georgian oil products consumption. With the closure of the Batumi refinery in 1995, Georgia has relied on imports to meet its oil products requirements. The recently opened small refinery near Tbilisi should alleviate some of this import dependence.

In 1997, transport was the largest oil product consuming sector (53% of total consumption, with gasoline accounting for 40% of total consumption). The residential-commercial sector accounted for 30% of consumption, followed by the power sector (9%) and industry (7%). By comparison, the oil products consumption mix in 1990 saw the residential-commercial sector as the leading consumer (40%), followed by the power sector (31%), transport 26%) and refining (2.2%). Georgia's cash shortage in the 1990's seriously affected its import capacity for heavy-fuel oil (HFO) and natural gas to fuel power plants. In 1990, Georgian CHP plants used 1.42 mt of HFO and 1 bcm of gas. By 1997, electricity and CHP plants burnt merely 85,000 t of HFO and 0.37 bcm of gas.

Fuel for power generation will remain a crucial issue. It is being tackled e.g. by Frontera, whose small refinery will supply the Gardabani power plant. The mooted refinery at Supsa should also supply heavy products suitable for power generation. With conversion capacity less of a priority, Georgia may remain dependent on gasoline imports to meet incremental demand in the transport sector for the foreseeable future.

Since 1992, all retail filling stations have been privatised, predominantly to Georgian investors, although a small number of foreign companies have opened filling stations – Lukoil (one station) and EKO (Greece) (five stations). Georgia has a requirement for 90, 92 and 95 octane gasoline (the Batumi refinery was only able to produce low octane gasoline, estimated at 72%).

The Georgian Energy Research Institute forecasts a rapid recovery in oil products consumption to between 2.6 mt (low-case scenario) and 3.1 mt (high-case scenario) in 2000. By 2010, consumption is prognosticated at between 3 mt (low case) or 4 mt (high case). These figures, especially the near-term ones, seem very high.

Oil Pricing

Crude and oil products prices are free (market prices). Pipeline transit tariffs are set by the Ministry of Fuels and Energy. Chevron (TCO) has reduced its fees for the Georgian leg of its Trans-Caucasus rail-pipeline export route from $1.06/bbl to $0.68/bbl.

NATURAL GAS

Natural Gas Policy

The policy priorities for the natural gas sector are largely the same as those for oil. The key elements of government policy for natural gas are: promotion of gas transit and diversification of gas supplies; rehabilitation of the distribution network; and encouragement of foreign investment. Georgia has considerable gas infrastructure already in place, including some idle transit capacity, and investment in this may prove as important in the short term as investment in new transit links.

Gas Industry Restructuring

The Georgian government has started the restructuring and privatisation of parts of the natural gas industry, similar to the model used for the electricity sector. However, liberalisation of the domestic natural gas industry is not expected to be as high a priority as development of a transit role and diversification of supply. The most important companies involved in the natural gas sector are:

- Saktransgas (high-pressure transmission);
- Georgian International Gas Company (GIGC; high-pressure transmission and transit);
- Itera[1] (trade);
- Intergaz (distribution).

1. Itera is a US-registered company with close ties with Gazprom. It trades Gazprom gas on FSU markets.

Saktransgas is responsible for around 2000 km of high-pressure gas pipeline, with a design capacity of 55 mcm per day. The main supply pipeline coming from Russia crosses the Caucasus at an altitude of up to 2700 m. Privatisation in the gas industry is not planned for transmission: Saktransgas is classified as a strategic company which is not to be offered for sale.

In 1997 the ownership of the 8000 km of low-pressure distribution grid was transferred to municipalities. Seven of the local gas distribution entities were sold to Intergaz, which is a joint venture owned 45% by Gazprom, 45% by the Georgian Government, and 10% by the gas trading company Itera. Further municipal distribution companies could be privatised.

In August 1998, Intergaz won an international tender for a 76% stake in the Tbilisi gas network (Tbilgas), but the deal was never finalised. The 76% stake was re-offered in September 1999. The remaining 24% will be distributed among employees. Before independence, Tbilgas supplied natural gas to about 30% of Georgia's population. Tbilgas planned to invest up to $30 million within two years to install gas meters in apartments and restore gas supplies in the region.

The monopoly gas supplier to Georgia is Gazprom, which sells gas through the trading company Itera. Volumes and prices are agreed annually with Itera. Gas is imported from Russia (from Itera) by five buyers – the chemical industry, the metal industry, power generation (essentially the Gardabani power plant which is the only fully operational thermal power plant in Georgia), the cement industry, and Intergaz.

Turkmenistan used to supply natural gas (via Kazakhstan and Russia) to Georgia until 1997. Deliveries were halted in 1997 due to payment problems and Russia's unwillingness to let Turkmen gas transit through its system. By July 1999, Georgia still owed Turkmenistan $400 million, accounting for nearly 22% of the country's entire foreign debt.

In 1997 the Government created the Georgian International Gas Company (GIGC), as a gas industry equivalent to the GIOC (oil). The aim of GIGC is to promote foreign investment in the gas transmission network. GIGC's current role, however, is uncertain. It is highly dependent on Saktransgas, which pays its salaries. It has been suggested that the government may give the high-pressure network to GIGC, which would in turn lease it to Saktransgas. The idea would be to strengthen GIGC's position to attract foreign investment.

A further complication is the role of Gruzrusgazprom, which would be a joint venture between Gazprom and Saktransgaz. If the ownership for this proposed joint venture is the same in Georgia as has already been agreed in neighbouring Armenia, this arrangement would give Gazprom control of Georgia's transmission system. Although the creation of the venture has been supported by a presidential decree, Saktransgas doubts that it would enhance Georgia's position as a transit country. Too much Russian control over Georgia's transmission system could hamper the country's supply diversification efforts by blocking gas imports from Azerbaijan and possibly Iran[1].

There is no effective competition in the Georgian natural gas market. Gazprom is the only supplier, with a high level of control over the supply chain right through to the industry or household consumers.

---

1.   Iran exported gas to Georgia (and the wider Caucasus region of the USSR) until 1979.

Gas Infrastructure and Transit

Georgia's pipeline system has a transit capacity of about 20 bcm/year, but it has been designed for trade flows that existed before the break-up of the Soviet Union. In 1997, it only transited 2.5 bcm from Russia to Armenia. Today, Georgia is enthusiastically promoting its role as a transit country for future westward natural gas stream from Azerbaijan and Turkmenistan or for Russian gas supplies to Turkey. Higher gas transit would earn Georgia significant revenues in transit fees, attract foreign investment to upgrade its infrastructure and diversify its gas supplies (See Map 5: Trans-Caucasus Oil and Gas Infrastructure).

There are two gas pipelines leading into Georgia: one line coming from Baku, which has a capacity of 8 bcm/year (which is currently used at less than 35% of capacity) and the Mozdok-Tbilisi line, which crosses the Caucasus mountains and has a capacity of 20 bcm/year. This line runs further into Armenia.

There are plans to expand the capacity of the Mozdok-Tbilisi-Armenia line and to extend it into eastern Turkey so as to export up to 8.5 bcm/year of Russian gas to Armenia and Turkey. The present pipeline presently carries between 1.5 and 3.5 bcm a year, depending on Armenian demand. GIGC estimates project costs at $500 million. Competition against this line comes from the "Blue Stream" project (See Chapter on Regional Energy Trade and Transit for more details).

Gas Pricing

Gas prices for industry and power generators is a reported $60/1000 m^3. Prices are effectively determined by Itera. Collections for the gas industry remain a problem, although much progress has been made. The collection increased from a mere 3% in 1994 to 76% at the end of 1997. Metering, accounting software and leakage detection system have been installed with donors' aid. In the industrial sector a portion of supplies are still not paid for in cash, but rather through barter of the produced goods. In the areas where low-pressure gas supply has been restored, residential consumers must pay for the meter in order to be reconnected.

Georgia has experienced difficulties in paying for gas imports. Itera has reduced gas deliveries to Georgia due to non-payment problems. In March 1999, after payment of some of the dues, gas deliveries to the Tbilisi power plant were increased from 2 to 4 million m^3/day. Gas deliveries to the Rustavi industrial complex were suspended between November 1998 and June 1999 because of non-payment. In October 1999, Russian gas supplies to the Gardabani power plant and to Tbilisi were suspended again after Georgia had accumulated $60 million of gas debt.

Gas Consumption

Georgian gas consumption dropped from 5.4 bcm in 1990 (99% of which were imported) to 0.94 bcm in 1997. Gazprom through Itera was scheduled to supply about 2 bcm to Georgia in 1999.

In Soviet times Georgia was highly gasified – around 70% of the population were connected to gas grid. The operability of the gas grid has been diminished after the demise of the Soviet Union and the conflicts in South Ossetia and Abkhazia. As a consequence, gas consumption by the residential-commecial sector dwindled from 4.4 bcm in 1990 (81% of total gas supplied) to 0.13 bcm in 1997 (15% of gas supplied). Gas consumption by the power sector (i.e. the Gardabani plant) declined less steeply, from 1 bcm in 1990 to 0.37 bcm in 1997. Rehabilitation of the domestic distribution system has started. In Tbilisi about 10% (30,000 dwellings) are again receiving natural gas – still only 10% of the 300,000 dwellings that were connected in the early 1990's. In Georgia as a whole, the number of dwellings now receiving gas is around 6-7%. Intergaz has invested to resume local supplies in the seven networks that it bought.

With GDP growth of over 11% in 1996 and 1997 expected to continue, consumption of natural gas is also expected to rise, although, in the period up to 2010, it is unlikely to exceed the levels reached in the early 1990's. The Georgian Energy Research Institute expects gas consumption to rise from 1.2 bcm in 2000 to 2.2 bcm in 2005 and 2.8 bcm in 2010 under a low-case scenario. A high-case scenario foresees consumption as high as 4 bcm in 2005 and 4.8 bcm in 2010. Some 70% of households have natural gas connections, so that there is strong long-term growth potential in residential as well as industrial demand.

ELECTRICITY[1]

Electricity Industry Structure

During the Soviet area, the Georgian electricity system was integrated with those of Azerbaijan and Armenia in a Transcaucasus network, which in turn was linked to the Soviet grid. Sector planning was done in Moscow and fuel was supplied from Russia. With the collapse of the Soviet system, the Transcaucasus network broke into its national parts, which now operate independently.

Transformation of the Georgian power sector began in 1995. The process included the creation of a Committee on Restructuring of the Power Sector, the unbundling of the electricity industry, the passing of the Electricity Law in June 1997, and the formal creation of the National Electricity Regulatory Commission (NERC) in July 1997.

The electricity market reform was a pre-condition for further aid by international organisations such as USAID and the World Bank. The wholesale market began operations in mid-1999 on a limited scale with a few operators.

The structure of the electricity industry is largely defined by the Electricity Law. The Electricity Law allows the market to operate primarily under a single-buyer scheme where the dispatcher has the right to purchase and resell wholesale power and to contract transmission services. However, it also allows distributors and large users to purchase power directly from local suppliers and abroad. NERC has the authority to determine who qualifies as eligible customer for direct power purchases. Generators have the right to sell to the dispatcher, distributors, direct consumers, brokers or to export.

In July 1996, the electricity sector was unbundled into power generation (under SakGen), transmission (SakTrans) and regional distribution companies. In summer 1998 the dispatching functions were transferred to a separate company.

Most of Georgia's hydro and thermal generation units have become 100%-owned subsidiaries of SakGen. Except for Abkhazia and South Ossetia, the distribution networks were transformed in 1995 into joint-stock companies controlled by local municipalities. Distribution companies were the first major assets sold to strategic investors, starting with Telasi, the company serving Tbilisi (*see below*).

---

1. This section draws on information obtained from numerous reports prepared by Hagler Bailly that have been funded by USAID and the World Bank.

There are about 150 utilities in Georgia (including in Abkhazia and South Ossetia), including 89 distribution companies, 1 transmission, 1 dispatcher and the rest generators, most of them in the holding company SakGen. The number of customers is approximately 1.2 million, approximately 1.1 million of which are metered. 98% of customers are residential customers. The distribution companies vary by size. Telasi serves over 340,000 customers in the capital, while eight distribution companies in the mountainous regions serve less than 5,000. The small size of the distribution companies outside Tbilisi makes them unattractive to private investors. That's why the government plans to consolidate the 66 distributors outside Abkhazia and South Ossetia into eight or fewer companies.

Georgia: Proposed consolidation of distribution companies

Grouping	Population (1000)	Customers (1000)	GWh 1996	MWh/customer
Adjara	256	64	272	4.25
Guria, Samegrelo, Zemo, Svaneti	532	130	326	2.51
Imeret, Lechkhumi, Kvemo Svaneti	595	150	788	5.25
Javakheti	236	59	129	2.19
Shida Kartli	298	75	183	2.44
Kvemo Kartli, Mtskheta-Tianeti and Kazbegi	789	198	415	2.10
Karkheti	381	96	89	0.93
Tbilisi	1247	342	1982	5.80
Total	4334	1114	4184	

Twenty-three distribution networks are in South Ossetia and Abkhazia. Those in Ossetia are served directly by Russia, who also supply power to north-western Abkhazia. The remainder of Abkhazia is connected to the Georgian network.

The Government is planning to establish a wholesale market for electricity. Until that happens, SakTrans is the sole buyer and sells to distribution companies. Some issues related to the operation of wholesale markets, such as the type of model that will be implemented (e.g. Single Buyer, Electricity Pool, hybrid system), the rules that will govern electricity trade and the contractual arrangements between suppliers, wholesaler and distributor remain to be clarified. It was proposed that all electricity should be traded through a power pool, with the exception of direct sales. NERC has the authority to set the percentage of generation, which may be sold directly to "eligible consumers" by generators. The difficulties are exacerbated by low cash flow in the system and power shortages leading to rationing. The chronical power shortage forced Fuel & Energy Minister T. Giorgadze to resign in November 1999.

Privatisation

In 1996 the Ministry of State Property adopted a privatisation programme for most of the electricity industry, with the exception of transmission. The World Bank is financing the services of Merrill Lynch, which was selected to implement the privatisation plan. Prior to 1996, a mass-privatisation scheme had resulted in the sale of small hydro-power plants, mainly Georgian citizens.

Seven major hydro-power plants, one thermal power station and distribution companies were earmarked for sale in the privatisation programme. Distribution companies were chosen for privatisation to improve collection and thus enhance the value of the generating companies.

The first significant privatisation took place in the second half of 1998 with the tendering of **Telasi**, the distributor for the Tbilisi area. In January 1999, **AES** (US) won the tender (against an EDF-led Georgian-French consortium) with a bid of $25.5 million for 75% of the company. AES pledged to invest $84 million and assumed $10 million of Telasi's debt. Telasi buys about two-thirds of its electricity from Sakenergo and the rest from hydro-power stations. In October 1999, AES was declared preferred bidder for three of these power stations with a combined capacity of 1200 MW.

Telasi supplies 370,000 customers, equivalent to 40% of the country's consumption. AES was inheriting a distribution company with chronic power outages during the winter, massive illegal connections and power stealing and endemic corruption amongst personnel. Collections were less than 10%, largely because customers did not receive bills. AES embarked upon a 3-year programme to re-meter and retrofit its 370,000 customers, raise collection to 90% and increase safety levels at its installations[1].

Although Sakenergo was committed to supply electricity to Telasi, it could not deliver power to Telasi in March and April 1999 at the agreed price of 2.5 tetri/kWh. Telasi was forced to import electricity from Armenia at 5 tetri/kWh. These higher purchase prices forced Telasi to increase end-user prices of 6 tetri/kWh by 25% in May 1999. Telasi is reducing its workforce of about 2,200 by 600 through voluntary redundancies.

The first year of operation of Telasi under AES management can be viewed as successful. In November 1999, however, the company suffered some set-backs, due to delays in installing meters. Telasi had to cut back power deliveries to 5-8 hours per day.

Some issues need to be resolved before generating companies can be de-nationalised. Among these are excess capacity (unless exported) which limit the market potential, lack of regulatory clarity, uncertainty about future market rules, the financial risks related to non-payment and securing reliable fuel supply for thermal power stations.

Assets in Abkhazia, which hosts about one-third of the country's generation capacity, will not be privatised until full Georgian jurisdiction is restored. Assets include hydro-power plants (the Vardivili cascade, the Sukhumi HPP, the country's largest hydro-power plant at Inguri (1,300 MW), and the Tkvarchelli thermal power station (220 MW).

Electricity Generation

Georgia's total nameplate generating capacity is about 5,000 MW: 2,088 MW are concentrated in three thermal power plants (Gardabani, Tkvarchelli and the Tbilisi CHP plant), about 2,700 MW is in hydro and about 5 MW are diesel units. The hydro-power capacity consists of 6 large storage plants, 17 large run-of-river plants and the rest are small run-of-river plants (see Table on page 113).

As of January 1998, only 1,575 MW of effective capacity was available in Georgia: of that, 400 MW was thermal capacity at Gardabani, and the rest was hydro-power. This reflected technical problems at the thermal power plants due to poor maintenance and damage by the civil war, as well as difficulties in purchasing imported fuels. Consequently, Sakenergo had

---

1.   By October 1999, 30,000 metering installations were done, 90% of customers receive their bills and 50% of customers pay their bills.

to ration electricity supply, in particular during winter[1]. Hagler-Bailly estimated that the unconstrained peak would be more than 1.7 GW.

Thermal Plants

The Gardabani thermal power station is the only one operating, with only about 400 MW of the total 1,850 MW available. The units can burn gas and fuel oil. With less than 20% the plant's thermal efficiency is extremely low. One of the plant's two 300 MW units has been restored to full capacity with funds by EBRD and KfW. Despite its young age (1993), the second 300 MW unit is scheduled for significant rehabilitation following a control room fire in 1995. The Tkvarchelli thermal plant in Abkhazia is shut down at present due to war damages.

Hydro-Power Plants

Hydro-power has been developed in Georgia since the 1920's. There are about 180 generating units in 103 plants. Fifty-four of the plants make up about 2.7 GW, the remaining plants are small HPPs. Of these 54 plants, 38 are connected to the main network and 16 serve isolated grids. Four large stations, Inguri, Vardivili, Ladzanuri and Vartsikhi, represent about 70% of the hydro-power capacity.

By far the largest hydro-power plant is Inguri with a name-plate capacity of 1,300 MW, but it has been down-rated to 1,100 MW due to difficulties with the generators. The dam is located at the border to Abkhazia and the turbine house is situated downstream inside Abkhazia. Rehabilitation of the plant is estimated at $50 million, partly to be funded by EBRD. The Khudoni hydro-power plant (700 MW) is partly constructed. Civil works are almost completed, but construction has been halted due to lack of funds.

About 20 smaller hydro-power plants ranging from 1 to 21 MW and totalling 90 MW were privatised before a mass privatisation process was halted in 1995. Four hydro-power plants (180 MW) have been leased to private operators (Jinvali, Atskuri/Adjaris-Tskali, Zahesi/Avchala and Ortachala). These plants generate about 10% of Georgia's electricity supply.

In the 1990's, the importance of hydro-power has steadily increased at the expense of thermal generation due to increased fuel costs. The hydro-power plants were originally designed as a source of peak power within the Soviet Transcaucasus network, but have been operated to meet Georgia's base load. This has placed many of the major hydro plants, in particular Inguri which provides one quarter of total capacity, under significant strain. Nominal annual generation at Inguri is 4.3 TWh, but actual generation has well fallen below this (2.1 TWh in 1997).

Georgia: Electric Power Capacity

Capacity (1996)	MW
Thermal (Sakenergo)	2088
Storage (Sakenergo)	1883
Run-of-river (Sakenergo)	832
Small hydro-power (Sakenergo)	30
Small hydro-power (private)	100
Small hydro-power (Min. Agriculture)	5
Total	**4938**

Source: Hagler Bailly.

---

1. Difficulties in securing fuel supplies for district heating plants and damage caused by the civil war resulted in a complete break-down of the municipal heat supply system. Consequently, a significant share of the heating demand in cities is met by electricity.

Electricity Production and Consumption

Since 1988 electricity production and consumption have declined dramatically. Overall electricity consumption dropped from 17,600 GWh in 1988 to 6,200 GWh in 1997. The decrease was caused primarily by the collapse of industrial energy demand. Industrial electricity consumption contracted from 7,800 GWh in 1990 to 828 GWh in 1997. Demand, however, is restricted and statistics are of poor reliability, due to frequent power cuts and frequency variations. The residential-commercial sector witnessed a less steep decline, from 6,300 GWh in 1990 to 5,140 GWh in 1997.

In spite of the contraction in demand, the domestic electricity industry cannot meet the country's electricity needs. Electricity supply is rationed, mostly in the winter period, due to cut-back gas imports since 1994 and poor maintenance of thermal power stations.

The decline in consumption is accompanied by significant shifts in the fuel pattern and a concentration of production in low-cost hydro-power. In 1990, about half the electricity was generated in thermal power stations. By 1998, about 85% were produced in hydro-power plants. In summer, hydro-power plants are practically the only source of electricity production.

In 1996, distribution companies accounted for 58% of the transmission system's total supplies (with Telasi accounting for 47% of these supplies). Purchases by large customers accounted for 15% of supplies, Abkhazia and South Ossetia supplies for 13%, and transmission losses for 14%.

There are 13 high voltage customers: nine industrial clients and four urban distribution companies (Telasi, Kutaisi, Rustavi and Sukhumi). SakTrans provides power to two other groups of consumers: 21 large industrial customers and 74 electricity distribution networks (of which 23 are in Abkhazia and South Ossetia). South Ossetia and parts of Abkhazia receive power from Russia, while Adjaria is supplied from the Turkish system. Part of the province of Kakheti in eastern Georgia is connected to the Azerbaijan grid.

Georgia: Electricity Production and Consumption

Production (GWh)	1990	1991	1996	1997
Sakenergo production	14200	12987	7146	7163
– thermal	n.a.	5568	1105	1129
– hydro	n.a.	7419	6041	6034
Autoproduction	0	0	80	9
Imports	4500	2554	221	653
– Russia	n.a.	n.a.	221	306
– Azerbaijan	n.a.	n.a.	0	337
– Armenia	n.a.	n.a.	0	10
Exports	1300	0	135	462
– Turkey	n.a.	0	121	462
– Azerbaijan	n.a.	0	14	0
Supply	17400	15541	7312	7363
Industry consumption	5943	4483	805	768
Household consumption	2320	2682	2639	2593
Public sector consumption	1200	2120	1490	1711
Agriculture consumption	n.a.	992	26	14
Other users (incl. commercial sector)	n.a.	2097	794	753
Own use & distribution losses	n.a.	3167	1558	1524

Electricity Network and Interconnections

The Georgian transmission system consists of 600 km of 500 kV lines, 20 km of 330 kV and a 6000 km loop of 220 kV and 110 kV lines. The medium-voltage network consists of 3360 km of 35 kV lines. Most of the 220 kV system was constructed in the 1950's, while the 500 kV grid was built in the 1970's and 1980's (See Map 6: Trans-Caucasus Power System).

The Georgian distribution system of lines operating at 0.4 to 500 kV is unusually long, totalling over 100,000 km. There are 455 substations of 35 kV and higher voltage, and over 10,000 transforming stations of 6-10 kV. It is divided into 74 distribution areas and is fed from the transmission system via 21 major substations.

The Georgian electricity system is connected with Russia, Turkey, Armenia and Azerbaijan. The major inter-connections with Russia consists are one 500 kV (operational capability 1000 MW) and one 220 kV (operational capability 100 MW) line. According to the World Bank the design capacities are higher, but stability considerations limit the power transfer. There are also several 110 kV and 35 kV links with Russia, with a combined capacity of about 100 MW. The line to Russia crosses the Caucasus at 2,100 meters altitude and is exposed to damage caused by harsh meteorological conditions. Nonetheless, the 500 kV line linking Russia, Georgia (through Abkhazia) and Azerbaijan – with a planned extension to Turkey - is a regional transmission backbone. The line to Russia is managed by a joint-venture of UES – the Russian power utility – and SakTrans. The line has been restored, but no exchanges have taken place yet due to payment arrears. An equity swap in return for repair work allowed UES to increase its share in the joint-venture.

In addition to the 500 kV line, there is a 330 kV line link to Azerbaijan with a capacity of about 500 MW. Both lines are operational and are used for occasional power exchange.

The inter-connections with Armenia are one 220 kV line (250 MW capacity) and one 110 kV line (35 kV capacity)[1]. The 110 kV line serves a railroad and provides local supplies, and is therefore of limited importance for regional electricity trade.

Inter-connections with Turkey are one 220 kV line with a capacity of about 200 MW. The line is operational and is used for occasional exchange in radial (Island) regime.

Financial Characteristics

Georgia's non-privatised power system is operating at a financial loss. This is mainly due to low energy tariffs and the government's inability to collect payments from consumers, both residential and commercial. Ageing equipment, little or no maintenance, war damage and fuel shortages have wreaked havoc on systems operation and reliability of power supply.

Collection ratios have improved to 80-85% at retail level, compared with less than 20% in 1995 (but industrial collection rates are still lower[2]. Tariffs that are below full costs are another reason for the precarious financial situation of the electricity industry. Although the Electricity Law stipulates that tariffs should reflect costs, electricity prices for all consumer groups have not yet reached levels that would allow the electricity industry to become financially viable.

---

1. The 220 kV interconnection with Armenia was interrupted, as 6-7 km of wire were stolen in October 1999.
2. Some independent experts doubt that collection rates are actually that high. A noteworthy pilot project was carried out in the town of Rustavi with USAID funds. Individual and controlled meters and billing systems were installed, resulting in a sharp improvement of collection rates, from 10% in 1998 to 95% in 1999. Power consumption declined 35% during the same period. AES plans to follow the same scheme for Telasi.

Since October 1998 distribution companies pay between 3.1. and 3.3 Tetri/kWh for the wholesale purchase of power from Sakenergo, depending on the voltage level. The wholesale electricity purchase price paid by Sakenergo to the state-owned generation enterprises is 5.4 Tetri/kWh for thermal and 1.3 Tetri/kWh for hydro power stations. These wholesale prices will have to increase if hydro-power plants were to be privatised successfully, and in order to adjust to the evolution of the load curve with a tariff structure that takes account of seasonal variations in the demand/supply balance.

Independent producers (i.e. privatised and leased hydro-power plants) can, however, sell directly to customers at freely negotiated price. Their fees are slightly above the prices for state-owned hydro-power plants.

NERC has stated that before 2000 electricity prices at the generation, transmission and distribution stage should reflect full costs and assure a reasonable rate of return. Household tariffs increased in 1996 and 1997 closer to industry level, thus reducing the level of cross-subsidy from industry to households. In October 1998 NERC increased the retail price for all consumers that are supplied from the 380/220 kV grid, including industry, to 6 Tetri/kWh. In June 1999 NERC further raised electricity prices to 9 Tetri/kWh (equivalent to 4.5 UScents/kWh). According to the World Bank, these retail prices would be sufficient to recover full production costs. The government also plans to introduce seasonal tariffs but that would require to change the meters.

Electricity Trade and Transit

Regional demand for exported Georgian hydro-power should be significant. Turkey has a major deficit in electricity and could therefore be a major electricity importer. The flexibility of hydro-power, with its peaking capabilities, is an opportunity for daily and seasonal electricity trade with Armenia, Azerbaijan and Russia to complement their predominantly base-load plants. About 40 TWh could be produced economically in Georgian hydro-power plants for exports. There would also be the possibility to increase electricity transit, for example from gas-based generation in Azerbaijan to Turkey. Organisational and technical problems (overloads, frequency variation) must still be overcome before trans-border electricity trade can really happen.

The capacity of the inter-connections between Georgia and its neighbouring countries exceeds 3,000 MW, i.e. about three times the 1998 peak demand. This provides significant potential for exports as well as trading within the region.

At present, net electricity trade is minimal, only about 3% is imported, whereas in 1990 net imports accounted for about 20% of domestic supplies. Turkey supplies a capacity of 15 MW to the Adjaria. Payment is made as exchange; Georgia supplies power in summer, and Turkey in winter. Russia supplies the network in Abkhazia which is de-coupled from the Georgian grid. In September 1998 Georgia signed an agreement with Armenia to buy electricity over a six-month period, and the agreement was to be extended in a long-term accord.

The Sakenergo/UES agreement is intended to supply up to 300 MW to Georgia at a price that ranges from 3 to 5.5 UScents/kWh, subject to peak variations. A further objective of the joint-venture is to wheel power from Russia through Georgia to Turkey and Armenia.

Investment   Georgia's electricity generating, transmission and distribution infrastructure has been deteriorating since the late 1980's. Limited financial resources combined with increasingly challenging operating conditions have crippled many of the power plants, which are among the oldest in the former Soviet Union. Inadequate maintenance and the use of untreated water in boilers have damaged many thermal generating units. Hydro units have also suffered from neglect. Dams have experienced silting which reduces water impoundment, and lack of maintenance caused damage to the irrigation system. As a consequence, rehabilitation of the entire system has become a priority for the government and for providers of international assistance.

According to World Bank estimates, the electricity sector would require $1.3 billion of rehabilitation investment over the next 5-10 years. AES's Telasi experience will be crucial to determine the level of confidence of private investors.

In addition to the sell-off of Talesi and other distribution companies, the government is considering a variety of investment projects, for which it seeks to attract private and foreign capital.

Proposed projects:

■ Rehabilitation of the Vartsikhi cascade, possibly financed by KfW (DM 83 million).

■ Completion of Khudoni hydro-power project of three 230 MW units in western Georgia ($500 million). About 30% of the work has been completed, including excavation and civil works.

■ Pilot privatisation and rehabilitation of the Jinvali HPP (130 MW).

■ Renovation of the Tbilisi CHP ($50 million), consisting of three generating units (6 MW each) connected to the Tbilisi distribution system.

■ Rehabilitation of inoperable generation units at Gardabani thermal plant and construction of unit 11 originally planned to be 300 MW gas-fired condensing unit. Ultimately, installation of a combined cycle facility of 200-250 MW is being considered in place of unit 11.

■ Completion of a high voltage electricity transmission line (Gardabani-Kars): $140 million (government estimate). The construction started during the Soviet area.

■ Construction of a 150-200 MW coal-fired plant operating on indigenous fuel in Tkibuli.

Ongoing projects:

■ Rehabilitation of Lajanuri and Khrami-2 hydro-power stations; dispatch centres of Tbilisi and Kutaisi, and communication systems. Financed by the Overseas Economic Cooperation Fund (OECF): ¥5.332 billion.

■ EBRD-financed renovation of the Inguri hydro plant, with five units of 260 MW each with a total potential production of 4,100 GWh, and rehabilitation of Vardivili-1 hydro station ($62.65 million).

■ EBRD-financed rehabilitation of the Rioni HPP and the Gardabani thermal plant, including the installation of a new water treatment plant ($18.1 million).

■ The World Bank finances the rehabilitation of a 300 MW unit (unit 10) at the Gardabani plant and provides working capital for increasing fuel reserves ($52.3 million).

■ UNDP and the EU-Tacis Energy Efficiency Centre in Tbilisi undertake a feasibility study for the rehabilitation and extension of small HPPs in the Tbilisi region.

In total there are about 1.1 GW of HPP capacity under construction, the largest being the completion of the Khudoni HPP. According to various studies, the technical potential of hydro-power is about 80 TWh, and about 30 to 40 TWh could be exploited economically at a tariff of about 4 UScents/kWh. Only about 20% of that potential has been exploited so far.

The EU-Tacis Energy Efficiency Centre in Tbilisi has analysed the options for renewable energy. In recent years, economic difficulties and disruptions in energy supplies have paradoxically increased the use of renewable energy: wood fuel and hydro-power represent about half of the energy supplies. These are exceptional circumstances with little indication for the long-term potential for renewable sources of energy. Favourable conditions for wind power exist along the Black Sea coast (Poti and Batumi areas), in Sabueti in central Georgia, in the suburbs of Tbilisi and in over 160 meteorological sights in Georgia used for measuring wind velocity.

Tacis estimates the total economic potential of renewable energy at 900 MW, with the following priorities:

■ Rehabilitation of existing small hydro-power plants is the most cost-effective option, with an average unit cost of $520/kW for an estimated 70 MW of capacity.

■ Biomass (mainly wood) and waste constitutes some 15% (140 MW) of the total potential of renewable energy. The risk is improper forest management and ensuing environmental damages.

■ Construction of new small hydro-power plants bears the largest potential – some 400 MW (45% of the total potential of renewables). Investments have been calculated at $1,500/kW.

■ Solar energy is a market niche in the services sector (water heaters).

■ Wind power represents a total potential of some 180 MW, but low electricity prices and unstable power transmission are obstacles to the development of wind power in the medium term.

■ The geothermal potential is small (20 MW) and restrained by the rehabilitation of existing wells and networks.

Georgia: Potential for Renewable Sources of Energy

	Technical Potential		Economic Potential		Cost Ratio $/kW	Total market (M $)
	Installed capacity (MW)	Energy generation (GWh)	Installed capacity (MW)	Energy generation (GWh)		
New building of SHHP	1,300	6,700	400	2,000	1,525	610
Rehabilitation of SHHP	130	700	70	270	520	36.4
Solar		18		3	2,500	1
Wind power	530	1,450	180	493	1,100	198
Wood and wood waste		2,530	140	422	1,500	210
Other (biogas, waste)		2,054	86	258	1,500	129
Geothermal	100	700	20	140	700	14
Total	2,060	14,152	896	3,586		1,198

Source: EU-Tacis Energy Efficiency Centre, Tbilisi.

DISTRICT HEATING

District heating was highly developed in Georgia under the former Soviet Union. District heating systems existed in all major towns, and overall district heating accounted for between 40-50% of heat demand for space heating and domestic hot water in the residential sector. These district heating networks are now totally out of use, causing major problems for the economics of the electricity sector. Firstly, CHP units which are no longer used for heating will be operating at sub-optimal efficiency for electricity production only, and secondly, the lack of district heating (and gas) have caused a significant increase in the residential demand for electricity. Given the relatively mild climate and short heating season, many experts consider the renovation of district heating systems appears not to be cost-effective.

Studies have been carried out by the IFC on the cost and feasibility of rehabilitating the district heating network. The renovation of the Tbilisi CHP plant, which supplied the district heating network of the city, is estimated to cost $50 million (3 × 6 MW units).

Annex Georgia: Hydro-Power Plants in Georgia – Installed Capacity and Production, 1997

Name	River	Year 1st unit Commissioned	Installed Capacity (MW)	Operating Capacity 1997	Rated Annual Generation (GWh)	Annual Generation 1997	Total & Useful Reservoir Capacity (hm³)	Number of Units	Max. Head (m)	Water Discharge (m³/s)
WESTERN GEORGIA										
INGURI (s)	Inguri	78	1300	650	4,340	2109.1	1100 - 676	5	360	450
VARDIVILI-1 (s)	Eristskali-Inguri	71	220	60	1,091	386.8	145 - 7	3	59	425
VARDIVILI-2 to 4 (s)	Eristskali -Inguri	71	120	–	–	–	–	3	35	425
VARTSIKHI-1 to 4 (s)	Rioni	76-78-80-88	184	113.4	1,000	794.4	14,6 - 2	8	60	350
LADJANURI (s)	Tskhenis Tskali	58-56	111.6	47.3	517	329.1	24,6 - 8,5	3	135	101.4
TKIBULI (s)	Tribuli	56	80	20.5	174	153.9	80 - 65	4	310	34
GUMATI-1&2 (s)	Rioni	56-58	66.5	47.9	394	216.3	19 - 13	7	37.4	214
RIONI (s)	Rioni	33	48	36	317	283.9	3 - 0,5	4	60	100
SHAORI (s)	Shaori	56	38.4	15	149	131.9	90 - 87	4	478	10
SUKHUMI	Gumista (East)	48	19.3	–	120	–	–	3	215	11
ATSKURI (l)	Adjaris tskali	37	16	10.9	103	66.2	–	2	46	45
BJUJA (p)	Bjuja	57	12.24	9	70	51.5	–	3	300	5
Sub-total			2,216	1,010	8,275	4,523		49		
EASTERN & SOUTHERN GEORGIA (Kura and its tributaries)										
JINVALI (l)	Aragvi	85	130	60	484	522.2	520 - 370	4	133.5	115
KHRAMI-1 (s)	Khrami	47	112.8	69.9	217	265.5	312 - 292	4	370	36
KHRAMI-2 (s)	Khrami	61	110	67.5	370	262.2	0,2 - 0	2	324	42
ZAHESI/ZEMO-AVCHALA (l)	Mtkvari (Zura)	27	36.8	29.8	203	157.8	–	6	20	235
CHITAKHEVI (p)	Mtkvari (Zura)	49	21	12.8	109	97.3	–	3	33	66.4
ORTACHALA (l)	Mtkvari (Zura)	54	18	12.4	90	55.9	–	3	10	225
SIONI (p)	Iori	64	9	4	33	26.0	300	2	48	23
SAMGORI CASCADE			31.4	10	173	67.2	–	5	283	39
SATSKHENISI (p)	Iori - Channel	52	14	–	86	32.7	–	2	128	13
TETRIKHEVI (p)	Iori - Channel	53	13.6	–	73	29	–	2	120	13
MARTKOBI (p)	Iori - Channel	53	3.8	–	14	5.5	–	1	35	13
Sub-total			469	266	1,679	1,454		29		
Total large HPPs			**2,685**	**1,276**	**9,954**	**5,977**		**78**		
Small HPPs			20	17	120	70.1				
Total Hydro-power Plants			**2,705**	**1,293**	**10,074**	**6,047**				

Source: EU-Tacis Energy Efficiency Centre.

Small HPPs (p): Alazani, Ritseula, Chkhorotskhu, Abasha, Kabali, Dashbash, Tirifoni, Misaktsiell, Okuri, Igoeti, Dmanisi, Kurzu, Arbo, Kazbegi

(s): HPP Sakenergo; (l): Leased HPP; (p): Privatised HPP.

VI. BULGARIA

BULGARIA AT A GLANCE

Population	8.25 million
Area	110,000 km²
Capital	Sofia
President	Petar Stoyanov (next election 2001)
Currency	The Lev is fixed against the DM (Lv 1: DM 1)
	$ = Lev 1.906 (Oct 1999)
	Euro = Lev 1.955

Bulgaria has been recovering from economic recession since 1998, even as the Kosovo war has cost the country one percentage point of GDP growth in 1999. EU accession is a prime goal of the current government, who has launched a reform of the energy sector. Bowing to EU pressure, Bulgaria has agreed to an early closure (2002) of its oldest two VVER-type reactors at Kozloduy. The closing date for two other VVER reactors will be set once Bulgaria adopts a new energy strategy in 2002. The EU and Euratom will honour Bulgaria's early retirement programme by funding Euro 450 million for modernising two 1000 MW reactors at Kozloduy. The four operating VVER reactors at Kozloduy, which have been upgraded with western aid, account for 22.5% of TPES (1997 statistics). Bulgaria has made progress in privatising and introducing Euro-compatible legislation. The legislative cornerstone is the July 1999 Law on Energy and Energy Efficiency. Energy prices are to be totally freed by 2001. Some improvements are still required on gas and electricity market deregulation and reducing state intervention in the coal sector. No clear timetable has yet been set for the unbundling and privatisation of the power monopoly NEK. The Burgas Neftochim refinery was sold to Lukoil. Some $2.5 billion are being invested in the power sector (mostly coal-fired) and lignite mines. Bulgaria's energy strategy foresees continued reliance on domestic lignite as a main fuel for its electricity plants (domestic and imported coal account for 36.3% of TPES). The country also tries to position itself as an energy transit route by upgrading its pipelines for Russian gas supplies to Turkey, FYROM and Greece. Longer term, Bulgaria proposes to channel Caspian oil through a pipeline bypassing the Bosphorus and Caspian gas exports via Turkey to Europe. This is part of a wider effort to diversify its heavy dependence on Russian oil and gas imports (29% and 18.7% of TPES respectively).

ECONOMIC AND POLITICAL OVERVIEW

Recent Economic Developments

Under the communist regime, Bulgaria's economic and foreign policy was fully aligned with the Soviet Union and followed strict central planning. The first free elections in June 1990 were won by the Bulgarian Socialist Party, the successor of the communists. Until spring 1997, the country was governed by changing coalition and socialist governments, which were only half-heartedly committed to reform. Bulgaria's economy was slow to adapt, and between 1990 and 1993 alone, it contracted by one third.

The last Socialist government, which came to power in 1995 led the country into a deep economic crisis. By early 1997, faced with hyper-inflation, capital flight, a banking system crippled by bad debts, virtually bankrupt state enterprises, and a plummeting living standard, the government had no other choice than to resign.

The call for anticipated elections and the successful negotiation of a currency board[1] by the caretaker government substantially improved political stability and paved the way to recovery. Ivan Kostov, who became prime minister in May 1997, and President Stoyanov, who was elected in November 1996, declared their intention to lead the country towards closer integration with the west, and eventually EU and NATO membership. The Government's further priorities include completing the privatisation process, attracting large-scale foreign investment and fighting corruption.

The present coalition government is expected to stay in power until the next parliamentary elections scheduled for April 2001, although ongoing closures of uneconomic enterprises and virtually no GDP growth in 1999 will further contribute to popularity losses. The war in Kosovo cost Bulgaria one percentage point of GDP growth in 1999, thereby delaying the country's economic recovery, after two years of GDP contraction in 1996-97 and modest growth (3.5%) in 1998.

The economic slowdown and disrupted transport routes due to the Yugoslav crisis have had a negative impact on trade performance, with a current-account deficit expected to exceed 6% of GDP. On the positive side, the currency board will maintain a cap on inflation and GDP is expected to grow again at a rate of 3% in 2000. The government has also had some success in reducing the share of the shadow economy, whose size is now estimated at between 20-40% of the official economy.

The IMF and World Bank have been lauding Bulgaria's economic turnabout and willingness for reform. In February 1999, the IMF approved a $860 million loan to reduce the balance-of-payments deficit and to foster further reform. Although Bulgaria is still regarded as a risk country, investors' confidence has risen over the past year.

Main Economic Indicators

	Unit	1997	1998	1999*
GDP growth	%	–6.9	3.5	–1.0
GDP	$ million	9,370	11,855	
GDP per capita	$ per person	1135	1495	
Unemployment rate	%	13.7	12.2	13.7
Inflation (CPI) (year avg.)	%	1,082	22.3	
Foreign Direct Investment	$ million	636	478	n.a.
FDI	$	467	376	**220

Source: EBRD, OECD, EIU.
* Preliminary figure.
** First-half 1999.

---

1.   Bulgaria opted for the DM as the reserve currency used to back-up domestic money supply, which reflects primarily the strategic objective of joining the EU. The government has announced its intention to maintain indefinitely the currency board and the existing exchange of 1,000 Lev to the DM.

Privatisation and Restructuring

Bulgaria's privatisation programme picked up speed after the present government under Prime Minister Kostov came to power in 1997. Although the Privatisation Law had been enacted in 1992 already, only an estimated 20% of state assets were spun off between 1991 and 1997. The Kostov government boosted sales of small assets under a low-price privatisation programme. Larger and more attractive assets were retained by the government until investors' confidence would build up.

By end-1998, the private-sector share of GDP had increased to 62%, and was expected to increase to 70% by end-1999. Cumulative foreign direct investment (FDI) amounted to $1.9 billion for the period 1992 to 1998, with more than 70% invested in the years 1996 to 1998. The Foreign Investment Agency (FIA) expected foreign direct investment (FDI) in 1999 to reach $1 billion for the first time in the country's history. Bulgaria's FDI requirements are pegged at $1.5-2 billion by the FIA. The FIA predicts a structural shift in FDI in 2000-01, as infrastructure investments will become proportionally more important at the expense of capital inflows linked to privatisation.

Prominent privatised companies include the telephone monopoly BTC (finalisation of the $510 million acquisition by Dutch and Greek telephone companies of a 51% stake was still pending in late 1999) and the provisional sale of the financially ailing Kremikovtsi steel works to a Bulgarian trading firm for $310 million. The sale of Bulbank, the country's flagship bank, did not take place as initially expected before the end of 1999. Other important sale, albeit not in revenue terms for the government, included deeply indebted national carrier Balkan Airlines, four pharmaceutical companies, compact disc manufacturer DZU, and the Chimco nitrogen fertiliser plant.

The sale of Chimco, which took place in April 1999, had a noteworthy energy market aspect to it. After four unsuccessful tenders between 1994 and 1998, Chimco was finally sold to IBE Trans. The US-based company induced Bulgargaz into reducing the Lv70 million debt owed to it by Chimco. Also, Bulgargaz would deliver Russian gas to the plant at a reduced price (to be negotiated between IBE Trans and Gazprom).

In October 1999, Russia's Lukoil bought a majority stake in Bulgaria's largest refinery **Neftochim** at **Burgas**. Lukoil was to pay $101 million for 58% equity, invest $408.3 million[1], and take on the refinery's debt which is equivalent to $229 million. There were two other short-listed bidders[2]. Lukoil is freed of all liability with regards to environmental damage at the complex. The Bulgarian government was negotiating a $30 million loan with the World Bank for a clean-up. Observers believe that Burgas refinery could benefit from shortages arising in Kosovo and the Federal Republic of Yugoslavia by supplying these markets.

The sale of the **Petrol AD** gasoline retailer was understood to be closed by late 1999. In April 1999, Russia's **Yukos** signed a preliminary agreement to buy – through a Cyprus-based subsidiary – a 51% stake of Petrol for $50 million. The deal rceived a green-light by the

1. Actually, only $268 million are to be spent on the refinery per se, mainly for a new catalytic reformer due to start operations in 2003. The remaining $140 million will be invested in developing Lukoil oil reserves in Russia, which will secure feedstock for the refinery. Furthermore, the Bulgarian Government wrote off Neftochim's debts equivalent to $172.4 million.
2. The other bidders were: Balkan Oil Consortium (which includes ICB – see following footnote – and several Russian companies); and offshore company Logomat Services.

country's anti-trust authorities in July 1999, under the condition that ICB[1] should continue to buy certain quota of oil products from the Burgas Neftochim refinery over a period of three years. Petrol AD has a network of 450 stations. The sale of Petrol AD was made easier by a new law, which freed gasoline prices as from July 1999. Previously, prices were fixed by the Neftochim refinery.

Energy stands out prominently among infrastructure projects, for which the FIA plans to attract foreign investments. Three such projects – the **Upper Arda** hydroelectric power station[2], and the **Maritza (Iztok) East 1** and **Maritza East 3** thermal power plants – require a total of $1.5 billion investment[3].

Other energy sectors will be only partly privatised. The state gas company **Bulgargaz** will maintain a monopoly over gas imports and transit to Turkey, Greece and Macedonia until 2006[4]. Non-transit gas transport and distribution are not earmarked for denationalisation for the time being. It is planned to create a company for high-pressure gas pipelines and regional low-pressure distribution companies in August 2000. Bulgargaz is expected to contribute its network assets as minority stakes in future joint venture companies, which will hopefully include foreign partners, as well as domestic ones (e.g. municipalities).

The financial turnabout of Bulgargaz in view of partial privatisation is underway. Tax debts are being written off and Lev 158 million debts re-scheduled, whilst Bulgargaz is spelling out a stringent program to collect about Lev 500 million debts from 28 corporate customers. Bulgargaz will have to pay back its Lev 230 million tax arrears over three years. Bulgargaz' largest debtors are the recently privatised **Kremikovtsi** steel works, four fertiliser plants and several district heating companies. Bulgargaz seems determined to cut gas supplies on defaulting customers, as it already once demonstrated at the expense of the Kremikovtsi works.

The Privatisation Agency has been trying to sell 22 small hydro-power plants since late 1998, using several foreign advisors. Technical work on the sale, known as the NEK-1 stage, should be completed in spring 2000. The lack of success of NEK-1 so far is imputed to tensions between the Privatisation Agency and the erstwhile Energy Committee (now the State Agency for Energy and Energy Resources, *see below*) on the one hand, and uncooperative behaviour of the state electricity company NEK.

1. ICB (International Consortium of Bulgaria) is jointly owned by Yukos, Austria's OMV and MEBO – an employee-management buy-out of Petrol. Yukos assigned its rights to Petrol shares to ICB.
2. In October 1999, Bulgaria's national electricity company NEK and Turkey's **Ceylan Holding** formed a 50:50 joint venture to build a $220 million cascade of three hydro-power plants at **Gorna Arda** river. The plant will have a capacity of 170 MW to produce 466 million kWh per year, some 12% of which is earmarked for exports to Turkey. Completion of the plant is scheduled for 2006.
3. Germany's **RWE** is mulling investing up to DM1 billion in the **Maritza Iztok** mines and in the rehabilitation of the **Maritza East 2** thermal power plant. Other sources reported investments of $400 million for the power plant and $150 million for the mine.
4. US company **Enron** is positioning itself for the times when Bulgargaz's monopoly will end, by signing a memorandum of co-operation with Bulgargaz in October 1999.

THE ENERGY SECTOR

Energy Overview

Main Energy Indicators

		1995	**1996**	**1997**
TPES	mtoe	22.904	22.598	20.616
Net Imports	mtoe	13.301	12.949	10.944
Net Oil Imports	mtoe	6.559	5.856	5.019
Net Gas Imports	mtoe	4.561	4.729	3.851
Electricity Production	GWh	40719	41472	41560
TPES/GDP	toe per thousand 90 $ PPP	0.476	0.523	0.512
TPES/Population	toe per capita	2.73	2.69	2.48
CO_2 emission from fuel combustion	mt of CO_2	56.88	55.03	51.00
CO_2/TPES	t CO_2 per toe	2.48	2.43	2.47
CO_2/GDP	t CO_2 per 1990 $ PPP	1.18	1.27	1.27
CO_2/Population	t CO_2 per capita	6.77	6.59	6.14

Source: IEA.

Figure 13   Bulgaria Energy Balance (1997)

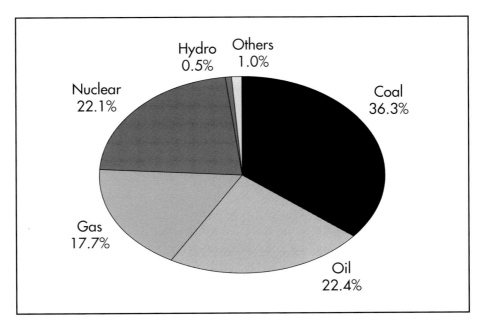

Source: IEA.

Figure 14   **Bulgaria TPES (1990-97)**

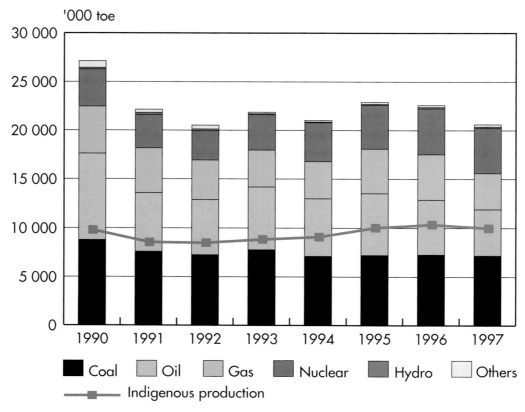

Source: IEA.

Energy Policy   The priorities in energy policy matters are clearly spelled out in an Energy Strategy, which was adopted by the Government in August 1998 and approved by Parliament in spring 1999[1]. The main goals are:

■ Reliable and cost-competitive energy supplies.

■ Nuclear safety.

■ Enhancement of the country's self-sufficiency.

■ Environmentally friendly development of the energy sector.

■ Establishment of a competitive domestic energy market.

■ Integration of the national system and market in the wider European markets.

In order to achieve the goals, the following measures are envisaged:

■ Harmonising the domestic regulatory framework with EU legislation.

■ Structural reform and privatisation to create a competitive market in the energy sector, structural reform in the electricity and gas sectors.

---

1.   "National Strategy for Development of Energy and Energy Efficiency until 2010", State Energy and Energy Resources Agency, August 1998, www.doe.bg/pages/strateg_engl.html. The Strategy is to be updated every year.

The Bulgarian authorities are aware that they will need foreign investment and technology to further develop the country's hydrocarbon potential. The lion's share of E&P is currently undertaken by domestic operator PDNG. Terms for foreign investors are therefore expected to be flexible enough to attract more exploration funds into the country.

Refining

Bulgaria has three refineries, but only the Neftochim complex at Burgas is active.

The integrated **Neftochim** complex has a crude throughput capacity of 6.6 million tons/year, and is one of the largest in Eastern Europe. Cracking capacity of 1.2 million tons/year is equivalent to 19% of crude and catalytic reforming capacity is equivalent to 5% of crude capacity. The refinery is chiefly fed by Russian crude oil. Until now, deliveries have been through intermediaries at a cost of some $140/metric ton. With **Lukoil** taking over 58% of the ownership of the refinery (See above), oil deliveries will be priced at an estimated $70/metric ton. Neftochim has been in operation since 1964. It comprises a refinery, a petrochemical and a polymer plant.

Burgas Refinery Capacity 1998

	'000 tons/year	% of crude
Air distillation	6,648	100
Catalytic cracking	1,235	19
Cat-hydro cracking	0	0
Catalytic reforming	319	5

Source: O&GJ, December 1998.

The apparent complexity of the refinery has improved over the 1990s. However, this is the result of a fall in air distillation capacity, from 12 mt in 1990 to less than 7 mt in 1998, rather than an increase in conversion capacity.

Over 1998, the refinery made progress in reducing its once considerable debt. However, the refinery's export sales apparently have suffered from hostilities in the FR of Yugoslavia. In addition, progressive lowering of import barriers threatens its long-term position on the domestic market. The refinery supplies about 60% of the Bulgarian market. In the past, it has lost market shares to importers, mainly from Greece and Romania. Most of the refinery's products are sold to the recently privatised retailer **Petrol**, who had to guarantee to continue buying Neftochim products (See Chapter Privatisation above). In a bid to help the refinery, the Government suspended early in 1999 the remaining 5% import duty on crude oil.

There is only one products pipeline in Bulgaria, connecting Burgas to Pleven. Neftochim exports some oil products to FYROM (FYR of Macedonia) by road haulage.

The **Pleven**[1] and **Russe** refineries (both located at Pleven) became inactive in the 1990's. The new owner of the Pleven refinery has indicated that the refinery will be at full capacity (1.2 mt) by mid-1999. The refinery used to supply some 80% of the local lubricant market. Without investment of between $20 to 40 million, the plant will not be able to produce oil products that meet EU standards.

---

1. Ownership of the refinery, which had been scheduled for liquidation in 1996 amidst much controversy, was finally granted to a group of investors who agreed to assume the plant's enormous debts. Since this time, the plant has been idle and wages have not been paid. In 1998 the district court declared the company insolvent, but in November 1999, a Swiss-Norwegian consortium acquired the rights an obligations of previous owners Euroenergy.

Oil Products Output and Consumption

Bulgaria: Oil Products Output and Consumption (million tons)

	1990	**1991**	**1992**	**1993**	**1994**	**1995**	**1996**	**1997**
Domestic supply	8500	5672	5539	5993	5438	5499	5310	4557
Imports	1024	1653	3241	1494	900	573	465	634
Exports	709	34	164	556	1887	2034	1608	1518
Consumption	8480	5581	5683	5906	5506	5299	5298	4570

Source: IEA.

Bulgaria has changed from a net importer of oil products in 1990 to a net products exporter in 1994. This was mainly a result of a 3 million tonnes a year fall in consumption in the early 1990's, due to economic decline. The Bulgarian economy shrank by 26% between 1991 and 1996, despite a slight recovery in 1994/95. However, the foreseeable economic recovery should lead to a resumption of growth in demand for oil products and a corresponding fall in exports.

Bulgarian Oil Products Balance 1997 (thousand tons)

	Production	**Consumption**	**Import requirement*/ Export surplus**
LPG and ethane	84	87	−1
Gasoline	1112	641	451
Jet fuel	152	228	−58
Diesel and HGO	2040	1013	868
Heavy fuel oil	1477	1538	−292
Naphtha	615	673	−58
Other	227	253	−26
Total**	5830	4557	1518

Source: IEA.
* Negative figure indicates imports.
** Totals do not add up, difference due to int'l marine bunkers, stock changes.

In 1997, a total of 1.02 million tons of gasoline, diesel and jet fuel were consumed in the transport sector, accounting for 23% of total oil products consumption. HFO is mainly consumed in power generation (heat and CHP plants), with limited use in industry.

Industry consumption of oil products was 1.34 million tons in 1997, accounting for 30% of total oil products consumption. Naphtha is the most important petrochemicals feedstock, with 673,000 tonnes consumed in 1997.

The Government is selling a 51% stake in the state-owned filling station chain, **Petrol**, which supplies about 30% of the domestic refined products market and owns about 450 filling stations (See Chapter Privatisation above).

The resumption of economic growth as from 1998 should lead to a rising trend for oil products consumption through to 2010. According to Bulgarian forecasts, consumption of oil products is projected to rise from 4.8 mt in 1996 to an estimated 6.6 mt in 2010, on the assumption that real GDP growth averages 3% per year. The strongest growth will be for transport fuels, with combined demand for gasoline, diesel and jet fuel expected to grow by 79% from

Figure 15   Bulgaria Oil Product Consumption (1997)

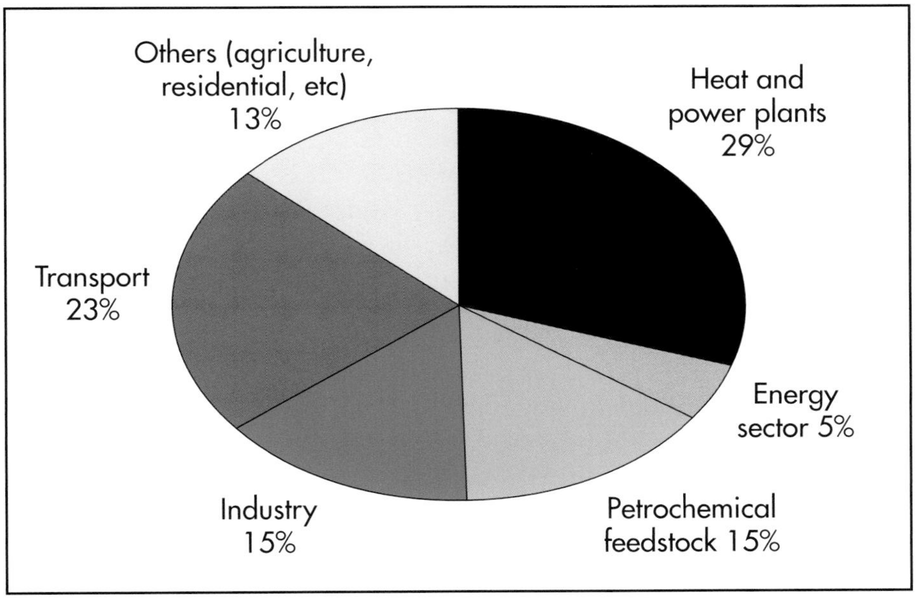

Source: IEA.

1.4 million tons in 1996 to 2.8 million tons in 2010. Bulgaria at present has low car ownership by EU standards and a fast growing car fleet. Expansion of smaller, private sector businesses is expected to lead to strong growth in road haulage.

Oil Infrastructure

Bulgaria's only existing oil pipeline network was built to transport oil from the Tyulenovo-Shabla field (on northeastern coast) to the Pleven refinery (See Map 7: Bulgaria, Romania – Oil and Gas Infrastructure).

Two oil transit projects are competing for investment, as part of the Bulgarian policy to develop its energy transit role. There are, however, numerous other proposed export routes for Caspian oil that would bypass Bulgaria.

■ A Burgas – Alexandroupolis transit pipeline would transport Caspian oil delivered by sea to the Black Sea port of Burgas (Bulgaria) and then onward to Alexandroupolis (Greece). The aim is to by-pass the Bosphorus. The initial capacity under discussion is 15 mt/year, increasing to 40 mt/year. Bulgarian, Greek and Russian companies have combined to form the Transbalkanneft joint venture to promote the construction of the pipeline.

■ The second pipeline (AMBO project) would transit Russian gas through Burgas to Vlore in Albania. This project is in the study stage, but it has the advantage of providing a port at Vlore, which could be upgraded to accommodate supertankers.

Legislation for the management and financing of strategic oil stocks is under preparation. It will part from the current regime, which declares data relating to oil stocks a state secret.

NATURAL GAS

Gas Supply and Consumption

Most of Bulgaria's natural gas needs are supplied from imports from Russia. In 1998, it imported 3.8 bcm of natural gas. Domestic gas production was only some 40 million m³ in 1998. Current consumption is about 4.5 bcm and confined mainly to power and industry. In 1997, 2.29 bcm of natural gas was used in power generation and 2.15 bcm in industry.

Residential and small industry demand has been severely constrained by lack of availability of gas and high gas prices. Residential heating requirements are currently met partly by district heating. Considerable investment is required in the gas distribution network in order to improve the availability of natural gas for domestic users.

Assuming an economic recovery with stable GDP growth averaging 3% per year through to 2010, natural gas consumption is assumed to increase to 6.1 bcm by 2010, an increase of slightly less than 1 bcm. This includes gas inputs to power generation required to meet incremental demand for power. However, it does not include fuel switching. This implies that the actual requirement for natural gas in power generation could be considerably higher. The development of new gas-fired power plants, or the conversion of old thermal plants to natural gas will depend on restructuring in the electricity sector, including regulations on IPPs, network access, tariff and competition issues.

The Energy Strategy presents a projection for the development of residential gas distribution, which foresees that by 2010 255,000 residential consumers (dwellings) can be supplied with gas. Growth in industrial demand will be limited by energy efficiency improvements and the decline of large, energy intensive industries.

Projection of the Development of Residential Gas Distribution

	Units	1997-2005	2006-2010
Apartments supplied	Thousands	110	145
Residents supplied	Thousands	300	400
Gas consumption	Million m³/annum	193	257

Natural Gas Policy

The major gas policy priority is the diversification of gas sources, to include suppliers other than Russia. The prospects for considerable non-Russian gas to be delivered to Bulgaria in a foreseeable future appear to be slim. Perhaps the most realistic alternative supplies could come from the North Sea, since Romania pursues the same diversification goal as Bulgaria and is looking at linking its gas network to Hungary's and thereby western Europe. Longer-term, Bulgaria could become a transit route for Azeri and/or Turkmen gas transiting via Turkey to Europe. LNG imports seems unlikely, because of traffic constraints through the Bosphorus. Another distant possibility is the supply of Libyan gas, if a pipeline from Libya is extended to Greece.

Gas Industry Structure

The gas sector is at present operated by a state-owned vertically integrated monopoly, **Bulgargaz**, which is under the control of the State Agency for Energy and Energy Resources (former Committee for Energy). The Government is planning a slow and cautious break-up of the gas monopoly, in a way that takes into account the strong position of Gazprom. Under the current restructuring plan, Bulgargaz would retain a monopoly of transmission and imports until 2006. The Government appears to have secured IMF backing for this not very investor-friendly decision. The Government will retain control of Bulgargaz and recently raised the company's working capital from Lv 83 million to Lv 370 million. It also intends to re-schedule Bulgargaz' debts until mid-2002.

The only step the Government is willing to make in the near term is to break up Bulgargaz's local distribution network. By March 2000, an international tender will open to create local gas distribution companies. The Government is likely to welcome associations between foreign investors, municipalities and Bulgargaz, which will bring in its existing infrastructure as assets to the new entities. Later in 2000, some additional Bulgargaz assets, including storage and transmission, may be floated.

The Energy Law sets out a new regulatory regime for natural gas and introduces some degree of competition. However, the extent to which this will enable market opening is unclear and secondary legislation will be required to deal with access, tariff, regulation and other important issues.

The main provisions of the Energy Law with an impact on the natural gas sector are:

- Separation of policy and regulatory functions including those pertaining to gas. The State Commission for Energy Regulation (SERC) reports directly to the Council of Ministers. Its responsibilities will include tariffs and prices, auditing of accounts and licensing issues.

- A single buyer model for gas to break the hold of Gazprom and the Overgas import company. Overgas, a joint venture between Gazprom and Bulgargaz, is under investigation for fraudulent practices. There are no firm plans for third party access rights to networks.

While the stated objective of the Government in the reorganisation of the gas sector is to meet the terms of the EU gas single market directive, the issues of market opening are yet to be fully clarified.

Gazprom and Overgas at present have a virtual stranglehold over the Bulgarian natural gas market. Not only do they control gas imports, but they also have shareholdings in the majority of distribution companies, raising some questions about the potential for de-monopolisation of the industry. This results from the sale by municipalities of their shares in distribution companies to private investors. At present only 2% of gas sales are by distributors. Households and small industrial consumers have limited access to gas due to the lack of low and medium pressure pipes.

Gas Infrastructure and Transit

Bulgaria has a current transit capacity of 10.5 bcm per year. Russian gas is supplied to Turkey through eastern Thrace. Transit to Greece has been limited by slow development of the Greek transmission and distribution network. The construction of a spur off the main line in 1997 has facilitated supply of natural gas to Skopje (FYR of Macedonia).

Bulgaria has the ambition to expand its current role and become a transit hub for Russian and Caspian gas sold to the Balkans and Central Europe. If Bulgaria succeeds in its ambition of becoming a transit hub, this should lead to greater diversification of supply and remove one of the stumbling blocks to greater gasification. Bulgaria also has insufficient storage capacity for effective peak demand management.

Bulgaria's own gas grid is underdeveloped. The network is a ring structure that supplies large consumers, such as chemicals plants, power generators and a handful of distributors prepared to build low pressure infrastructure for towns near the pipeline.

The key planned infrastructure to facilitate gas transit are:

■ A gas supply framework agreement with Russia calls for an increase in imports from 6 bcm to 19 bcm by 2010, with the bulk of supplies destined for Turkey, Greece and FYR of Macedonia. By mid-1999, Bulgargaz was about twelve months behind schedule in expanding its gas transit system under an agreement initially reached with Gazprom in 1997. The pact was re-visited, and Russian gas transit through Bulgaria are now scheduled to reach 17.9 bcm by 2002, including 14 bcm destined for the Turkish market. Ultimately, the gas transit capacity will be expanded from 10.5 bcm to 20 bcm per annum.

■ Gas storage capacity is confined to 1.2 bcm at Chiren. It will be expanded to 1.7 bcm.

■ A mooted LNG terminal on the Black Sea is unlikely due to the problems associated with shipments through the Bosphorus.

■ Preliminary talks have taken place with Shell and Botas about a new pipeline from Turkmenistan through Iran, Turkey, Bulgaria and into Central Europe. Another proposal would link Bulgaria with North Sea gas through Romania.

Gas Pricing

Bulgarian gas prices are regulated and tend to be high due to monopolist rents imposed by Gazprom and transit fees through Romania. These prices discourage some potential consumers. The pricing structure is over-simplified and unrelated to real costs, especially in the transport, distribution and service parts of the supply chain. Industry consumers cross-subsidise households. Current prices are based on the import price plus 11% to cover exploitation costs, capital costs and profit. Cost based prices were to be phased in from January 1999.

COAL

Coal Production and Reserves

Bulgaria produced some 31.95 mt of coal in 1997. Almost 85% of output is low-quality brown coal. Furthermore, the country imported 3.9 mt of coking and other bituminous coal in 1997, largely from Ukraine. Coal is the largest primary energy source in Bulgaria, accounting for 36% of TPES in 1997. Lignite production plummeted from a peak of at 36.6 mt in 1987 to a level of 25-26 mt in the years 1991-94, before increasing back to 28.1 mt in 1996. The 1997 economic downturn took its toll on lignite output, which dropped back to 26.9 mt. Bulgaria's reserves are estimated at some 2.5 billion tons of lignite and 200 mt of sub-bituminous coal.

Most of the coal is used to fuel power and CHP plants[1]. Bulgaria's coal-fired capacity is 6,556 MWe, including CHP.

---

1.   51% of coal was used at power plants, 31% at CHP plants in 1997. Other important coal consumers are the residential sector (6.4% in 1997) and the metallurgy (5.1%).

State-owned utility **NEK** owns 11,062 MW of capacity (87.9% of total), including 4590 MW of TPP's, and all nuclear, hydro and pumped-storage capacities. Independent producers are mainly district heating companies and large industrial enterprises, who own a total of 1606 MW of capacity (including CHP plants).

There are seven thermal power plants in Bulgaria. All of them are coal-fired and generate an estimated 38% of the electricity produced by NEK.

Coal imports for thermal power plants are limited in order to support nuclear energy and the use of indigenous coal. Plants using imported coal are Bobov Dol, Rousse and Varna. Coal is extracted mainly from the Maritza deposits in southern Bulgaria. There are four thermal power plants in proximity to these reserves: **Maritza-1** and **Maritza East 1-3**.

Between 1994 and 1999, Bulgaria completed the four stages of the largest pumped-storage hydroelectric power station in the country, **Chaira**. Total installed capacity consists of 4 reversible sets of 864 MW (generating mode) and 788 MW (pump mode).

Bulgaria has one nuclear power plant, **Kozloduy**, which consists of six units using Russian-designed VVER reactors. Units 1-4 were commissioned in the 1970s and early 1980s. Units 5 and 6 were commissioned in 1988 and 1993. Total capacity of Kozloduy is 3760 MW and the plant currently generates almost 42% of Bulgaria's total electricity needs.

Bulgarian Power Stations

Power Station	Type	Capacity (MWe)	Year Commissioned
Maritza East 1	Lignite	4 × 50 (200)	1958-61
Maritza East 2	Lignite	4 × 150, 2 × 210, 2 × 215 (1450)	1966-95
Maritza East 3	Lignite	4 × 210 (840)	1977-80
Bobov Dol	Brown coal	3 × 210 (630)	1973-75
Maritza 3	lignite	2 × 25, 1 × 120 (170)	1951-54
Varna	imported coal/gas	6 × 210 (1,260)	1966-76
Ruse	imported coal	2 × 30, 2 × 110, 2 × 60 (400)	1964-85
Belmeken-Sestrimo cascade	hydro	735	1974-76
Chaira PSP	PSP-hydro	864	1994-99
Vacha cascade	hydro	401	1933-84
Batak	hydro	231	1957-59
Arda cascade	hydro	274	1958-65
Iskar cascade	hydro	85.5	1927-57
Sandanska Bistritsa cascade	hydro	54.7	1969-71
Prinska Bistritsa cascade	hydro	47	1981-92
Kozloduy 1-4	nuclear	4 × 440	1974-82
Kozloduy 5-6	nuclear	2 × 1000 (3760)	1988-93

Source: NEK.

Electricity Supply and Demand Outlook

The projected electricity demand and maximum electricity power supply loads – as presented in the Energy Strategy – are shown in the table below:

Electricity Demand Projections

Year	Basic Scenario		Minimum scenario	
	GWh	MW	GWh	MW
1996	42352	7923	42352	7923
1997	38309	7115	38309	7115
1998	42580	7892	38780	7201
1999	44809	8297	40809	7570
2000	46660	8634	42660	7906
2001	48731	9010	44731	8283
2002	51414	9498	47114	8716
2003	53337	9848	48837	9029
2004	55021	10154	50521	9336
2005	56479	10419	51979	9601
2006	57750	10650	53250	9832
2007	58754	10832	54254	10014
2008	59567	10980	55067	10162
2009	60586	11166	55886	10311
2010	61696	11368	56996	10513

The Energy Strategy foresees a "quite rapid" consumption growth with the onset of economic recovery, although industrial capacity is presently operating at only 50-60%. It is argued that economic growth will lead to an increase in demand in the residential sector.

An increased demand of anywhere between 49% and 61% in the coming decade, as foreseen by the Energy Strategy, is questionable. The foreseen increase in industrial power demand is unlikely to happen, given that much of this projected demand comes from inefficient heavy industry, which must face restructuring and rationalisation.

The Strategy believes that a large part of the present generating capacity can be cost-effectively rehabilitated, extending the design life of the capacity. Some older capacity, however, is earmarked for de-commissioning (1420 MW until 2010; a further 1200 MW between 2010 and 2015). Based on the projected demand growth, the following new generating capacity is foreseen:

Bulgaria: New Power Generation Capacity

	1999-2005	2006-2010
Chaira pumped storage station	430	–
Rehabilitation of existing thermal power plants	430	–
Replacement capacity at Maritza East 1 TPP	900	–
New TPP capacity with imported coal	–	–
New nuclear	–	600
New hydro-electric capacity	–	600
Combustion-turbine backfits on DH plants	240	280
Peak-load combustion-turbine capacity	100	250
Total	2100	1730

The share of thermal power (using mainly domestic coal) is to increase gradually during the first decade at the expense of nuclear power. The Energy Strategy envisions the Maritza East TPP's and the nuclear plant to cater for base-load capacity, with capacity utilisations of 6000-7000 hrs per annum. Power generation from the Maritza East TPP's is forecast to grow from 11.8 TWh in 1998 to 19.5 TWh in 2005 and 21 TWh in 2010. Consumption of lignite from the Maritza East mines is forecast to grow from 23 mt in 1998 to 36 mt in 2005 and 38 mt in 2010.

In the period 2003-2005, about 900 MW are planned to be commissioned at Maritza East 1 (three 300 MW units). The government expects a new 600 MW nuclear unit to become necessary at **Belene** after 2006.

Shoulder-load capacity will be provided by combustion turbines (240 MW at **Devnya** TPP and 250 MW at **Sofia** TPP) and by 600 MW of new TPP capacity fired by imported coal. The annual utilisation rate of these plants is planned to be in the range 3000-4500 hours per annum.

Peak load capacity will be provided by hydro-electric capacity, pumped storage, and peaking combustion-turbine capacity, with utilisations of less than 2500 hours per annum. This capacity plan will give a reserve margin of 18-21% (in line with UCTE requirements), with technical power losses of 1200 MW.

Capital investment requirements are estimated at some $7.3 billion until 2010, as shown in the table below:

Bulgaria: Power Sector Investment Requirements (million $)

	Until 2001	**2002-2005**	**2006-2010**
Upgrading of Kozloduy NPP	216	184	270
TPP rehabilitation	434	262	30
Replacement capacity at Maritza East 1 TPP	285	1064	–
Combustion-turbine backfits on DH plants	145	150	–
New TPP's fired with natural gas and imported coal	–	–	1090
New nuclear capacity	–	700	1220
Pumped storage, and new hydro-electric capacity	147	270	18
Transmission and distribution	231	350	215
Total	1458	2980	2843

The following major investment priorities have been identified in Bulgaria's power sector:

■ **Varna** Thermal Power Plant (TPP): A proposal is being discussed for the Varna plant to be operated on a concession basis for a period of 15 years by a private operator. Upgrade of the Varna plant is to be addressed within the World Bank's Energy Loan II. Three units of the power station, which were designed for Ukrainian anthracite, are to be upgraded to use various grades of coal.

EBRD Power Sector Refurbishment Project includes:

■ Rehabilitation of the **Maritza East 3** thermal power station (units 1-4, 210 MW); US company **Entergy** is planning a $400 million rehabilitation project for the station.

■ Upgrade of the high-voltage transmission network;

■ Installation of domestic and industrial meters.

■ Negotiations are underway with EBRD and EIB for the funding of a € 200 million modernisation programme of the country's power transmission system.

Power Transmission, Trade and Interconnections

The high-voltage transit network and the distribution networks are owned and operated by NEK. There are 85 km of 750 kV lines, 1862 km of 400 kV lines, 2296 km of 200 kV lines, and 8165 km of 110 kV lines (See Map 8: Bulgaria, Romania – Power System).

The Bulgarian power system will be interconnected with the countries in the region[1], including Ukraine (one 750 kV line[2]), Moldova (one 400 kV line), Romania (one 750 kV line, two 400 kV lines, one 220 kV line), Turkey (one 400 kV), Greece (one 400 kV), and former Yugoslavia (one 400 kV).

Bulgaria's power system operates in parallel (synchronised) with Romania and the UCTE members former Yugoslavia and Greece. The completion of the improved control system for NEK, which has been financed by the World Bank, will facilitate Bulgaria's eventual membership in UCTE.

Independent Power and Cogeneration Projects

Most major cities in Bulgaria have district heating cogeneration systems. The heating plants generate 22% of Bulgaria's household heat consumption (hot water) and about 58% of industrial heat needs (hot water and steam).

The district heating systems use mostly natural gas and some fuel oil. Those units using natural gas are candidates for conversion to gas turbines. Plants, which could be turned into combined cycle, are Sofia (Sofia, Sofia Iztok), Pernik, Plovdiv, Pleven and Shumen.

There are nine state industrial enterprises with cogeneration capacity greater than 10 MW. These include large petroleum and petrochemical plants (Neftochim, Plama), chemical facilities (Devnya and Svishtov), a metallurgical plant (Kremikovtsi), a tire plant (Vida), fabric plants (Stara Zagora and Gabrovo) and a fertiliser plant (Chimco in Vratsa). The plants use gas, coal and fuel oil and primarily produce steam for the factories and power. Some of these co-generators sell surplus electricity back to the NEK grid. The current sales terms with NEK may not be sufficiently attractive to induce investments in new co-generation capacity.

Opportunities are emerging for independent power suppliers. As NEK's monopoly recedes, independent power producers will capture more markets. The government's Concession Law permits concessions to be issued in power generation and transmission.

---

1. A 400 kV line is to be built to connect the power systems of Bulgaria and FY of Macedonia. The 100 km line will run from Chervena Mogila (Bulgaria) to Dubrovo (FYROM). Its cost is estimated at $23 million.
2. In the past, about 800 MW could be imported from Ukraine at periods of peak demand, with about 4-5 TWh imported each year. Ukraine may be unable or unwilling to provide the energy and capacity that was previously supplied and for which the 750 kV transmission line was originally installed.

NUCLEAR POWER

General Background

Bulgaria operates six nuclear power units at **Kozloduy**; all of them are VVER-type reactors of Soviet design. This type of reactor offers many similarities with Western pressurised water reactors (PWRs), but their early designs present grave safety deficiencies. Kozloduy-1 and 2, two VVER-440 reactors (Model 230) completed in the mid-1970s, are considered the least safe of the six reactors at the Kozloduy station. Kozloduy-3 and 4 are later versions of the V-230, completed in the early 1980s, which feature an improved emergency core cooling system (ECCS). Kozloduy-5 and 6 are more recently designed VVER-1000 units. The Kozloduy site, which has a total installed capacity of 3,760 MWe (3,538 MWe net), is located on the Danube some 125 km north of Sofia.

A second nuclear power plant site was chosen in the early 1980's at **Belene**, near the town of Svishtov on the Danube. The original project called for the construction of two units, with another four units to be built at a later date. The site was prepared with all the necessary infrastructure to host six VVER-1000 reactors. Construction of the first unit began in 1986. It was about 50% complete in 1990 (including the pressure vessel and the steam generators, in storage in the Czech Republic), when construction was stopped because of lack of funds. By that time, Bulgaria had invested around $1 billion at the site.

To meet projected demand – especially when Kozloduy-1 to 4 will be shut down – and taking the position that Bulgaria has no alternative to nuclear power, government bodies and NEK have repeatedly proposed completion of Belene-1. Feasibility studies have been undertaken, and discussions have been held between relevant Bulgarian and Russian ministries. No decision has yet been taken.

An alternative and more recent proposal is to write off the Belene investment and to construct a seventh unit on the Kozloduy site, making use of Belene-1 components.

Since 1975, nuclear power has been consistently gaining ground in the overall production of electricity in the country. In recent years, Kozloduy's output has been growing at an annual rate of around 4.75%. The 1997 nuclear share in total electricity production was 42.7% (17.75 TWh gross electric power), down slightly on the previous year's figure. In the past, the share of nuclear power has often risen to 50% because of thermal plant inefficiency, fuel shortages and insufficient rainfall for hydropower.

The load factor of the 440 MW units has been reasonably high (up to 80% or more for Unit4) in the 1980s. After 1991, because of the long outages needed for modernisation, load factors decreased to 60% or less. The 1000 MW units operate with a load factor, which is determined by the specific requirements of the grid.

Regulatory Structure for Nuclear Power

Kozloduy is operated by state-owned **NEK**. Article 18 of the Constitution of Bulgaria and the Law on the Use of Atomic Energy for Peaceful Purposes vest ownership of nuclear power plants with the State. The electricity re-structuring programme unequivocally states that nuclear facilities will remain under state control in the future.

The State Committee on the Use of Atomic Energy for Peaceful Purposes (CUAEPP), set up in 1985, is the nuclear regulatory authority with jurisdiction over nuclear matters, including the implementation of national policy.

CUAEPP is made up of ministerial representatives, together with representatives from other administrations involved in the safe use of nuclear energy, and is under the control of the Council of Ministers. One of its entities is the Inspectorate for the Safe Use of Atomic Energy. The Inspectorate is responsible for establishing safety requirements that all nuclear licensees must meet, verifying that the requirements are met, establishing licensing requirements, processing license applications and issuing licenses. One of the Inspectorate's units provides on-site inspectors; there are six such inspectors at the Kozloduy plant and CUAEPP's Emergency Response Centre. CUAEPP grants annual operating licenses for all six Kozloduy units, each time after an inspection.

A consortium of European safety authorities[1] is helping the Bulgarian authorities to set up a western-style licensing procedure. Using funding from the European Commission's PHARE programme, the consortium has looked at the legal and regulatory framework in Bulgaria. Under the PHARE programme, Bulgaria has also received an ECU 7 million loan to fund the work of the country's nuclear regulator. The International Atomic Energy Agency (IAEA) completed a review of Bulgaria's nuclear regulatory authority. The Bulgarian Government ponders splitting Kozloduy from NEK.

Kozloduy and EU Accession

The four older units of Kozloduy have been overshadowing Bulgaria's planned accession to the EU. The European Commission has made it clear that Bulgaria must present an acceptable timetable for decommissioning the four older reactor before accession talks can begin. The timetable initially set forth in Bulgaria's Energy Strategy paper[2] is too protracted in the opinion of the European Commission. The Agenda 2000 of the EU Commission called for Units 1 and 2 to close in 2001 and Units 3 and 4 in 2001/02.

In November 1999, Bulgaria gave in to EU pressure. Reactors 1 and 2 will be closed in 2002. The closing dates for reactors 3 and 4 will be definitively set in 2002, when the country will adopt a revised energy strategy. The EU expects these two reactors to be retired by 2006 at the latest. To compensate for the early retirement of the reactors, the EU will disburse a non-refundable Euro 200 million from its PHARE programme. The second tranche of this aid will be disbursed in 2002, conditional on the decision to close reactors 3 and 4. Furthermore, a Euro 250 million Euratom credit will be made available for the modernisation of Kozloduy reactors 5 and 6.

Before the agreement was reached, Bulgaria had argued that alternative energy sources and financing must be found before closing the four reactors. Furthermore, it was pointed out that the safety standards of units 1 to 4 have been enhanced through concerted international aid since 1993 to an internationally acceptable level, as was concluded by the 1999 missions of the IAEA and the Western European Nuclear Regulators' Association (WENRA). Modernisation of the four units has absorbed Euro 130 million since 1991, and the programme is scheduled to go on until 2001. The more stringent EU demands are imputed to the promises made by the Berov Government in 1993 to the EBRD, which called for closing Units 1 and 2 by spring 1997 and Units 3 and 4 by late 1998. Furthermore, closure of the units hinged on alternative energy supplies being available in the form of the Chaira pumped-storage power

---

1. The consortium is comprised of IPSN (Institut de Protection et de Sûreté Nucléaire, France) and including GRS (Gesellschaft für Anlagen- und Reaktorsicherheit mbH, Germany), HSE (Health and Safety Executive, United Kingdom) and AVN (AIB-Vinçotte Nucléaire, Belgium).
2. Unit 1 to be shut down in 2003, Unit 2 in 2005, Unit 3 in 2008, Unit 4 in 2010.

station, Kozloduy Units 5 and 6, and the Maritza East and Varna thermal power plants having been modernised. None of these substitution energy supplies are ready by now[1]. Proponents of continued operations of the Kozloduy units argue that the cost of Kozloduy power is 20% below the cost of power generated by power plants fired by domestic coal.

Nuclear Units in Bulgaria

Name	Type	Capacity MWe		Commercial Operation start-up
		Net	**Gross**	
Kozloduy-1	VVER-230	408	440	Jul 1974
Kozloduy-2	VVER-230	408	440	Nov 1975
Kozloduy-3	VVER-230	408	440	Jan 1981
Kozloduy-4	VVER-230	408	440	Jun 1982
Kozloduy-5	VVER-320	953	1000	Sept 1988
Kozloduy-6	VVER-320	953	1000	Dec 1993

Nuclear Safety Aspects

Kozloduy-1, 2, 3 and 4

Kozloduy-1 and 2, two early-design VVER-440 reactors (Model V-230), are considered the least safe of the six reactors at the Kozloduy station. Kozloduy-3 and 4 are later versions of the V-230 which feature an improved emergency core cooling system (ECCS) and improved leak tightness. All four V-230s were shut down in 1991 following an IAEA-sponsored examination, which revealed severe safety problems in design, management and quality assurance.

The weak points of the Kozloduy VVER-440/V-230 reactors were mainly of two types.

■ First, there were weak points inherent to the design. These were essentially the lack of redundancy of safety circuits, under-sized emergency cooling systems, the problem posed by pressure vessel embrittlement, the lack of a containment able to withstand a primary circuit pipe rupture and insufficient confinement of radioactive fission products in the event of an accident, considerable vulnerability in the case of fire or flooding, and faulty evaluation of earthquake-related risks. These shortcomings are, however, compensated by design safety margins larger than those used in Western-type reactors, by great robustness of the equipment, and simplicity of operation.

■ The second weak point of the Kozloduy plants was that the maintenance program was long delayed, and that plant organisation and management were too far from good practices and quality assurance rules. This situation had been aggravated by the departure in 1990 of the Russian experts working at the plant and Bulgaria's limited industrial and scientific infrastructures.

Although Western experts regard VVER-440/230 reactors as insufficiently safe, Bulgarian authorities left little doubt that, in the face of the country's continued need for power, they would rather improve Kozloduy so that the country would no longer have to choose between blackouts and nuclear safety.

---

1. Chaira is completed, but, being designed to provide peak load capacity, it cannot be considered as substitution to the nuclear base-load capacity. Also, it cannot operate more than 8.5 hours/day because of reservoir restrictions.

Several nuclear operators agreed to help as from 1991[1]. In June 1993 Bulgaria received 24 million ECU (about $29 million) from the Nuclear Safety Account administered by the European Bank for Reconstruction and Development (EBRD) to purchase safety-related equipment.

As European experts did not expect the plants to be operated for more than a few years, they made no recommendation for large-scale back-fitting. In return, Bulgaria pledged to follow an alternative energy path that might allow closure of the four units by the end of 1998. Closure of the old VVERs hinged on rehabilitation of the Bulgarian energy sector, including planning for investment in new electricity sources and the necessity to modernise the newer units, Kozloduy-5 and 6. The 1993 agreement indicated that Kozloduy-1 and 2 should be closed by the spring of 1997, when the upgrade of Kozloduy-5 or 6 and construction of the Chaira pumped-storage hydro plant should be completed. The closure of Units 3 and 4 was scheduled for the end of 1998, when Kozloduy-5 and 6, as well as three district heating co-generation units should have been upgraded.

Annealing of Kozloduy-2's pressure vessel was done in April 1992. Analysis of samples from the vessel after treatment showed that embrittlement had been largely reversed. The condition of the vessel at Kozloduy-1 was considered more problematic, in particular because there were differences in the phosphorus and copper content and in the tensile qualities. A controversy developed between Western organisations on the one side, and Bulgarian organisations and the Russian engineering bureau Gidropres on the other side. In 1995 NEK proposed an operating program for Kozloduy-1 limited to six months, with a special base-load-only operating regime, and including preparations for taking samples of, or annealing, the pressure vessel at the conclusion of the cycle. The proposal was accepted by the CUAEPP.

Mechanical analysis of Kozloduy-1 pressure vessel samples was done during the second half of 1996. It gave results very different from those obtained in 1995 through chemical analysis, and raised fundamental questions about the computer codes used to calculate vessel embrittlement for all VVERs and potential effects of annealing. As a result of improvements made in Russia in the analysis of the rate of re-embrittlement following annealing, international experts agreed that risk of brittle rupture of the pressure vessel was sufficiently low for Kozloduy-1 to operate safely most likely to the end of its design life in 2004. Kozloduy-1 was reconnected to the Bulgarian grid at the beginning of 1997.

The Nuclear Safety Account's first major initiative ended in December 1997 without accomplishing its prime goal of shutting down the first-generation Kozloduy VVER-440s. Because of delays and limited experience on the Bulgarian side, not all the safety equipment on site was actually installed. It became evident that early closure of Kozloduy-1 to 4 was no longer feasible by 2000. The EBRD's position was that Bulgaria was legally bound by the NSA agreement to shut down the four units once the agreed replacement capacity was in place.

---

1. Électricité de France (EDF) agreed in June 1991 to "twin" Kozloduy and EDF's Bugey nuclear power plant. In September 1991 Germany sent $11 million worth of spares to Kozloduy from VVER-440s at the closed East German Greifswald plant. The consortium of Western European safety expert organisations, together with WANO (World Association of Nuclear Operators), and their Bulgarian counterparts, agreed on a three-year outage management program for plant restoration, engineering, documentation, creation of a safety committee, and training. One hundred thirty-seven priority backfits were to be implemented both on Kozloduy-1 and Kozloduy-2. Part of the financing was provided by the Bulgarian Government ($10 million) and the European Commission ($15 million). Funded by the EC, experts from the IPSN and the GRS worked together with Bulgarian safety regulators in a program to evaluate the safety of each unit. GRS/IPSN experts also carried out a complete examination of material quality for pressure-boundary components, and repair and partial replacement of main isolation valves in the primary circuit. Other measures were taken to improve the reliability of safety systems, such as installation of interlocks on ECCS, replacement of valves on the feed lines of ECCS pumps, and improvement of the emergency power supply for sprinkler system pumps.

The Bulgarian Government decided to negotiate with the EBRD an extension of the operation of Kozloduy-1 and -2, using the two following arguments: firstly, Bulgaria could not afford to spend $800 million to shut down and replace these two units; secondly, stopping the two reactors would have a catastrophic effect on the Bulgarian economy as no replacement capacity has been built yet. The position of the Bulgarian authorities was that each of the units should be allowed to operate to the end of its design life: 2004 for Unit 1, 2005 for Unit 2, 2011 for Unit 3, and 2012 for Unit 4. Any plant lifetime extension beyond the design life would be excluded.

A positive reply by the EBRD would have amounted to a relaxation in the policy on old VVERs adopted by the G7 in Munich in 1992. It was argued that, given the delays in deploying replacement capacity, the Kozloduy-1 to 4 decommissioning dates could be extended without renegotiation of the 1993 agreement with the EBRD, although NEK would have to demonstrate that the old reactors were really needed and were a least-cost solution. On several occasions the European Commission had expressed concern about the safety of Kozloduy-1 to 4, and recalled that adequate nuclear safety standards is one of the conditions imposed by the European Union to accept new members.

Negotiations between the EBRD and NEK in June 1998 failed to reach agreement on a target date for closing the four units. As a result, the NSA donors asked NEK to propose realistic closure dates, which could be appended to the 1993 agreement. In September 1998 the Bulgarian Government announced that it would agree to close Kozloduy-1 and 2 in 2004 and 2005 respectively, coinciding with the completion of large-scale upgrading and modernisation work at Kozloduy-5 and 6. The Government's closure timetable would then see Kozloduy-3 and 4 shutting down in the period 2008-2012.

NEK planned to invest up to $370 million by the end of 1998 to revitalise Bulgaria's ageing power installations, including the Chaira pumped storage plant, safety reconstruction of all six Kozloduy units, and a sulphur reduction installation for a new coal-fired power plant at the Maritza power complex.

With respect to Kozloduy-1 to 4, NEK launched with EDF a "Comprehensive Program" to bring them to international standards and to operate the units to the end of their design life, considering that previous work had resolved most design deficiencies. The programme included inputs from Siemens, Framatome, Atomenergoexport, and various Bulgarian organisations. The Comprehensive Program has been reviewed by the IAEA. It aims at eliminating the remaining plant deficiencies by 2001-2002. This means, among other things, addressing all so-called category IV safety issues, the most serious VVER-440/230 defects identified by IAEA experts, such as separation of instrumentation and control systems and confinement upgrades.

Kozloduy-5 and 6

The Kozloduy-5 and -6 units are of VVER-1000 Model 320 design. This design is generally consistent with standard international safety practices. Western governments have generally favoured the continued operation of the VVER-1000 nuclear power plants, provided they are retrofitted with instrumentation and control systems more reliable than the original Soviet systems. At the request of NEK, EDF and the Russian design and engineering association MOHT developed a joint project defining a generic reference upgrade program for VVER-1000 reactors called "Generic Reference Program for the Modernisation of the VVER-1000 Model V-320". It was the first to introduce Western-style methodology for selecting, classifying, and prioritising the hundreds of modifications considered necessary or desirable for safety, availability, and operability. The upgrade document was coherent with Russia's own modernisation program for VVER-1000/320 reactors. The modernisation proposals were favourably reviewed by an IAEA mission to Kozloduy-5 and 6. CUAEPP approved the program.

Tenders were put out at the end of 1996. The work was to focus on long-term cooling of the reactors, radiation and fire protection, instrumentation and control and emergency power supply, and enhancing plant operating reliability and availability. It was to include improvements in the units' seismic stability, the performance of safety and mechanical analyses, the installation of diagnostic equipment, and the improvement of components on the secondary side. In addition, the Kozloduy plant was funding a four-phase project to upgrade the autonomous radiation control system at Units 5 and 6. The program – estimated to cost 270 million ECU ($325 million) – was planned to take four years, although it was so intensive that there were fears that it might run longer. The work, which entailed 135 different items, would take place in two phases: first an engineering phase in which specifications were to be prepared for the equipment (likely to account for around a fifth of the 270 million ECU), and then the actual hardware. The first of the two preliminary engineering contracts, to prepare specifications for instrumentation and control equipment, was awarded to Westinghouse. The second contract, for basic engineering, was awarded to a consortium led by Siemens. The work will be carried out in yearly steps during annual outages, starting in 1999. The government decided to guarantee a $380 million loan ($77 million from Citibank, $80 million from Roseximbank, € 212.5 million from Euratom).

Staff Competence and Training

An IAEA safety review team, which visited Kozloduy in 1993, concluded that a renewed management drive was required in a number of directions, notably development and management of an overall training program and specific staff training in emergency response.

NEK management now pays serious attention to staff selection, training and retraining. Kozloduy has put an on-site training centre into place, where classroom instruction is given to operators. The UK Government has provided equipment for training centre. Plant operators and shift supervisors spend two and a half to five years in training, and must renew their licenses every five years. A training simulator that can handle up to design-basis accidents, and that is based on Kozloduy-3, has been provided under EC's PHARE program but is not operational; operators of the Kozloduy VVER-400 units can train on the simulator at the Novovoronezh plant in Russia. NEK has signed a contract with a US firm for the supply of a full-scope, VVER-1000 simulator. The IAEA organises training seminars in Bulgaria.

Nuclear Fuel Cycle

Until 1990, when the Soviet Union stopped purchases, all Bulgarian uranium production was sold to the USSR through barter trade arrangements. Since 1990, stocks in Bulgaria have accumulated to about 650 metric tons. Uranium mining ended in 1994 following a Government decision to close the uranium production industry. No further production is planned as all production facilities have been closed. Uranium exploration has also been stopped. The Bulgarian uranium occurrences contain ore of low grade and mining was extremely scattered. "Reasonably Assured Resources" with a production cost of less than $130/kgU amount to 7,820 tons, "Category I Estimated Additional Resources" with the same production cost limit to 8,400 tons. Current Bulgarian annual uranium requirements are of the order of 850 tons.

VII. ROMANIA

ROMANIA AT A GLANCE

Population	22.5 million
Area	238,391 km²
Capital	Bucharest 2.037 million
President	Emil Constantinescu (next election 2000)
Currency	US$ = Lei 17,840 (November 1999)

Romanian GDP is expected to resume growth in 2000 or 2001 after a decade-long decline. Energy demand (TPES), which has declined some 30% (from 61.1 mtoe in 1990 to 44.1 mtoe in 1997), is not expected to rebound parallel to GDP, because potential gains in energy efficiency. Primary fuel demand for electricity could be reduced by a factor of 2.5 to 3 if infrastructure were brought to a West European level. Romania's energy supplies rely heavily on gas (36% in 1997), oil (29%) and coal (21%). The share of imported primary fuels (35% in 1997) will increase in the future, since domestic oil and gas production is declining and uneconomic coal mines are being shut. Domestic nuclear energy from Cernavoda, which went into operation in 1996, contributes only 3% of TPES. A consequence of the past years' slump is an excess capacity in electric generation. The country has become a net electricity exporter, in spite of national power company Conel using only some 50% of its installed generation capacity. Romanian electricity exports hope to get a boost from the closure of nuclear power facilities at Kozloduy (Bulgaria) and Chernobyl (Ukraine). Romania also has surplus refining capacity, leading to standstills. The country hopes that some of its refineries, once modernised, will win an important market share in SE Europe. The promotion of a pipeline for Caspian oil from Constanta to Trieste underpins Bucharest's regional energy ambitions. Romania's legislative progress in the field of energy, privatisation and regulation have won the country good marks in the latest EU accession review. Further efforts are to be made to liberalise the gas and electricity markets, to abolish cross-subsidies for households and hard coal. Foreign investment in the energy sector has been timorous until now, the single largest investment being the sale of 51% of Ploiesti – the country's third largest refinery – to Lukoil/OMV for $300 million. The planned privatisation of national oil company Petrom (possibly in 2000 with an IPO of no less than $500 million) will be a test case for Romania's appeal to investors. Gas company Romgaz and parts of electric utility Conel are also earmarked for privatisation. But contrary to Petrom, they will not be sold in one block, and further re-structuring is needed before gas or electric utilities will be offered to investors.

POLITICAL AND ECONOMIC OVERVIEW

Recent Economic Developments

Since the overthrow of the Ceausescu regime in December 1989, Romania has seen a number of centre-left and centre-right governments that implemented reform measures at varied speed. This undermined investors' confidence and is one of the main reasons why the country has fallen behind other European transition economies.

The last parliamentary and presidential elections were won by a multi-party coalition in November 1996.

President Emil Constantinescu is committed to market reform and close ties with the west. The first coalition government under Victor Ciorbea tried to introduce a radical, market-oriented reform programme involving the removal of remaining price controls, and tighter monetary and fiscal policies. One of its key objectives – early accession to the EU and NATO – suffered a setback in summer 1997 when Romania failed to be listed as a candidate for the first round of enlargement in both institutions. The government's reform agenda ran into troubles in late 1997, ultimately causing one party to leave the government. Mr. Ciorbea's new coalition government again was soon undermined by internal dissent.

A new centre-right government was formed by Radu Vasile in April 1998 with a parliamentary mandate to accelerate reform. However, by December 1998 Mr Vasile's government faced yet another economic crisis, which was primarily caused by a failure to implement structural reforms.

There is a danger that speed of reform will stall again. Support for the governing coalition continues to fall ahead of the next elections due in late 2000. Opinion polls forebode that the centre-left Social-democrats and nationalists could beat the present coalition and president. The coalition's lost majority in the Senate is another impediment to a resolute implementation of reform. The government's pro-NATO stance during the Kosovo campaign has given it some difficulties, while strengthening its pro-Western credentials.

In the first half of the 1990s, governments made excessive use of Romania's low external debt levels to borrow from multilateral lenders and later from the international capital market. Rapid GDP growth in 1995 (7.1%) fuelled inflation, devaluation and industrial contraction, leading to a return to price and currency control. Reforms, including privatisation of about 4000 firms, was delayed by Parliament. Tighter monetary and fiscal policies contributed to contraction of GDP (–6.6% in 1997, –7.3% in 1998). The economy is expected to have contracted by 5% in 1999[1]. A modest 1% GDP growth is projected for 2000.

Inflation has been brought down from 155% in 1997 to 35% in early 1999. One cause for these still high rates were the increase in energy prices with electricity prices rising by some 125% in 1998, and natural gas by 100%, reflecting the government efforts to bring these closer to market levels.

According to government figures, FDI up to the beginning of 1999 was $5.17 billion, of which $1.5 billion was invested through privatisation agreed between 1993 and October 1998. In 1999, Romania intended to attract at least $500 million, much of it through privatisation.

In 1997, the government adopted legal and fiscal incentives for foreign investment. The lack of transparent procedures, however, often discouraged foreign investment. In February 1999, the Government, in an effort to service its debt, decided to suspend retroactively, for one year, certain tax breaks for foreign investors.

---

1. The Kosovo crisis has contributed to recession. The Romanian Government estimates Kosovo-induced losses at $850 million, largely lost trade and disrupted navigation on the Danube. Power generation at the jointly owned Romanian-Yugoslav Iron Gates hydro-plant on the Danube was disrupted. Power from the Yugoslav half of the plant had to be taken by Romania (because of damaged transmission lines) with part of this power supplied to Yugoslavia via Bulgaria, Greece and FYR of Macedonia (into Kosovo).

Privatisation and Restructuring

Romania has pursued various avenues for privatisation: management-employee buy-outs (for small- and medium-sized enterprises); direct sales by the State Ownership Fund (SOF) to strategic investors; voucher mass privatisation (starting in 1995); privatisation through the stock exchange; sales through an instalments system (an example of this is failed privatisation of the Petromidia refinery).

Privatisation proceeded slowly after the initial transfer of small enterprises and farms, with just 8% of the nominal capital of 6600 industrial enterprises in private hands at the end of 1995. A new scheme to mass-privatise almost 4000 firms (out of the 5000 still state-owned) through a combination of direct sales and the issue of vouchers to the population was staged in late 1995, largely to win the support of the IMF. Vouchers were widely dispersed and the scheme seemed to be designed to fragment ownership so that it would not interfere with management plans. In 1997, the Ciorbea Government launched another rapid privatisation programme, which came to a halt in early 1998[1]. The Vasile government sold stakes in more than 1600 enterprises out of a possible 2744 in 1998.

Since late 1998 final responsibility for privatisation rests with the Prime Minister and the State Ownership Fund (SOF). The Government's privatisation efforts were driven by three major sales as from December 1998[2]. Speedy privatisation was one of the government's leading priorities for 1999. No *regies autonomes* in the energy sector have yet been privatised. Until autumn 1999, it looked as if the first major privatisation in the energy sector would be **SNP Petrom**, the integrated oil company, but this plan may now be delayed because of internal wrangles. Some smaller refineries have been privatised, but the first landmark energy privatisation was to be the sale of the **Petromidia** oil refinery to a Turkish investor in January 1999. However, the SOF cancelled that sale later in the year as the Turkish company failed to meet certain obligations.

The process of restructuring and privatisation of public utilities (*regies autonomes*) started in 1997 through Ordinance 30/1997, subsequently ratified by Parliament as Law 207/1997 that decided the conversion of *regies autonomes* into state-owned joint stock companies for subsequent privatisation. A new Privatisation Law 88/1997 was voted by Parliament in January 1998 and is meant to create a more coherent and unified privatisation framework.

The creation of a vertically integrated oil corporation in 1997, SNP Petrom, incorporating two refineries, was meant as another step towards privatisation. The country's seven other refineries were to be sold off or closed. In 1998, the electricity monopoly RENEL was corporatised into **Conel** and the power sector partly unbundled. The corporatisation of *regies autonomes* meant that these were no longer protected from bankruptcy under the 1995 Bankruptcy Law.

In application of the Bankruptcy Law, the Government wanted to declare some 50 large state-owned companies bankrupt in 1999. The social disruption that is expected to accompany large-scale restructuring, in particular in the energy sector, has persuaded the Government

1. The programme called for privatising about 50 enterprises per week (2200 in all) so that 65% of GDP would be generated by the private sector by the end of 1997. These targets were not achieved: 1300 companies had been privatised and the private sector accounted for 58% of GDP by the end of 1997.
2. 35% of the state telephone monopoly, Romtelecom, were sold to the Greek company OTE. Renault acquired carmaker Dacia. 51% of the Romanian Development Bank were acquired by Société Générale (France). Furthermore, the SOF sold its holdings in about 1000 companies in the first four months of 1999 through a combination of direct sales, auctions, and sales of shares.

to hold back on some of its more radical plans to reshape Romanian industry. During 1999-2000, 110 mines were planned for closure (many have ended production but are on a care and maintenance basis) with tens of thousands of miners made redundant[1]. A protest by the Jiu valley miners in early 1999 has forced the Government to soften the ambitious restructuring plans for the hard coal sector.

The challenges that Romania faces today are maintaining political stability and to continuing economic reforms. Achieving the country's main policy objective, membership in the EU, will crucially depend on continued efforts to stabilise the economy.

Main Economic Indicators

	Unit	1997	1998	1999
GDP growth	%	−6.6	−7.3	−5.0
GDP	$ million	34,800	40,200	
GDP per capita	$ per person	1540	1786	
Industrial gross output growth	%	−7.4	−9.0	−7.5
Unemployment rate	%	8.8	10.3	11.5
Consumer Price (end year)	%	151.4	40.6	35.0
Foreign Direct Investment	$ million	1224	2040	1400
FDI per capita	$ per person	54	91	62

Source: EBRD, IMF, EIU.

THE ENERGY SECTOR

Energy Overview

Main Energy Indicators

		1995	1996	1997
TPES	mtoe	45.669	49.114	44.135
Net Imports	mtoe	13.986	14.399	14.212
Net Oil Imports	mtoe	6.461	6.215	6.982
Net Gas Imports	mtoe	4.793	5.663	4.029
Electricity Production	GWh	59,266	61,350	57,148
TPES/GDP	toe per thousand 90 $ PPP	1.33	1.38	1.32
TPES/Population	toe per capita	2.01	2.17	1.96
CO_2 emission from fuel comb.	mt of CO_2	123.80	123.22	110.69
CO_2/TPES	t CO_2 per toe	2.71	2.51	2.51
CO_2/GDP	t CO_2 per 1990 $ PPP	1.72	1.65	1.59
CO_2/Population	t CO_2 per capita	5.46	5.45	4.91

Source: IEA.

For most of the 1990s, the modernisation of the energy sector has been constrained by the preservation of state monopolies, continued subsidies to domestic consumers, and the failure to re-structure the energy industries. The economic downturn of the country after the overthrow

---

1.   In September 1999, the World Bank agreed to lend $44.5 million to help Romania close 29 unprofitable mines.

Figure 16   Romania Energy Balance (1997)

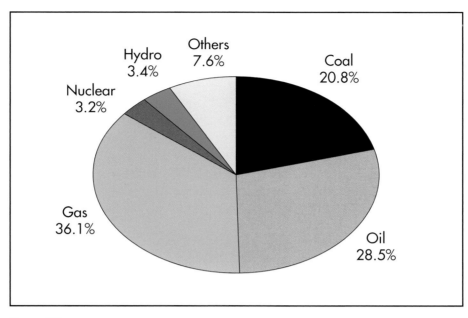

Source: IEA.

Figure 17   Romania TPES (1990-97)

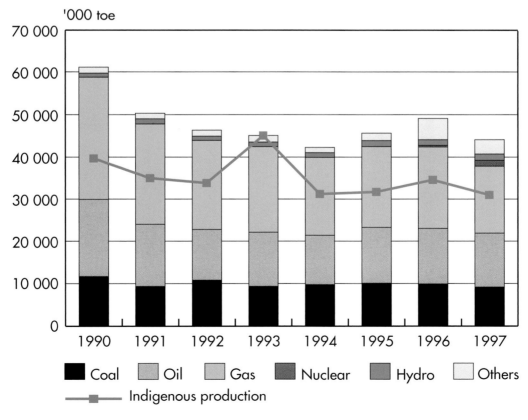

Source: IEA.

on the Ceausescu regime in 1989 also affected the energy industry, but there were earlier signs that the regime's failure to access modern production technologies severely diminished the country's ability to meet its energy needs.

Domestic oil and gas production have been declining since the late 1970s and early 1980s respectively.

Consumption of oil products peaked in 1990 at 17.978 mt, before it dropped by more than 25% to 13.428 mt in 1997. Refinery output declined accordingly, from a peak of 28.8 mt in 1988 to merely 12.3 mt in 1997. Electricity consumption peaked in 1989 at 79 TWh and then decreased 35% to 50.78 TWh in 1997. This enabled Romania to cut back on net electricity imports, from 9.47 TWh in 1990 to merely 0.2 TWh in 1997. Natural gas consumption witnessed the steepest drop of all fuels: 1997 consumption (414,000 TJ) was 60% below the plateau of 1.03-1.05 TJ, which had been attained in 1986-89.

Energy Policy

In mid-1997, the MIT prepared an Energy Strategy paper, which was approved by the Government in August 1998. Its main goals are:

- To increase energy efficiency in all parts of the energy chain – production, transport, distribution and end use, in order to reduce energy intensity in Romania to the level of "advanced economies" within 20 years;

- Diversification of supplies through the interconnection of natural gas and oil networks with West European networks, through the development of gas and oil interconnections in the Black Sea region and through membership of Romania in the UCTE electricity network;

- Increased energy security through the development of increased stocks of oil and gas;

- Reduction of environmental pollution and meeting EU norms and regulations and other international commitments;

- Technological modernisation by supporting research and development and attracting foreign investment;

- Development of an institutional and legal framework based on market economy principles;

- Promotion of competition in the energy sector.

Notwithstanding the Energy Strategy, energy policy making remains an institutional weakness in Romania. The different energy sectors are integrated in reporting terms only at the level of State Secretary (junior Minister). In addition the MIT has inadequate *integrated* energy policy-making expertise. An energy strategy blueprint, which has been prepared, needs further enhancement. An EU PHARE Programme funded "fuel sourcing study" (ECN, 1998) prepared scenarios of energy futures up to 2020. In addition, training in modelling and the models themselves were provided to the Energy Directorate of the Ministry of Industry and Trade (MIT).

The Electricity and Heat Law (passed as Emergency Ordinance No 63/98 in December 1998) contains, for the first time, both a definition of the content of an energy policy and the responsibilities for its preparation and approval. An energy policy must be submitted to Parliament by the Government in a concrete programme that contains the directives of the policy for a period of two years. The policy must give due attention to issues such as: safety of supply; forecasts of energy demand and trade; investment programmes in the energy sector; environmental protection and environmental recovery of sites affected by energy activities; transparent pricing and tariffs; energy efficiency; development of renewable energy; directions of research and development; proposals of specific regulations in the energy field.

The Electricity and Heat Law also clarifies the principal responsibilities of the MIT in relation to energy policy making. The Law specifically defines energy policy-making (including prioritising energy investments), as well as building and monitoring emergency fuel stocks as the Ministry's responsibility.

Energy Projections

Projections of primary energy production from 2000 to 2020 show a continued decrease in domestic production of natural gas and crude oil:

Forecast Primary Energy Production

	Unit	1995	2000	2005	2010	2015	2020
Total domestic production	mtoe	33.61	33.2	29.92	28.59	26.51	26.51
of which:							
Natural gas	Bcm	18.29	15.3	13.65	12	9.4	9.4
Crude oil	mt	6.7	5.9	4.9	4.9	4.9	4.9
Lignite*	mt	30	43.5	41	41	41	41
Hard coal*	mt	4.9	4.9	4.9	4.9	4.9	4.9

* Potential output that includes also some inefficient production capacities.
Source: Romania's Energy Strategy, 1997.

The strategy sets out three scenarios for the development of energy demand ("inertial", "restructuring" and "maximum development"):

Estimated Energy Demand

	Variant	1995	2000	2005	2010	2015	2020
Final commercial energy consumption (mtoe)	Minimum		30.1	33.46	36.75	40.04	44.17
	Average	31.76	30.1	34.02	37.5	42.35	47.67
	Maximum		30.1	34.93	40.46	46.76	51.59
Final energy consumption per inhabitant (kgoe/inhabitant)	Minimum		1337	1496	1654	2015	2054
	Average	1393	1337	1521	1699	1937	2217
	Maximum		1370	1562	1822	2140	2393
Final electricity consumption (Twh)	Minimum		45	51	57	63	68
	Average	46.46	45	53.5	62	70	79
	Maximum		47.5	58	71	85.5	100
Final electricity consumption per inhabitant (kWh/inhabitant)	Minimum		2000	2281	2567	2883	3162
	Average	2046	2000	2393	2792	3203	3674
	Maximum		2111	2595	3198	3913	4651
Ratio of electricity in the final energy consumption (%)	Minimum		12.3	13.1	13.4	13.5	13.6
	Average	12.7	12.9	13.5	14	14.1	14.2
	Maximum		13.5	14.3	14.3	15.4	15.9
Final consumption of thermal energy (PJ)	Minimum		445.44	445.44	455.91	489.82	538.38
	Average	393.51	451.3	453.39	471.81	516.61	568.1
	Maximum		454.23	465.53	496.93	549.86	606.62

Source: Romania's Energy Strategy, 1997.

Energy Efficiency

Energy efficiency policy making and programme implementation is the responsibility of the Romanian Agency for Energy Conservation (ARCE). It was set up in April 1991 by the Government Decree No. 327 as a semi-autonomous agency. In 1994 its status was changed to that of a department of the MIT under the co-ordination of the State Secretary for Energy. In addition to the Head Office in Bucharest, ARCE has 16 regional offices. ARCE employs 80 staff members. Administrative costs are covered within the budget of the Ministry and energy efficiency programme costs are provided predominantly by international donors. The State budget provides no funding for energy efficiency programme expenditures and a minimal level of support for research and development ($10,000 in 1998).

Technical assistance studies have identified weaknesses in ARCE, which limit the implementation of energy efficiency policy. Such deficiencies include the lack of a national strategy for energy efficiency and poor communications between ARCE and energy users. Moreover, the regional offices are not adequately involved.

Technical assistance studies have recommended that the policy making should be retained by the MIT and the programme implementation activities should be separated from the Ministry with the agency having an autonomous status.

Relevant documents on labelling and minimum energy efficiency standards have been adopted, in accordance with the EU *acquis communautaire*.

Energy Institutions

The Ministry of Industry and Trade (MIT) is responsible for the energy sector and for formulating and implementing the country's energy policy. Under the central planning system each energy sector formed a Ministry: Ministry of Electric Power; Ministry of Mining etc. The MIT was established in July 1990. During the same period, the status of *regie autonome* was given to the major energy enterprises (electricity, gas, coal mining, upstream and downstream oil). Under Law 15/1990, the *regie autonome* status means that the enterprise is a part of the ministry concerned (or Local Authority for local RAs – i.e. local district heating or water RAs) and the budget of the RA is included in the budget of the ministry.

Other important institutions in the energy sector are:

■ ANRM (Agency for Mineral Resources) oversees the petroleum and mineral resource sectors.

■ ARCE (Agency for Energy Conservation) is responsible for energy efficiency policy.

■ ANRE (National Regulatory Authority) is the regulator in the electricity and heat sectors. One year after its inception in October 1998, ANRE had merely 14 staff (vs 120 planned), which made it impossible for the regulator to carry out its role effectively. The government is planning to set up a separate regulatory authority for the gas sector.

■ Petrom, the national oil company, is earmarked for privatisation.

■ Romgaz, the national gas company.

■ Conel, the electricity monopoly.

These institutions are discussed in greater detail below.

There are currently 465 hydrocarbon fields with over 14,300 producing wells. Over 90% of petroleum and more than 95% of gas are produced onshore. Offshore production from the Lebada field in the Black Sea is from fixed platforms at water depths of about 50 metres.

In Romania, all mineral resources (according to both the Petroleum Law and the Mining Law) are the property of the State.

Crude oil production amounts to around 6.6 mt (1998). The country has been maturely explored and produced. The potential for new hydrocarbon discoveries is limited and insufficient to revert the production decline, which has been going on since the mid-1970's, when output exceeded 14 mt. Crude oil imports amount to around 2.2 mt (imported by Petrom). Upstream production of oil and gas is organised through 11 production branches (Videle, Ploiesti, Braila, Timisoara, Pitesti, Suplac, Moinesti, Tirguviste, Craiova, Tirgu Jiu and Constanta).

Oil and gas could be key areas for foreign investment. The hydrocarbon sector is operated inefficiently due to lack of investment and transfer of technology. Romania's efforts to attract foreign oil companies into its upstream sector since the early 1990's have not been particularly successful. Only a fraction of the country's prospective acreage has been licensed to foreign operators. Some oil majors, who had shown an initial interest as from 1992, have withdrawn from the country (except Elf), leaving a good dozen tiny foreign oil companies behind. Experts believe that upstream spending should concentrate on field rehabilitation and improved recovery schemes.

Privatisation of Petrom

Societate Nationala a Petrolului Petrom (SNP **Petrom**) was established with a capitalisation of $1.1. billion as the national oil company under Emergency Ordinance 49/09.15.1997, which was ratified by the Romanian Parliament in April 1998. Petrom was formed through the amalgamation of the upstream operations of exploration and production, 2 refineries (**Arpechim Pitesti** and **Petrobazi Ploiesti**), together with the distribution network of **PECO** (525 stations) as an integrated oil company. Petrom has a turnover of $3.5 billion and represents some 10% of the Romanian economy. It produces some 6.3 mt of oil and 5.6 bcm of gas per annum. It has 70 mt of proven oil reserves and 65 bcm of gas reserves on its books. Petrom has also some interests abroad, including Turkmenistan, Kazakhstan, Turkey and India. The state currently owns 93% of Petrom.

The privatisation of Petrom, which was decided in December 1998, is not proceeding as swiftly as declarations by the MIT would suggest. Contrary to Romgaz and Conel, Petrom will not be split up into smaller companies. In April 1999 the Government selected ABN Amro-Rothschild as privatisation advisors. The company has been trying to boost its market value through a $100 million cost-cutting exercise, which included reducing its bloated workforce of 103,000 by 30%. Ten strategic investors have shown interest in Petrom, according to Minister Berceanu. But the target of selling Petrom before the end of 1999 was not met. Advisor ABN-Amro has mentioned a sum of not less than $500 million for the IPO. Petrom's capital is to be increased by some 35% during the first stage of the privatisation. An international listing of Petrom is planned for September 2000. The company's investment needs have been pegged at some $4 billion.

Petroleum Infrastructure

Crude oil transportation has been split off into a separate pipeline company, **Compet**. Compet operates 4500 km of pipelines connecting the port of Constanta with the refineries. **Oil Terminal** operates seven berths at the port of Constanta and is responsible for handling of crude oil and product exports and imports. Refined product is distributed by **Petrotrans** (a subsidiary of Petrom), which is responsible for 2454 km of product pipelines and railway transportation[1] and distribution, and **Transpeco** (also a subsidiary of Petrom), which is responsible for road transportation (See Map 7: Bulgaria, Romania – Oil and Gas Infrastructure).

Oil Terminal is also responsible for port storage capacity of 1.7 million m³. This capacity was designed for an annual throughput of up to 24 mt of crude oil and 12 mt of oil products.

The retail sector suffers from poor locations and fragmentation. Petrom's subsidiary PECO owns 525 gasoline stations. Shell, Agip/ENI and MOL have small but expanding chains. PECO also operates 158 storage facilities.

The most important investment requirements are upstream in E&P and in refinery upgrades. Pipeline and other infrastructure projects will be relatively few in number.

A Caspian oil transit route through Constanta on the Black Sea to Trieste is under discussion (See Chapter on Regional Energy Trade and Transit). It could provide an additional option for Caspian oil exports, as an alternative for shipping oil through the Turkish Straits, the Baku-Cehyan line and the use of existing pipeline systems in Russia and eastern Europe. The cost of the project is estimated at $2 billion. Initial capacity would be 6-7 mt/year, and could ultimately reach 35 mt/year. The fate of the project will to some extent depend on international efforts to reconstruct infrastructure in southeastern Europe and the Balkans after the Kosovo crisis. The route would partly make use of existing pipelines and cross the territory of the Federal Republic of Yugoslavia.

In 1998, an international consortium, comprising three US companies (UGI Corporation, the largest US marketer of propane gas, Energy Transportation Group and North American World Trade) and three Romanian (Conel, Rompetrol and Romgaz), established the Black Sea LPG Romania SA. Some $180 million are to be invested for the construction of a 1 mt/year capacity LPG terminal. The project will be phased, starting with a planned 100,000 tonnes initially and reaching 600,000 after 3 years, provided an adequate LPG market can be proven.

The Constanta port has a capacity to handle 24 mt of crude oil and 10 mt of refined products per annum in seven berths. The port accommodates tankers up to 150,000 dwt. Current storage facilities at the oil terminal are 600,000 t of crude oil, and 300,000 t of refined products. There are plans to expand the terminal capacity to up to 3 mt per month of crude.

Refining

There are 10 refineries in Romania, with a total capacity of 34 mt/year. Romania's refining sector has a significant over-capacity, since demand is only 14-18 mt/year. But, based on Petrom and other industry sources, effective capacity is estimated to be no more than 26 mt/year. The industry suffers from surplus capacity (the current average utilisation rate is only 50% of operable capacity) and low margins.

---

1. Approximately 65% of oil products are moved by rail.

Petrom owns two refineries: **Arpechim Pitesti** and **Petrobazi Plioesti**, which together processed 5.5 mt of oil in 1997. Petrobazi processed 2.7 mt of exclusively domestic oil. Arpechim's run included over 2 mt of imported oil and some 0.8 mt of domestic crude. Nominal capacity of these two refineries amounts to approximately 14 mt. Petrom will retain the two refineries but halve their capacity to 7 mt/year. Investment in upgrading and conversion capacity (including additional isomerisation facilities) is recommended.

Petrom is negotiationg with the SOF to take over a third refinery, **Rafo Onesti**. The are reports about the loss-making Rafo being partly be closed with the loss of about 470 jobs of a total on 3,100. The SOF still has a 60% share in Rafo, which it failed to sell in 1998 after rejecting a bid from a domestic private company. It is estimated that the 3.5 mt capacity refinery, which has debts of $130 million, will require investment of $78 million for modernisation and compliance with environmental standards.

Two refineries have been sold through management/employee buyouts (using state-given vouchers): **Suplacu de Barcau** and **Lubrifin Brasov**. The SOF has put 66% of the **Darmanesti** refinery up for sale. Five investors have reportedly shown interest.

Fifty-one percent of shares of the country's third-largest refinery, **Petrotel Ploiesti** (4 mt/year capacity), were sold to Lukoil (Russia) and OMV (Austria) in 1998 for $300 million. This is one of the largest foreign investments in the country. Under the terms of the contract, Lukoil will supply Petrotel with around 3 mt/year of crude oil and will modernise the refinery.

In January 1999, the government signed an agreement to sell a 65% stake in the **Petromidia** refinery to Akmaya Sanayi Ve Ticaret (Turkey) in what had appeared to be the largest investment so far in post-communist Romania. This was the second attempt to sell the plant. The Turkish company was the only bidder. Petromidia is one of Romania's most recent refineries and has an annual capacity of 5.3 mt. However, it was also one of the biggest loss-makers in the economy. The Turkish company agreed to pay about $700 million, including cash payment, assumption of Petromidia's $260 million debt and an investment commitment.

Romania: Effective Refining Capacity, 1998 (thousand metric tons/year)

Refinery	Location	Atmos. dist.	Vacuum dist.	Coking	Catalytic cracking	Catalytic Reforming	Cat. Hydro cracking
Arpechim*	Pitesti	3,500	1,872	0	955	609	76
Astra	Ploiesti	2,789	468	428	0	0	0
Petrobazi*	Ploiesti	3,450	1,954	630	1,066	669	0
Petrolub	Bacau	398	259	0	0	0	0
Petromidia*	Midia	4,980	0	1,095	946	608	0
Petrotel*	Ploiesti	5,179	2,787	572	1,041	572	0
Rafinaria Darmanesti	Darmanesti	797	0	473	0	149	0
Rafo*	Onesti, Bacau	3,849	0	222	1,354	631	0
Steaua Romania	Cimpina	462	316	0	0	0	0
Vega	Ploiesti	576	187	0	0	0	0
Total		25,979	7,843	3,420	5,362	3,238	76

* Designed to handle imported sour crude. Arpechim, Petrobazi, Petromidia and Petrotel have fully integrated olefin and aromatics plants.
Sources: OGJ, Petrom, ERAS estimates.

But the Government later rescinded on earlier investment incentives, thereby increasing the price for Petromidia by some $120 million. The Turkish investor decided not to pursue the acquisition. The refinery was then closed for seven months until September 1999. Petromidia intends to sell 20% of its products domestically and export the remaining 80%. The Government is searching for a new investor.

The five more modern refineries (Arpechim, Petrobazi, Petromidia, Petrotel, Rafo) have conversion and secondary processing capacities, with similar levels of complexity to average Western European refineries. However, they suffer from technical and economic inefficiency and require investment in upgrading. These refineries represent 85% of total nominal processing capacity.

The five older, smaller, refineries were designed to run low-sulphur domestic crude. They have a low degree of complexity, without any significant conversion capacity. These plants have a nominal operating capacity of 4.9 mt per year, however, they are currently operating closer to 2.8 mt per year. The 5 small refineries have been privatised.

Oil Production and Consumption

Unlike natural gas, which has slid continuously throughout the 1990's, oil and condensate production has stabilised at between 6.5 and 7 mt since 1991. Domestic production provides about half the feedstock for local refineries. The potential for producing oil products from imported crude has been limited by the poor condition of many of Romania's refineries, some of which are not designed to run imported sour crude. The result has been a decline in oil products output, from more than 28 mt/year in the late 1980's to 12.3 mt in 1997.

Figure 18   Romania Oil Product Output and Consumption

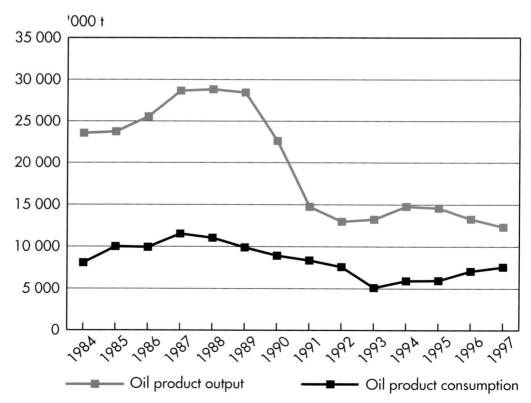

Domestic oil products consumption has also fallen sharply since the collapse of the command economy, although by a smaller amount than production. Romanian GDP shrank by 25% between 1990 and 1992, following negative growth in the late 1980s. There was a recovery between 1993 and 1996, however, the economy entered another deep recession in 1997 and this led to a further fall in consumption of oil products. The combined effect of declining consumption and an even steeper output drop resulted in Romania turning from a major oil products exporter into a small net importer in 1997.

The freeing of oil products prices is likely to accelerate this trend. Higher refining costs in Romania will erode the competitiveness of domestically produced oil products compared to imports. Romanian refineries, such as Lukoil-owned Petrotel, are investing in upgrades so as to enhance their competitive position.

Romania: Oil Products Consumption, 1997

'000 tonnes	Consumption	Share
LPG	259	2%
Gasoline	1,433	12%
Jet Fuel	312	3%
Diesel	2,554	22%
HGO	529	4%
HFO	4,214	36%
Lube Oils	292	2%
Naphtha	465	4%
Other	1,811	15%
Total	11,869	100%

Source: Ministry of Industry and Trade, ERAS estimates.

The transport market accounted for an estimated 24% of oil products consumption (including power generation). Unleaded gasoline consumption is currently low: according to Petrom, 90% of the 1.4 mt of gasoline sales in 1997 was leaded and only 10% unleaded. However, leaded gasoline will be phased out by 2003. There is a large diesel market. HFO is mainly consumed in power generation, which accounted for 29% of oil products consumption in 1997. Industrial consumption of 2.1 mt, mainly heavy products and naphtha, accounted for 18% of oil products consumption.

Romanian consumption of oil products is forecast to recover to an estimated 12 mt in 2050 and 14.2 mt in 2010, assuming that positive economic growth resumes as from the year 2000.

The transport sector should offer strong growth potential through to 2010, given that car ownership is still low (25% of the European average). The trend growth rate of the private car fleet is estimated at 12% per year. Until refineries are upgraded, Romania will have an increasing requirement for imports of unleaded and high-octane gasoline. The transport sector is forecast to account for 37% of oil products consumption in 2000 and 53% in 2010.

Demand for HFO is expected to decline, especially if imported natural gas manages to supplant HFO for use in power generation. Assuming that secure supplies of natural gas can be found,

Figure 19   Romania Oil Products Consumption by Sector

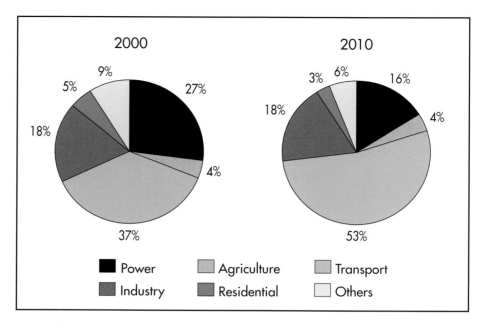

Source: ERAS Estimates.

it is forecast that power generation will account for only 16% of oil products consumption in 2010 (compared with 27% in 2000).

Oil Pricing

Oil product prices are no longer regulated, but ex-refinery prices are often higher than imports, due to relative inefficiency. Industry sources estimate that Petrom ex-refinery prices are considerably higher than import prices – the difference may be as much as $40 per tonne.

The implication is that imports of oil products will increase and Romanian refinery margins will be severely squeezed, adding impetus to restructuring and upgrading. There is no import duty on petroleum products.

Tariffs for access to the crude oil pipeline network are set by ANRM. In 1998, these were around $4-5 per tonne.

Oil Stocks

In addition to operational stocks held at the Constanta oil terminal and at the refineries, there are approximately 20 days of stocks held by the **National Administration of State Reserves**. This body is an independent government agency, set up under the Ceausescu regime. The exact level of stocks held by the Agency is considered to be secret.

In order to comply with EU Directives on minimum stocks and crisis management measures, it is necessary for Romania to establish a system for supervision and control of the stocks, including commercial stocks. It has been proposed that the National Agency for State Reserves should be given this responsibility.

NATURAL GAS

Gas Exploration and Production

The Transylvanian Depression is the main gas producing basin, accounting for more than 70% of total reserves, which are estimated at 450 bcm. The gas in these fields is nearly pure methane (99.8%), with only traces of ethane, propane and butane. The deeper, pre-salt section of the basin is deemed to hold a significant untapped gas potential.

Gas has been produced from over 150 fields and some 3700 wells. Peak production was achieved in 1986 (39 bcm). Since then production has been in sharp decline: in 1997 less than 15 bcm were produced.

Gas Industry Structure

The Romanian government plans extensive restructuring of the national gas company **Romgaz**. Romgaz is responsible for exploration, production[1], transportation, storage and sale of natural gas. It also imports gas and is responsible for international transit operations. The new company has the following structure:

Three subsidiaries are responsible for the exploration, production and storage of gas: Exprogaz-Medias, Exprogaz-Tirgu Mures, and Exprogaz-Ploiesti. Two subsidiaries are responsible for distribution: Distrigaz-Sud, based in Bucharest; Distrigaz-Nord, based in Tirgu Mures.

The Government plans to break up Romgaz before privatising it. It is likely that shares in distribution entities will be offered to investors. Under the terms of the Law on Public Property, gas transmission pipelines are perpetual public property, but concessions may be granted to operate the network.

Romgaz is the common carrier for all gas transport in Romania. In the view of some observers, unbundling of Romgaz is not the key issue for fostering competition in gas supply for two reasons: Firstly, even with existing legislation, Romgaz does not have a monopoly of end use supply. Large industrial users are presently able to contract for supplies with an alternative supplier. Secondly, although Romgaz is responsible for 75% of gas imports, 25% of gas imports (1998) were imported by other companies (including Arcom, Rompetrol and Wingas, a joint venture between Wintershall of Germany and Gazprom).

The principal problems which are restricting the development of competition for "eligible consumers" are:

■ A lack of information on the present legislation – i.e. large industrial users are often unaware that they have the right to third-party access to the transmission system.

■ There is a lack of secondary legislation, which should detail access to the gas network. The National Agency for Mineral Resources (ANRM) has the responsibility to develop secondary legislation, including model contracts.

In the case of gas, as in the case of electricity, there has been considerable debate among energy policy makers and Romgaz on the market structure of the gas sector. The key to the restructuring of the gas industry and also to new investments in electricity generation (with

1. Romgaz produces some 60% of Romanian gas, the remainder being produced by Petrom.

new IPP investments being predominantly gas-fired), is the development of a commercially independent transmission network. There is a danger that, without unbundling, Romgaz will impose technical conditions on access to the gas transmission network, which prevent open access to the gas grid. While in theory the National Agency for Mineral Resources (ANRM) will be responsible for monitoring access to the gas grid, in practice the Petroleum Law does not warrant equal access. In addition ANRM lacks the resources and expertise to develop the necessary secondary legislation. Actually Romgaz is preparing a draft secondary legislation for submission to ANRM.

Reform is still embryonic and will require further legislation. A new regulatory framework is planned, but legislation has not yet been adopted. The planned legislation will create a new regulatory agency and will follow EU legislation with respect to infrastructure investment and access to the network. This should lead to clearer rules and regulations on third party access and greater transparency on tariffs.

Declining Romanian production of natural gas has led to a search for alternative supplies, mainly from Russia. Purchases of imported natural gas to meet the supply shortfall by Romgaz have been constrained by a lack of foreign currency. This has encouraged large consumers of natural gas to seek alternative suppliers to Romgaz, which has contributed to market opening.

In 1998, market opening had reached an estimated 25% by volume.

Competition to Romgaz includes:

- Gas supplies are sourced from Gazprom as well as domestic producers including Petrom.
- Romgaz is the sole operator of the transport system, but it has an obligation to provide third-party access rights.
- Competition in marketing developed when Conel signed a supply agreement with Wingas.
- The national oil company Petrom has approval for direct sales of its gas to customers.

Gas Infrastructure

The existing gas infrastructure in Romania was designed largely for the transmission and distribution of domestically produced natural gas. Romania has a developed gas network to serve industrial and residential consumers. The network totals 36,000 km, including 11,000 km of transmission lines. The maximum transmission capacity is estimated at 135 million cm per day and 40 bcm per year. There are connections to the cities in all regions and household connections outside the major population centres are increasing rapidly (See Map 7: Bulgaria, Romania – Oil and Gas Infrastructure).

The network is operated by Romgaz, its transmission subsidiary and two distribution subsidiaries: one located in Bucharest to serve the southern half of the country, and the other located in Tirgu Mures, which serves the northern half of the country. The government's restructuring plan for the industry foresees that these subsidiaries will be spun off.

There has been some degradation of the network, including corrosion of pipelines which need replacing. Romgaz is upgrading the network with the help of World Bank and EIB loans, totalling $170 million.

Existing underground gas storage in depleted gas fields cover peak winter demand in the Bucharest region.

Romania: Underground Gas Storage Facilities

Location	Total volume (mcm)	Max withdrawal (mcm/day)	Status
Uriceni	60-120	0.45	existing
Balciuresti	600-1,200	5.7	existing
Balaceanca	50-60	0.3	existing
Sarmasel	20	2	existing
Roman Mar.	90	9	projected
Ghercesti	3,000	5	projected
Sub-total existing	1,400	8.5	
Sub-total projected	3,090	14.0	
Total	4,490	22.5	

Major investment in improving gas infrastructure are planned. The plans will boost transport and storage capacity and diversify supply sources. Expansion of interconnectors to allow higher imports will be a priority, in order to meet a supply shortfall due to declining domestic production of natural gas:

- The capacity of the main import line through the Ukraine will be expanded from 8 bcm to 14 bcm;

- An LNG project has been mooted at Constanta, but it is unlikely to materialise as it would require passage through the crowded Bosphorus;

- Connections with the Hungary pipeline grid would allow to import an initial 2 bcm/year of North Sea gas;

- Romania wants a Caspian gas route through their territory but plans are undeveloped;

- Underground storage capacity will be boosted from 1.4 bcm to 3.5 bcm by 2005.

Gas Pricing

Under the 1996 Petroleum Law, wellhead gas prices are established by ANRM. A two-tier structure is applied: one for domestic gas and one for imported gas, which allows for cross-subsidisation of domestic gas production. The price of imported gas is based on alternative fuel values but the price of domestic gas reflects cost calculations.

ANRM is also responsible for the transport and distribution tariffs, which are generally lower than real costs and West European levels. Romgaz states that the average tariff for transport and distribution is about \$9.50/'000 m^3 (The lack of separate accounts for transport, storage and distribution makes it difficult to calculate these charges).

Until the 30th of June 1998, consumer tariffs were set for industry and the residential sectors by the Office of Competition in consultation with the MIT. In the second quarter of 1998 industry prices were set to the equivalent of about \$95/'000 m^3 compared with residential prices of only \$30/'000 m^3. However, rapid exchange rate depreciation eroded these prices.

Since July 1, 1998 industry prices have been freed and a series of residential price increases have been scheduled in an effort to eliminate cross-subsidies to households. Once this phase-out is complete, low-income households will receive direct subsidies and thereby reduce supply side distortions. In August 1998 industrial prices averaged about $83/'000 m³ and residential prices increased to about $40/'000 m³. (The industrial gas price per thousand cubic metres includes $10 for royalties, $4.5 for transport and $5 for distribution, but not VAT).

In June 1999, prices for both for industry and households increased to Lei 900/m³ (with the exception of the fertiliser industry, which receives a reduction to $40/1000 m³) for 50% of its gas needs. Applying the June exchange rate that domestic price would yield $57/1000 m³. These changes followed an increase in February 1999 for households from 450 to 575 Lei/m³ and from 677.7 to 840 Lei/m³ for industry.

In consultation with Romgaz the ANRM is preparing a new binomial pricing system that is intended to reflect true costs across the gas chain. The new tariffs will include capacity and volumetric consumption charges and take into account transport distance. The need for such a system is underlined further by the fact that some 25% of gas transported by Romgaz is for third parties.

Romgaz proposes its prices based on costs to the MIT and the Competition Office. In future this approval will be the task of a regulatory body, which is expected to take a more active role.

The pricing structure is over-simplified and unrelated to real costs, especially in the transport, distribution and service parts of the supply chain. Industry consumers cross subsidise households.

Gas Production and Consumption

Romania has been a major producer and consumer of natural gas since the early part of the 20th Century.

However, there has been a severe decline of production and consumption of natural gas in the 1990s and an increase in import dependence. Production of natural gas fell to 14 bcm in 1997, a decline of 36% from a production level of 22 bcm in 1991. This is a result of the failure to replace reserves, which are falling by 5-8% per year according to industry estimates. The MIT forecasts a continuing decline in production of natural gas as fields become further depleted. Official estimates predict a fall in production to 13.5 bcm in 2000 and 8.5 bcm in 2015. However, fresh investment and technological upgrades could slow down the decline.

Romania has a high level of gasification in the industry and household sectors. In 1997 gas consumption was about 18.5 bcm, of which 14.7 bcm was from domestic production. The balance was imported from Russia.

Consumption of natural gas has been severely affected by the shrinking of the Romanian economy since the revolution, falling 42% from 1990 consumption of 32 bcm. The most important features of current demand trends are:

■ Industrial gas demand has declined, in spite of freed and falling delivered cost of gas in the second half of 1998;

■ Rising consumer demand for natural gas, with 700,000 households connected. This is in spite of rising gas prices for households.

In 1997, the power sector consumed 26.5% of gas. Other large gas consumers were the chemical and petrochemical industry (16.4%), households (12.9%), heat plants (9.9%) and the metallurgical industry (7.1%). Household demand is expected to continue. The MIT expects household and commercial demand to account for 40% of demand in 2015. A recent EU Synergy study on the Balkans concludes that industrial demand for gas will remain practically stable in spite of industry growth, i.e. 8.8 bcm in 1995 and 8.7 bcm in 2015. As the economy recovers, overall natural gas is expected to stabilise at 25-26 bcm/year.

Gas imports will have to rise steeply to meet the projected shortfall in supply. Russia will remain the dominant supplier, providing up to 14 bcm/year once the capacity of Romania's main import line through the Ukraine has been increased to this level.

As dependence on imports increases, security of supply will become an ever more important issue. The MIT forecasts 3.5 bcm of supplies from sources outside Russia in 2015. Diversification of supplies will depend on the development of new infrastructure, such as the mooted connection with the Hungarian network which would afford gas imports from the North Sea.

In April 1998, Romania signed an agreement with Ruhrgas, calling for the supply of 0.5 bcm/year of gas transiting through Austria and Hungary for 15 to 20 years, starting in the winter of 1999/2000. The agreement provides for the possibility of a gradual increase to 2 bcm by 2005.

Romania: Natural Gas Import Requirement Forecasts

Bcm/year	1995	2000	2005	2010	2015
Russian Federation	5.0	12.0	13.0	14.0	14.0
Western Suppliers	0.0	0.5	1.0	1.5	1.5
Central Asia	0.0	0.0	0.0	1.0	2.0
Total	5.0	12.5	14.0	16.5	17.5

Source: Ministry of Industry and Trade.

COAL

Industry Structure

The coal industry was fostered by the Communist regime as a way to reduce energy imports. It is now facing severe difficulties in adapting to a market economy. Lignite accounts for 80% of domestic coal output. There are three state-owned coal mining companies, all of which have been converted from the status of *regie autonome* to commercial (and still fully state-owned) companies. The MIT exercises the right of ownership over the mining companies. The three companies are:

- Compania Nationala a Lignitului Oltenia, based in Tirgu Jiu (CNLO) – formerly RALO;
- Compania Nationala a Huilei, based in Petrosani (CNH) – formerly RAH;
- Societatea Nationala a Carbunelui, based in Ploiesti (SNCP) – formerly RACP.

The government's coal policy has been to rationalise, re-structure and finally privatise the three state-owned coal mining companies. The following steps have already been taken: an emergency ordinance was adopted in August 1997 offering severance packages for miners willing to take voluntary redundancy (Ordinances 9 and 22). Miners were offered up to 22 monthly salaries. As a result, employment in the coal mining industry has fallen from 109,000 in August 1997 to 52,000 at the beginning of 1999.

Romania: Employment in the Coal Mining Sector

	01.01.1997	01.08.1997	01.01.1998	01.01.1999
CNH, Petrosani	45,134	43,029	23,496	20,735
CNLO, Tirgu Jiu	51,044	49,668	23,124	21,000
SNCP, Ploiesti	17,220	16,208	10,145	9,323

The 1998 Mining Law created the necessary legal framework for private investors to obtain licences to produce coal and lignite. Most significant deposits are being exploited by the three state companies, which are, however, anxious to form joint ventures or to divest loss-making mines. Although subsidies have been substantially reduced in the last two years, about 50% of coal production is still subsidised.

Coal demand and output

CNLO is the primary producer of lignite in Romania, with production being sold almost exclusively for power and heat generation. CNLO accounts for 92% of total output of lignite, with the remainder being produced by SNCP Ploiesti. CNLO mines lignite and brown coal in three areas – Oltenia (accounting for the bulk of production), the central basin of Berbesti and a basin in the West of Romania centered around Mehedinti.

SNCP Ploiesti is the secondary producer of lignite and brown coal, with mines in the southeast, central and northwest Romania. The power plants at Brasov, Oradea, Zalau and Doicesti absorb most of SNCP's annual production of 3 mt (1998).

The demand for lignite for power generation has been reduced in both 1997 and 1998 because of high stocks at the power stations in 1998, a mild winter, and a higher than average rainfall leading to higher production from hydro-power stations. Conel reduced their demand for lignite in the first quarter of 1998 by about 5 million tons to 26.5 million tons, primarily from the CNLO mine.

Lignite

Demand for lignite in the medium to long term will depend on a number of factors, including:

■ The delivered fuel costs to individual power and heat generating stations.

■ Decisions relating to the rehabilitation and conversion of power stations. Some cogeneration plants, particularly those that are distant from their lignite source (e.g. Iasi, Suceava), are likely to be converted to other fuels. Given the high cost of transporting lignite to remote stations, CNLO is unlikely to deliver lignite at an economic price in the future. The rehabilitation of lignite-fired condensing plants is closely linked to the expected future price of lignite.

■ Construction of new electricity and heat generating capacity, and the reform of the electricity sector. At present there is considerable excess capacity in the Romanian power system.

Romania: Major Thermal Power Stations

Thermal Power Station	Installed Capacity (MW)	Primary Fuel	Commissioned (Year)
Turceni	7 × 330 (2,310)	lignite	1978-87
Rovinari	4 × 330, 2 × 220 (1,720)	lignite	1972-79
Mintia	6 × 210 (1,260)	black coal	1969-80
Craiova	2 × 315, 2 × 100, 1 × 55, 3 × 50 (1,035)	lignite	1965-76
Braila	1 × 330, 3 × 210 (960)	oil/gas	1973-79
Brazi	2 × 200, 2 × 105, 6 × 50 (910)	oil/gas	1961-86
Ludus	2 × 200, 4 × 100 (800)	gas	1963-67
Borzesti	2 × 210, 1 × 60, 2 × 50, 3 × 25 (655)	oil/gas	1955-69
Bucuresti Sud	2 × 125, 2 × 100, 2 × 50 (550)	oil/gas	1956-75
Galati	3 × 105, 1 × 100, 2 × 60 (535)	gas/coke & furnace gas	1969-84
Doicesti	2 × 200, 6 × 20 (520)	lignite	1952-78
Paroseni	1 × 150, 3 × 50 (300)	coal	1956-64
Fintinele	1 × 100, 1 × 50, 4 × 25 (250)	gas	1954-66

Source: Conel.

Romania: Major Hydro Power Stations

River	Installed capacity MW	Maximum output MW	River	Installed capacity MW	Maximum output MW
Arges-Vidraru	220	220	Riul Mare upstream	335	200
Arges - upstream and downstream	197.2	190	Riul Mare downstream	148.3	140
Riul Tirgului	24.8	12	Ruieni	140	60
Dimbovita	69	32	Olt Cascade I	85.2	37
Ialomita upstream	12	10	Olt Cascade II	383.8	260
Ialomita downstream	33	20	Olt Cascade III	396	253
Teleajen	10	8	Danube Portile de Fier I	1050	1030
Buzau upstream	42	40	Danube Portile de Fier II	270	220
Buzau downstream	35	25	Cerna	50	40
Somesul Cald upstream	265	258	Tismana	106	90
Somesul Cald downstream	35	32	Tismana downstream	13	10
Bistrita	21	17	Jiu	21	13
Crisul Repede	46	30	Bistrita upstream	210	180
Dragan	158	148	Bistrita downstream I	67	62
Lotru	643	510	Bistrita downstream II	78	71
Chem small hydro	127	85	Bistria downstream III	99	91
Sebes upstream	300	260	Siret	162.05	146
Sebes downstream	46	40	Total Hydro-electric	5898.35	4840

Source: Least cost development study 1998, Tractebel, funded under the EU-PHARE programme.

The most recent capacity addition was Unit 1 of the Cernavoda Nuclear Power Station (which is based on Canadian design and involved Atomic Energy of Canada Ltd. and Ansaldo (Italy)). It came on-line in 1996.

Domestic production covers more than 99% of the country's electricity needs; only about
470 GWh were imported in 1998. In the first six months of 1999, Romania even exported
more electricity than it imported. Hydro-power production accounts for more than one
third of production, followed by coal-fired stations (30%). Conel supplies almost 90% of the
domestic electricity production. The remainder is produced by the Cernavoda NPP (10%),
and industrial co-generation plants or local communities (4%).

Romania: Electricity Production by Source, 1998

Generation source	GWh	%
Hydro	18,798	35.2%
Coal (hard coal and lignite)	15,885	29.8%
Oil and gas	11,360	21.3%
Nuclear	5,307	9.9%
Autoproducers	1,095	2.0%
Independent generators	940	1.8%
Total generation	53,385	100%

Source: Conel Annual Report 1998.

Romania tries to optimise the use of power stations with the lowest operational costs. Between
1997 and 1998, electricity production in hydro-power stations increased by about 8%,
while the production in coal-fired stations declined by 14.5%. Due to exceptional hydrological
conditions, output from hydro-power generation was 18.8 TWh in 1998, as compared to
17 TWh in 1997 and 15.3 TWh in 1996.

Most technology in Conel's thermal plants dates from the 1960's and early 1970's. Many
plants have exceeded their operating life, although others have been decommissioned or
mothballed due to declining demand. Only the more efficient plants are operated.

Electricity consumption in 1998 was 42.5 TWh, of which two thirds were used by industry.

Romania: Electricity Consumption, 1998

	GWh	%
Industry	28,100	66.1%
Agriculture and services	4,300	10.1%
Residential	7,900	18.6%
Transport	2,200	5.2%
Total consumption	42,500	100.0%

Source: Conel Annual Report 1998.

Romania: Electricity Imports and Exports

	1997	1998	1999
Imports	1,038	1,181	673
Exports	817	715	1,045
Net Imports	221	466	–372

Source: Conel.

Given the continued decline in electricity demand and the availability of low-cost electricity generated in hydro-power stations and of nuclear power, Conel intends to increase its revenues by exporting electricity to neighbouring countries[1]. Spare capacity is significant, as peak demand in 1998 fell to 9 GW (or 50% of the installed capacity).

In the first quarter of 1999, Conel exported 554 GWh to Turkey, Greece, Italy, Bosnia and Hercegovina, and FR of Yugoslavia. Limited transmission capacity in Hungary and quantitative restrictions in Bulgaria prevent Conel from exporting more. In June 1999 Conel signed a preliminary export agreement with Turkey for 500 MW, but deliveries have not started because no transit agreement has yet been reached with Bulgaria.

Romania: Electricity Trade by Country

	1998 Trade (GWh)	
	Import	Export
Bulgaria	332	325
FR of Yugoslavia	684	258
Moldova	27	132
Hungary	138	0
Total	1,181	715

Power Transmission System

Romania has an extensive interconnected power transmission and distribution network with an overall length of about 313,000 km. The national grid operates on 750 kV, 400 kV and 220 kV for transmission and 20 kV, 10 kV, 6 kV, 1 kV and 0.4 kV for distribution (See Map 8: Bulgaria, Romania – Power System).

Traditionally, Romania has had strong interconnections with Ukraine and Bulgaria and the FR Yugoslavia and weaker links to Moldova and Hungary. Conel is currently operating the Romanian network in parallel with the electric power systems of Bulgaria, Greece and Albania and is working to become fully integrated into the UCTE system.

The CONEL system is interconnected with neighbouring countries as follows:

750 kV:	through Isaccea to South Ukraine, and to Varna to Bulgaria.
400 kV:	– Rosiori to Mukacevo in the Ukraine; – Portile de Fier (Iron Gates) to Djerdap in the FR of Yugoslavia; – Iintareni to Kozloduy in Bulgaria; – Arad to Sandorfalva/Szeged in Hungary (rated at 400 kV but operating at 200 kV)
220 kV:	Isalnita to Kozloduy in Bulgaria
110 kV:	– Stinca to Costesti, Tutora to Ungheni, and Husi to Cloara in Moldova; – Jimbolia to Kikinda, Cura Vaii to Sip, and Ostrovul Mare to Kusijak in Yugoslavia.

International trading over these lines has been only moderate in recent years. The technical requirements for a full membership of Romania in the UCTE are currently discussed between Conel and the UCTE. No date has been set for UCTE membership. A 1994 EU Interconnection

---

1. Electricity exports to Moldova have been overshadowed by that country's solvency problems. Moldova still owes Conel $9 million for exports in 1998. Romania temporarily stopped electricity supplies to Moldova in autumn 1999 because of non-payment. Conel, however, resumed supplies in November, in spite of Moldova's outstanding debt.

Feasibility Study indicated the importance of completing the 400 kV network in North Transylvania through construction of a line from Arad to Oradea. The study also suggested that a 400 kV connection between Oradea and Bekescsaba or Rosiori-Mukachevo-Albertisza would contribute towards improved security in North Transylvania.

Because of the recent war in the Federal Republic of Yugoslavia, many previously proposed interconnections proposals for Southeastern Europe are now invalid, at least in the short term. This may shift Romania to a key position for interconnecting Greece, Bulgaria, and Romania with Western Europe. The relevant existing lines are the Rosiori-Mukachevo and the Arad-Sandorfalva 400 kV lines. The value of the Portile de Fier (Iron Gates) – Djerdap (in the Federal Republic of Yugoslavia) 400 kV line for interconnection with Western Europe is presently unclear.

Electricity Prices and Tariffs

Conel has faced two major financial problems: firstly the historically lower level of residential prices, and the political and social difficulties associated with price increases. The second major problem relates to the low level of cash collections, with major difficulties concerning the industrial sector.

Concerning the price structure, significant progress has been made in eliminating cross-subsidies between the industrial and the residential sectors. Residential electricity prices have been increased several times over the past years. The last price hike in October 1999 reduced the subsidy for households to 3%[1]. The price for the commercial sector has been increased by 24% and for households by 17.4%. Tariffs for households consuming more than 50 kWh/month have been increased to 610 Lei/kWh, and for those consuming less than 50 kWh/month to 500 Lei/kWh (social tariff). Residential consumers can choose between three tariffs: a social tariff without a fixed charge for consumption below 50 kWh, a standard tariff and a time-of use tariff.

Romania: Residential Electricity Tariffs, June 1999

	Social Tariff		Standard Tariff lei/kWh	Standard Tariff (time of use)	
	0-50 kWh/month (lei/kWh)	> 50 kWh/month (lei/kWh)		day time (lei/kWh)	night time (lei/kWh)
Low voltage (0 - 1 kV)	500	1,951	610	740	480
Medium Voltage (above 1kV)	–	–	500	600	400

Tariffs for industrial clients are differentiated according to voltage levels, contracted power and time of use. Demand charges range from 291 lei/kWh (above 110 kV during off-peak period) to 2,003 lei/kWh (between 0.1 and 1 kV during peak period).

Conel collects approximately 50% of revenues in cash, 25% in "compensation coupons" and 25% remain as debts (promises to pay). Compensation coupons are issued by Conel to suppliers for a fixed value of electricity (i.e. in debts to Electrica)[2]. However, since the coupons were

---

1. Prices for households were last increased 9% to 870 Lei/kWh (standard tariff) and 572 Lei/kWh ("social tariff" for up to 70 kWh/month). Prices for industry were increased to 602.9 Lei/kWh (ab. $0.037/kWh).
2. In July 1999, difficulties to pay outstanding debt to the foreign consortium that constructed Cernavoda NPP nearly required Nuclearelectrica to close the plant.

like cash, with a face value, and without the name of the companies involved, they were traded (at a discount of 10% of face value) between companies with urgent debts. Conel is now issuing compensation coupons only for a specific debt and to specific companies, so that trading in coupons is no longer possible. Cash collections come predominantly from the residential sector. A disproportionate percentage of cash collected is generated by the Bucharest distribution utility (45% of the total).

Investment Plans

Generation

The projected development of the power generation system in Romania foresees that a total of 8.3 GW of generation be retired by 2020. In parallel, rehabilitation and greenfield projects should add 3.4 GW of capacity by 2005 and a further 3.5 GW of capacity by 2010. These projections are made by Conel on the assumption that the electricity market in Romania will become sufficiently attractive for outside investors to encourage this level of investment in generation.

Romania: Plant Retirement Programme

Year	MW
1999 - 2010	5,724
2011 - 2015	865
2016 - 2020	1,674

Source: Conel Annual Report 1998.

In the short term the following generation investments are planned or underway:

- Upgrading of coal-fired plants running on medium- and low-grade lignite. A World Bank loan has already been granted for the $345 million project.

- Completion of Unit 2 of the Cernavoda Nuclear Power Station. Efforts to find financing for this plant have been underway since 1998. The likelihood that financing will be found and construction restart in the short term is small.

- In 1998 Hidrolectrica contracted with a consortium led by Sulzer Hydro (Switzerland) for the rehabilitation and modernisation of one of six units of the Portile de Fier I (Iron Gates) plant. Efforts are currently underway to secure financing for the other five units of this plant. Each unit is to be upgraded from 175 MW to 190 MW rated power, with the capacity to increase output to 200 MW for short periods. The reconstruction of unit 6 is planned to be completed in the first half of 2000.

- There are 33 unfinished hydro-electric power plants with a capacity of 1,400 MW, of which 14 would be finished by Hidroelectrica.

- Grozavesti thermal power plant (TPP): The project calls for installing 2 × 40 MW gas turbines and 2 × 106 Gcal/hour recovery type boilers, and the rehabilitation of two 50 MW units by June 2000. An $80 million tender was awarded to a consortium including General Electric, Eizenberg (Israel) and Elin (Austria). In April 1998, Tomen Power (Japan) and United Development (Israel) each took a 25% stake in Grozavesti Electric and Thermal Power Co.

- Bucharest North TPP: Commissioning of 3 × 40 MW gas turbines, 3 × 106 GCal/hour recovery type boilers, and 6 × 100 Gcal/hour peak hot water boilers using fuel oil. This new

TPP is to be financed under "built and operate" or "build and transfer" schemes through foreign equity investment. The tender will be organised by the Bucharest municipality, which will own and operate the plant. The value of the project is $180 million.

■ Bucharest West TPP: Two 125 MW units to be financed through a build and transfer scheme, plus two 100 Gcal/hour hot-water boilers.

■ Progresul TPP: Rehabilitation of a 50 MW unit and four 420 tons/hour steam boilers (possibly to be financed directly by Conel), plus three 100 Gcal/hour peak hot-water boilers.

■ Bucharest South TPP: Rehabilitation of six of the sixteen 100 Gcal/hour hot-water boilers (financed by Conel), plus the rehabilitation of two 100 MW units (number 3 and 4), financed by an EIB loan.

■ In March 1998, Combined Energy Companies (US) and state-owned aluminium producer Aldro Slatina SA signed a 25-year power purchase agreement. Enron has recently joined the project. The planned 320 MW plant will be fueled by gas supplied by Romgaz. Tentative completion date is 2002. The $300 million project is partly financed by the IFC.

Transmission System The investment needs in the transmission system focus on the rehabilitation of substations and overhead lines; the installation of metering and a market settlements system; telecommunications, and the completion of the 400 kV network with the "closure" of an open 400 kV ring in Northern Transylvania. A EU PHARE project will prepare (starting in the fourth quarter of 1999) a business plan for the transmission and dispatch functions of a standalone "national grid company".

Present transmission system planning is based on Conel's generation plans. Different transmission requirement may result from the emergence of a competitive market in generation and the entry of Independent Power Producers (IPPs). This could affect the flows in the transmission system.

The objective of the re-structuring of the electricity system is to create a market in which electricity will be traded between suppliers and distributors and/or consumers through the transmission network of Conel (as a national grid company). This will require the transmission company to have the capacity (including telecommunications) to operate the trading and settlement process. In addition Conel would need systems for the operation and settlement of ancillary services (frequency control, voltage control, reactive power) and for constraints costs and losses. The total investment needs are approximately $970 million.

A joint $150 million EBRD/EIB loan for transmission system investments is being negotiated. The loan would cover the most urgent investments (metering and market settlement systems, telecommunications, and overhead line replacement).

NUCLEAR POWER

Structure of the Nuclear Utility

Romania operates one nuclear power plant, a Canadian-technology CANDU-6 pressurised heavy-water reactor (PHWR). This type of nuclear reactor uses natural uranium fuel to create the nuclear reaction and heavy water as the neutron moderator and reactor coolant. The plant, located at Cernavoda, some 150 km east of Bucharest on the Danube, has a net electrical capacity of 650 MWe. It was put into commercial operation in December 1996. During the first full year of operation it produced 5.40 TWh, ten percent of the total Romanian electricity generation. Its load factor throughout 1997 was 87.27%.

Cernavoda is run by Societatea Nationala "Nuclearelectrica" S.A, which emerged from the split-up of the *regie autonome* Renel. Nuclearelectrica has three subsidiaries: CNE-Prod, headquartered at the Cernavoda nuclear plant, responsible for electricity production; CNE-Invest, responsible for future developments of the nuclear sector; and FCN (Filiala de Combustibil Nuclear), responsible for nuclear fuel fabrication at Pitesti.

Another product of the Renel de-merger is the state-owned corporation for nuclear activities (Regia Autonoma pentru Activitati Nucleare, RAAN). RAAN includes the heavy water production plant (ROMAG and its associated thermal plant), the Center of Technology and Engineering for Nuclear Projects (CITON) and the Institute for Nuclear Research (Institutul de Cercetari Nucleare, ICN) in Pitesti. CITON and ICN are to be converted into separate commercial enterprises before being privatised. The plan was approved by Parliament in August 1998. It is expected to take two years to implement.

The National Commission for the Control of Nuclear Activities (Comisia Nationala pentru Controlul Activitatilor Nucleare, CNCAN) is the regulatory body for the use and development of nuclear energy. CNCAN is headed by a President who holds the rank of Secretary of State and reports directly to the Prime Minister. The duties of CNCAN include:

■ Regulations, technical documents, standards and instructions for the safe operation of nuclear installations and power plants; for the protection of workers, the public and the environment against undue radiological hazards; and for physical protection, safeguards, transport, import, export and transit of radioactive materials;

■ Issuing and revoking licenses, and approval of emergency preparedness plans;

■ Verification of compliance with regulations and procedures during design, construction, commissioning and operation of nuclear power plants.

CNCAN is also responsible for developing international co-operation in the nuclear field. CNCAN was restructured during the first half of 1998 (Law 16/1998 and Government Decision No. 287/27.05.98). It is now composed of four general divisions: Nuclear Power Plants and Fuel Cycle, Applications of Ionizing Radiation, Surveillance of Environment Radioactivity and Resource and Development.

Since its creation in 1990, CNCAN has suffered from a lack of resources and from salaries five times lower than those paid by industry. The staff of the commission was increased significantly at the end of May 1998, from 27 to 307 positions (of these, 202 are manning the environmental radiation monitoring network). The budget, which is based on state allocations and on fees derived from regulations, was increased. Additional staff was hired and preparation of new regulations was sped up. CNCAN's new organisational structure is in line with EU practices. The commission expected to complete the harmonisation of Romanian nuclear legislation and regulations with the EU's "acquis communautaire" by 1999.

A 1998 review of CNCAN by an International Regulatory Review Teams (IRRT) of the International Atomic Energy Agency (IAEA) concluded that considerable progress had been made in recent years towards the establishment of an independent and competent nuclear regulatory authority in Romania. The basic structures to regulate nuclear and radiation safety are in place; a number of good practices have been recognised. Nevertheless, substantial resources are needed to complete the transition as planned. In particular, the need to provide adequate resources was identified in all areas, including: provision of an adequate budget, recruitment and retention of competent and experienced staff, provision of adequate salaries and training of staff. The EU commented in its late-1999 accession report that the capacity of the CNCAN needs to be reinforced.

Nuclear Safety   Construction of the five nuclear units (all CANDU-type reactors) on the Cernavoda site began in the 1980's. Only Unit 1 is in operation. There are plans to complete Unit 2, while further work on Units 3 to 5 has been postponed indefinitely.

Romania's choice of a Western technology, which led to the signing of contracts with Atomic Energy of Canada Ltd (AECL) and Ansaldo (Italy), was motivated by safety concerns, and the use of natural uranium as fuel and heavy water as coolant and moderator, possibly to be manufactured in Romania. Furthermore, the process equipment for CANDU nuclear stations does not generally require as large an investment in sophisticated manufacturing plants as that for other types of nuclear stations.

Romania concluded engineering, procurement and financial assistance agreements with AECL in 1979 for nuclear steam plant and with Ansaldo for the supply of equipment related to the balance of plant and for the turbine generator. In 1990, AECL-Ansaldo Consortium (AAC) was formed. Romanian efforts were stepped up to manufacture many components within the country.

Under the Ceausescu regime, quality control during the construction of Cernavoda-1 was at times inadequate. Exaggerated focus on "hard" areas (such as concrete poured, equipment installed, welds done, etc.) at the expense of "soft" areas such as quality procedures, project planning, etc. resulted in rework and delays. AAC thoroughly reorganised the project in 1991. The legacy of poor-quality workmanship was rectified and CNCAN is now confident about component reliability at Cernavoda-1. The unit has also been carefully examined by IAEA experts.

The spare parts situation at Cernavoda-1 requires careful management to overcome shortages of critical equipment. Some of the CANDU-6 equipment designed in the late seventies is no longer available. To complete Cernavoda-1, Renel partly "cannibalised" Cernavoda-2.

The utility has invested $17 million in a full-scope simulator and a modern, well-furnished training centre on the reactor site. A comprehensive training program has been underway

Turkey has the potential to grow very fast, if the obstacles to better resource allocation are removed, particularly with respect to infrastructure. Energy, transport and telecommunication are key sectors. The investment needs in infrastructure are significant, in particular in the energy sector, and a slow-down in economic recovery could severely jeopardise large-scale infrastructure projects, which are in need of private capital. In August 1999, Turkey adopted four constitutional amendments that could resolve many of the problems faced by private power developers. The amendments provide a legal basis for private ownership of electrical generation and distribution assets and grant foreign owners of electrical assets the right to call upon international arbitration. Implementing legislation for these constitutional amendments was passed in January 2000. The denial of access to international arbitration has been a major obstacle to foreign investment in the Turkish electricity sector in the past. Investors are also waiting for a law to clarify the status of projects run under the build-operate model, based under the 1984 BOT Law and ensuing laws, including the 1997 BO Law.

Privatisation and restructuring of state enterprises, including in the energy sector are a priority. The Ministry of Energy foresees that total energy demand will double over the next ten years; electricity consumption will increase even more rapidly. The electricity sector, which has been traditionally dominated by the state, faces two major challenges: improving efficiency of its existing infrastructure and expanding supply capacity. In both cases, the government's strategy has been to involve the private sector. Long-term electricity sales agreements have been signed with several foreign investors, who wish to construct more than 5 GW of additional generation capacity. Another key objective is to ensure reliable gas supplies for power generation and industry. A growing role of Turkey as a market and transit corridor for Caspian oil and gas is seen as an important factor to strengthen Turkey's geopolitical weight.

Main Economic Indicators

	Unit	1997	1998	*1999
GDP	billion 90 $ PPP	448.7	461.3	467.7
GDP growth	%	7.5	2.8	1.4
GDP per capita	$ per person	7063	7144	7130
Industrial gross output	%	11.4	1.8	n.a
Unemployment rate	%	6.4	6.3	6.5
Consumer Price (end year)	%	85.7	84.6	64.3*
Foreign Direct Investment	US $ million	873	982	n.a.
FDI per capita	$ per person	14	15	n.a.

* June 1999, year-on-year percentage change.
Source: OECD.

THE ENERGY SECTOR

Energy Policy Objectives

Energy policy objectives are set out in five-year plans, the current one being the 1995-2000 plan. Energy objectives have changed little over the past five-year plans. The main objectives are:

■ To ensure sufficient, reliable and economic energy supplies to support economic and social development.

■ To maintain energy security of supply.

■ To encourage sufficient investments to meet growing energy demand.

In addition, environmental improvements, which do not jeopardise economic growth, have received increased attention in recent years. Current macroeconomic policies, and in particular price and tax reform as well as privatisation policy, have also had a large impact on the energy sector. Turkey is planning to augment its natural gas supplies with gas from new sources to further diversify its energy supplies. To this effect, the state-owned natural gas and oil transport company **Bota,s** has signed several contracts and memoranda with Russia, Algeria, Nigeria, Turkmenistan, Iran and others, and is negotiating additional contracts. Turkey has also offered several solutions to facilitate the transit of oil and natural gas from the Caspian area toward western markets, which should support its supply diversification effort.

Total primary energy supply (TPES) in 1997 totalled 71.27 mtoe. TPES has been growing at an average annual rate of 4.9% in the 1990's, but year-on-year growth has been erratic, ranging from a 2.3% decline in 1994 to a peak growth of 9.4% in 1995. Turkey imported 63% of its energy needs in 1997. Oil is the most important fuel in Turkey, contributing 43% of TPES, followed by coal (almost 30% of TPES) and gas (11.8%).

Final consumption (TFC) amounted to 53.62 mtoe in 1997. Industry was the largest consumer with almost 38% of TFC, followed by the residential sector (31%) and transport (23%).

Figure 20   Turkey Energy Balance (1997)

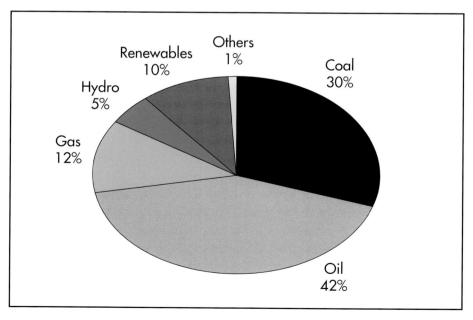

Source: IEA.

Main Energy Indicators

		1996	**1997**
TPES	mtoe	67.55	71.27
Net Imports	mtoe	41.54	43.34
Net Oil Imports	mtoe	28.52	27.47
Net Gas Imports	mtoe transfer to bcm	6.84	8.17
Electricity Production	GWh	94,862	103,296
TPES/GDP	toe per thousand 90 $ PPP	0.36	0.35
TPES/Population	toe per capita	1.08	1.11
CO_2 Emission from Fuel Comb.	mt of CO_2	176.75	187.49
CO_2/TPES	t CO_2 per toe	2.61	2.63
CO_2/GDP	t CO_2 per 90 $ PPP	0.42	0.42
CO_2/Population	t CO_2 per capita	2.82	2.94

Source: IEA.

Energy Administration and Industry

Energy issues are under the responsibility of the Ministry of Energy and Natural Resources (MENR). The Ministry of Environment is the main co-ordinating body for environmental issues. The State Planning Organisation (SPO), which reports directly to the Prime Minister, evaluates Turkish energy needs, including production and imports, after consultation with the relevant State Economic Enterprises (SEEs). The SPO makes investment decisions on an annual basis after consultation with the SEEs. The Privatisation Administration, which also reports to the Prime Minister, is responsible for enterprises, which are for sale and prepares them for privatisation.

The Turkish energy sector is still mainly state-owned with State Economic Enterprises for electricity (**TEAS** for generation and transport and **TEDAS** for distribution), oil (**TPAO** for the upstream sector, **Tupras**[1] for refining), coal (**TKI** for lignite and **TTK** for hard coal), and oil and natural gas transportation (**Botaş**). The planned sale of a 51% state-owned stake in **Petrol Ofisi**, the Turkish public oil distribution company, to a Turkish consortium led by Is Bankasi and Bayindir Holding for $1.6 billion, was cancelled. A new tender is planned in spring 2000.

Most of the SEEs have been dependent upon a capital endowment by the Treasury and state guarantees for investments. The state itself finances the building of dams. In addition, the Treasury compensates TTK for its large losses in the production of hard coal.

Energy Supply and Demand Projections

Following the growth in GDP, TPES has increased at a fast pace in recent years. Between 1990 and 1997, TPES increased 4.9% per year, slightly above Turkish GDP growth and well above the IEA European average energy demand growth of 0.8%. TPES is expected to continue to increase quickly, reaching 93 mtoe in 2000 (30% above 1997 level) and 179 mtoe (2.5 times more than in 1997) in 2010. The prediction for 2000, which implies persistent 9% annual growth rates, may be too high in light of preliminary figures for 1998 and early 1999.

Domestic energy production has grown only by 10% over the 1987-97 period, far less than demand. Consequently, energy imports in Turkey have almost doubled between 1987 and

---

1. Tupras has a small amount of private shareholding.

1997. In 1997, they reached 43.34 mtoe, i.e. over 60% of TPES, in comparison with 36% in 1973. Current forecasts indicate that the share of energy imports vs domestic production will stabilise if domestic lignite production will rapidly increase. However, lignite production has stabilised over the past decade, and production forecasts are currently being revised. Oil imports are expected to increase from 28.78 mtoe in 1997 to 29.8 mtoe in 2000, and natural gas imports are expected to increase from 8.17 mtoe to 18 mtoe over the same period.

Privatisation

The high rate of inflation and the rapid growth in the public debt are the two major economic problems faced by the Turkish Government. One cause for the large budget deficit are the losses of the State Economic Enterprises. There are about 35 SEEs, which are fully state-owned[1] and report to the Government. Eight SEEs, among them TEAS (electricity generation and transmission), TEDAS (electricity distribution), TDCI (iron and steel) and TTK (hard coal), accounted for the majority of the public sector losses. Since the mid-1990s, the reduction in SEE losses has been an important part of the government's stabilisation and structural reform plans.

The government plans to privatise most state enterprises and passed a privatisation law in 1986. In some cases, the government has implemented Transfer of Operating rights. The Government is also trying to attract private and foreign capital by implementing Build Operate Transfer (BOT) and Build Own Operate (BOO) programmes in various sectors of the economy, in particular the electricity sector. However, legal disputes have caused delays in this policy. In July 1997, a law on BOO programmes was adopted by Parliament.

In the energy sector, the government is working on a privatisation programme with the following aims:

■ Increasing budget revenues.

■ Increasing private capital participation in the investments needed to meet the projected demand, thus supplementing public enterprise investments.

■ Improving management and reducing the cost of supplying energy.

The privatisation programme has changed several times in scope, timing and organisation. At the beginning of 1997, it included the following actions for energy:

■ In the electricity sector, BOT/BOO programmes were created to allow private investors to build and run new generating plants for 20 to 30 years. Operating rights of some of TEAS' generating plants are currently being transferred to the private sector. TEDAS has been divided into 29 regional systems, with the operating rights of each system being transferred to the private sector.

■ In the oil sector, there are plans to privatise Tupras. As stated above, 51% of Petrol Ofisi is to be sold in 2000.

■ In the gas sector, Botas will remain a SEE, but the government envisages abolishing its legal monopoly on natural gas imports and transport. Eventually, the government plans to set up an independent regulator.

■ In the coal sector, two lignite mines have been transferred to the electricity plants they supply. The government is planning to transfer operating rights of lignite mines to the private sector.

---

1. With the exception of Tupras.

Energy Pricing Policy

Energy prices are set, in principle, by the SEEs, but all decisions concerning prices require government approval. As SEEs have the largest market share, prices set by private competitors are often at the same level as those set by SEEs.

The government has been using energy prices to promote social objectives. For example, although electricity prices for households have increased, they are still at about the same level as those for industries. In 1994, electricity prices in "Priority Development Areas" were set at 14% below the level of the rest of the country. Overall, prices are too low for electricity enterprises to make necessary investments.

In the hard-coal sector, energy prices do not cover the cost of supply. After years of operating losses, TKI made profit in 1995 due to price increases and cost reductions. In the oil sector, the government sets ex-refinery prices and does not systematically increase oil product prices following a depreciation in the Turkish lira or a rise in international oil prices. Both events should lead to a rise in ex-refinery prices. As a consequence, Tupras makes temporary losses. In the natural gas sector, there are cross-subsidies between industries and households in favour of the latter.

The ongoing reform process can lead to a partial rationalisation of this pricing system as follows:

■ In the electricity sector, private generators can be allowed by MENR to sell electricity to consumers at a negotiated price.

■ In the gas sector, under the new regulations being discussed, large consumers would be allowed to choose their suppliers using Botas' infrastructure.

■ In the oil sector, the Government has set a pricing mechanism in July 1998, which links domestic oil product prices to international prices. It also envisages selling Tupras' refineries to different buyers, so as to foster competition.

THE OIL SECTOR

Oil Consumption

Between 1973 and 1997, oil demand increased at an average annual rate of 4%. In 1997, final consumption of oil reached 26.65 mtoe (actually representing a 2.4% drop vs 1996) and accounted for just under 50% of final energy consumption.

The Ministry of Energy and Natural Resources (MENR) forecasts that final oil consumption will continue to increase, but at a slower pace. Consumption is forecast at 32.87 mtoe in 2000[1] and 44.50 mtoe in 2010. The highest oil consumption growth is expected in the transport sector. In the industry and commercial/residential sectors, oil consumption will increase more moderately, since these sectors are expected to increasingly cover their demands with coal and gas.

---

1. An annual growth of more than 7% would be needed in 1998, 1999 and 2000 to reach this forecast. This contradicts the official assumption that future oil consumption growth will flatten below the 4% of the past years.

State Companies

In Turkey, there are three state-owned companies in the oil sector:

■ The Turkish Petroleum Corporation (**TPAO**) is responsible for the upstream oil sector (production and exploration).

■ Petroleum refining is undertaken by the Turkish Petroleum Refinery Corporation (**Tupras**).

■ **Botas,** the oil and gas transport company, was a subsidiary of TPAO until 1995, but is now a State Economic Enterprise.

TPAO and Tupras are not monopolies but have the largest market share in Turkey. Botas has a legal monopoly status.

In the early 1990's, the government decided to privatise Tupras and Petrol Ofisi. In 1991, as a first stage, 2.17% of Tupras shares were sold to the public in the Istanbul market. By 1995, 3.59% of Tupras were privately owned. Other smaller private Turkish enterprises as well as foreign companies are involved in oil exploration, production, refining and distribution.

Oil Production, Imports, Refining and Distribution

Production

In 1997, oil production was 3.52 mtoe (12.7% of oil demand). Production has been declining since the early 1990's. Oil is produced mainly in the southeast of the country, where the fields produce heavy and high sulphur oil. There are some other fields in the European part of the country. In general, field reserves are small and production costs are high. Oil production is expected to decrease due to the natural depletion of the fields.

Imports

Net oil imports have increased more than threefold between 1973 and 1997 and have increased more than 25% since 1990, reaching 27.47 mtoe in 1997. Before 1990, Iraq was the largest oil supplier. After UN sanctions were imposed on Iraq, Turkey increased its crude oil purchases from Saudi Arabia and Iran. In the first quarter 1999, Saudi Arabia and Iran accounted for 45% of Turkish crude imports, followed by Libya (almost 15%) and Iraq (8.5%). As domestic oil production is expected to decline, oil imports should continue to increase to meet the rapid growth in demand.

Refining

There are five refineries in Turkey with a total capacity of 32 mt. Tupras owns four refineries and more than 85% of total capacity. Tupras' refineries are situated at Alliaga, Izmit, Kirikkale and Batman. Another refinery at Atas (Mersin) is a joint venture between Shell, Mobil, BP and Turk Petrol.

There has been over-capacity in the refining sector in Turkey since the completion of the Kirikkale refinery near Ankara in 1986. This over-capacity has diminished, however, due to the recent rapid increase in demand. The rate of utilisation of the refineries increased from 75% in 1988 to 85.2% in 1997.

The conversion capacity of refineries in Turkey is low in comparison with other IEA countries. In 1989, Tupras initiated a $1.8 billion modernisation plan to increase the conversion capacity of its plants and the quality of its oil products. The plan also calls for the production of unleaded gasoline, low-sulphur diesel and heavy fuel oil (*see table p. 205*).

The plan has been financed by Tupras (after approval by the State Planning Organisation) with the participation of long-term credits from international institutions. In addition, due to increasing oil demand, the MENR is planning to build two new 5 mt/year refineries before 2005.

Turkish Refineries

	Installed capacity, 1995 (mt)	Utilisation in 1995 (%)	Upgrades
Kirikkale	5	68.2	Hydrocracker (1993), isomerisation (1997)
Batman	1.1	50.6	
Izmit[1]	11.5	87.2	Hydrocracker (1996), catalytic reformer (1997), vacuum distillation (1997), isomerisation (1999)
Izmir (Aliaga)	10	90.2	Hydrocracker (1993), catalytic cracker (2000), isomerisation (2000)
Atas	4.4	91.7	

1. Operations stopped after the August 1999 earthquake.
Source: MENR.

Pipelines, Distribution and Storage

Crude oil pipelines are owned and operated by Botas. There are no oil product pipelines. The main pipelines are (See Map 1: Black Sea Oil Transport Infrastructure):

■ Two pipelines with a total capacity of 71mt/year from Iraq to Ceyhan. Economic sanctions against Iraq in 1990 led to the closure of these two pipelines. Turkey evaluated the direct losses caused by the closure of these pipelines to its economy at more than $30 billion over five years. After the UN vote on Resolution 986, which allowed Iraq to sell oil worth $2 billion over a period of six months, the pipelines were opened again in December 1996.

■ A 3.5 mt/year pipeline from the Batman fields to the port of Dortyol[1].

■ A 5 mt/ pipeline from Ceyhan to the Kirikkale refinery.

There are twelve distribution companies. In 1999, Petrol Ofisi had a market share ranging from 35% to 67% of the retail market, depending on the types of products. After Petrol Ofisi, Mobil and Shell are the main distributors.

Oil storage units are owned principally by Petrol Ofisi. Other companies, including foreign companies, are building oil storage units, mainly in the western part of Turkey, the fastest growing and main consuming area.

Legislation and Regulation

Upstream

To revitalise domestic oil exploration and production, the government plans to lower royalties, which amounted to 12.5% of production in 1996. New royalties should decrease proportionally with the production and should be lower for smaller fields.

Until 1990, domestic oil producers were obliged to sell their production to Tupras. In 1990, however, producers were allowed to export up to 35% of oil production from new reservoirs. The price of crude oil is set by the government, on a parity basis with the price of the same quality, and taking into account transport costs to the refineries of imported crude.

---

1.   A 42 km pipeline transports crude oil from the Selmo area to the Batman refinery.

Oil Product Prices

Domestic oil product prices were liberalised in 1989, but post-refinery oil product prices set by Tupras require government approval. Occasionally oil product prices, and in particular diesel prices, are not increased in the wake of a devaluation of the lira against the $ or a substantial increase in international oil prices. For instance, in the summer of 1996, when international oil prices rose, the Government asked Tupras not to increase ex-refinery prices. As a consequence, oil product prices at the refinery gate were below international prices. At the distribution level, prices of oil products are theoretically determined by the market. But, distributors competing against the dominant Petrol Ofisi, will not set their prices higher than the latter for fear of losing market share. These companies are also trying to increase throughput per outlet to reduce costs.

Transportation tariffs are negotiated between Botas and the users of the pipelines (TPAO and Iraq).

In July 1998, a formula to link the domestic price of oil products to the international price (Mediterranean FOB price) was set up. In addition, the oil product taxation system was simplified: several specific taxes were replaced by a single consumption tax.

Import and Export Regulation

Crude oil and product imports were liberalised in 1989. Import licences are granted to all refiners and retailers that have the minimum storage capacity required. During the summer of 1996, at the same time that domestic oil products prices were set at a lower level than the international prices, Atas experienced difficulties in getting administrative documents to export its products.

Oil Transit

Turkey is an almost inevitable transit country for Caspian oil. Traffic statistics through the Turkish Straits are shown in the chart below (See also Chapter on Regional Energy Trade and Transit).

In 1995, about 60-70 mt of Russian oil coming from Novorossyisk, Tuapse and Odessa transited the Bosphorus. Turkey has increasingly warned the international community about the environmental and safety risk that arises from the swelling traffic through the Turkish Straits. The number of vessel passages has soared almost 2.5 times since 1996, from a level of about 20,000 units per year to about 50,000 units. Tonnage transported through the Straits peaked at 167 mt in 1988. Because statistics since 1996 have been missing, one cannot determine if tonnage increased parallel to the vessel passages. In other words, it is not clear if more smaller vessels or "half-loaded" vessels (i.e. empty voyage one-way and loaded voyage the other way) have sailed through the Straits since 1996. It may be noted that vessel passages had stabilised at about 20,000 units/year since the early 1970's, notwithstanding considerable variations in tonnage. A major cause for the surge in vessel passages since 1996 is the opening of the Main-Danube canal. Russian and Caspian oil exports have not increased above the level of the late 1980's.

What is certain is that traffic through the Turkish Straits cannot increase indefinitely. At what traffic level and when saturation will be reached is not known. One can reasonably predict some 100-135 mt/year of oil to be evacuated through the Turkish Straits sometimes after 2005. This scenario is based on proven reserves and planned production profiles in Russia, Azerbaijan and Kazakhstan (and to a much lesser extent Turkmenistan) and on the assumption that no major pipeline system will be available to bypass the Turkish Straits by then. No doubt, the Turkish Straits will not be able to handle such a volume.

Figure 21   Turkish Straits Traffic

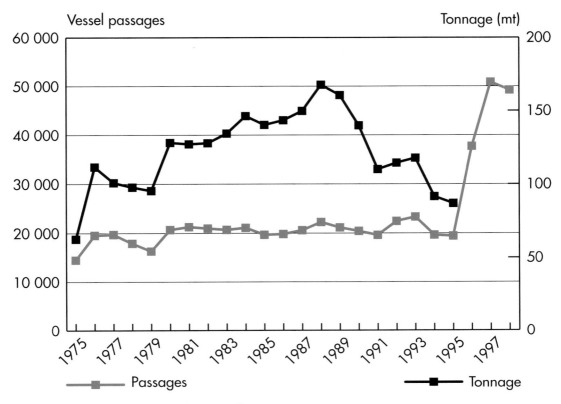

Source: Turkish Ministry of Foreign Affairs.
Note: Tonnage statistics as from 1996 are not available.

In anticipation of future traffic congestion, Turkey has been promoting a "main oil" pipeline from Baku (Azerbaijan) via Georgia to its Mediterranean terminal at Ceyhan (which is also the terminal for the Iraq pipeline system). A memorandum for the construction of this pipeline was signed by Turkey, Azerbaijan and Georgia at the OSCE summit in Istanbul in November 1999. The US, who have been supporting the Baku-Ceyhan line, witnessed the signature of the memorandum.

The signing of the Baku-Ceyhan memorandum has overshadowed construction of a pipeline along the Bosphorus. The cost of such a bypass line has been pegged at some $575 million. This pipeline would compete against the proposed Burgas-Alexandroupolis pipeline, which has been promoted by Russia, Bulgaria and Greece. A proposed 760 km, 40 mt/year, $760 million pipeline from Samsun on the Turkish north coast via the refinery at Kirikkale to Ceyhan has also fallen into oblivion.

NATURAL GAS

Natural Gas Consumption and Production

Natural gas consumption in Turkey commenced in 1976 and has increased quickly, particularly since the mid-1980s. In 1997, primary gas supply amounted to 8.34 mtoe, i.e. 11.7% of total primary energy supply.

Final consumption of natural gas also expanded rapidly and reached 4.07 mtoe in 1997, i.e. 7.6% of total final energy consumption. The largest consumers of gas in 1997 in were the electricity sector (44% of primary gas supply), industry (26%) and the residential sector (22%). In all sectors, gas has replaced oil and coal.

Domestic gas production, which commenced in 1976, reached 0.21 mtoe in 1997. There are seven fields, six of which are owned and operated by TPAO, the Turkish national upstream company, including the largest field (Hamitabat) in the Thrace basin on the European side of the country. Production from the first offshore field in the Marmara Sea began in 1997. As there are good prospects for further discoveries, the Ministry of Energy and Natural Resources forecasts that production will stabilise at its present level as new production will compensate for the depletion of the old fields.

Primary natural gas consumption is expected to increase rapidly over the next fifteen years.

Natural Gas Consumption by Sector (million m³ per year)

	Power	Fertiliser	Other Industry	Residential	Total
1987	671	0	64	0	735
1990	2556	493	320	49	3418
1995	3062	718	1624	993	6937
1996	4050	802	1364	1484	7700
1997	4900	734	1830	1955	9419
1998	9690	851	2758	2783	13352

Source: Botas.

The Turkish Government has released the following projections of gas consumption. Most outside experts consider these forecasts as too high.

Turkish Natural Gas Demand Forecast (bcm)

	Power	Industry	Residential	Total	Deficit
2000	12152	4959	3679	20790	957
2005	24520	11744	8337	44601	4671
2010	30520	13866	9167	53553	9151
2015	40520	14706	9576	64802	20400
2020	52520	17555	9925	80000	35598

Source: Botas.

Gas Import Contracts

Imports of natural gas started in 1987. Between 1987 and 1994, the former Soviet Union was the sole supplier of natural gas to Turkey. Imports from Algeria started in 1994 after the completion of the Marmara LNG terminal. In the first quarter 1999, Russia was still the main natural gas supplier with 61% of total imports, followed by Algeria (36%) and United Arab Emirates (3%).

State-owned monopoly Botas intends to contract increasing amounts of natural gas to meet the growing demand.

Contracts with Russia are as follows:

■ In 1986, Botas signed a contract with Soyuzgazexport for the purchase of natural gas for a period of 25 years starting in 1987 to be delivered via Ukraine, Romania and Bulgaria. The amount to be delivered increased gradually to its maximum of 5/6 bcm/year in 1993. According to this agreement, 70% of the amount paid for the supply of gas has to be used by Russia to purchase Turkish goods. According to Botas, the purchase price of Russian gas is lower than that of any other European country.

■ In December 1996 an agreement was signed with Gazprom for the delivery of additional natural gas over 25 years, reaching 8 bcm/year after 2002, to be delivered through the existing route along the western shore of the Black Sea. Upgrading of the existing pipeline is proceeding, albeit slower than planned.

■ A second overland route across Georgia into eastern Turkey to deliver 16 bcm/year after 2010 is being studied. This project, however, seems to have fallen from grace since the inception of the "Blue Stream" project.

■ ENI (Italy) and Gazprom signed a memorandum of understanding on the building of a $3 billion gas pipeline through the Black Sea from Dzhubga in Russia to Samsun in Turkey. The project (the "Blue Stream") is a 50/50 joint venture between the two companies. Initial plans, which obviously are no longer realistic, called for delivering 0.5 bcm to be delivered in 2000, rising gradually to 16 bcm in 2007. In spite of much publicity, and signing of various engineering contracts, no commercial gas marketing or financing agreement has been signed yet.

Contracts with Algeria are as follows:

■ In 1988, Botas signed a 20-year contract with Sonatrach, the Algerian oil and gas company, for the supply of LNG equivalent to 2 bcm/year of natural gas.

■ In October 1995, Botas signed an agreement with Sonatrach, for the supply of LNG equivalent to 1 bcm/year starting in 1997. An additional supply of 1 bcm/year of natural gas equivalent LNG starting in 1999 has also been confirmed.

In August 1996, Botas signed with the Iranian company NIGC a 23-year contract for the supply of 3 bcm/year of natural gas. Gas purchases could reach 10 bcm/year in 2005. A dedicated gas pipeline is being constructed from North-eastern Iran to Erzurum. By the end of 1999, Iran had completed its leg, whereas work on the Turkish side has been lagging. First gas was due to flow in mid-1999, but may now be delayed until 2001 according to Botas.

In November 1995, Botas signed a 20-year contract with the company Nigeria LNG Ltd. for the supply of 1.2 bcm/year of natural gas equivalent LNG, starting in 1999.

Other developments are listed below. It should be noted that these projects are at best at the stage of a memorandum of understanding and still far from being finalised as a commercial contract.

■ In January 1995, the government signed a memorandum of understanding with Qatar for the supply of 1 bcm/year of natural gas equivalent LNG by 2000. Botas is negotiating with Qatari enterprises for additional natural gas supplies.

■ In March 1999, and following several other similar agreements, Turkey signed a "pre-agreement" with Turkmenistan for the import of 16 bcm/year of gas.

■ Azerbaijan emerged as a potential gas supplier to Turkey with the discovery of the Shah Deniz field in mid-1999. Although appraisal of the discovery is still ongoing, start-up of gas exports to Turkey as from 2005 is already considered a likely possibility. Shah Deniz could supply as much as 16 bcm/year to Turkey.

■ In December 1996, a memorandum of understanding was signed with Yemen for the supply of 3.7 bcm/year of natural gas equivalent LNG starting in 2000-2001.

■ Negotiations are underway with Egypt for the supply of 4 bcm/year of natural gas equivalent LNG.

Figure 22   Turkey Projected Gas Demand and Supplies

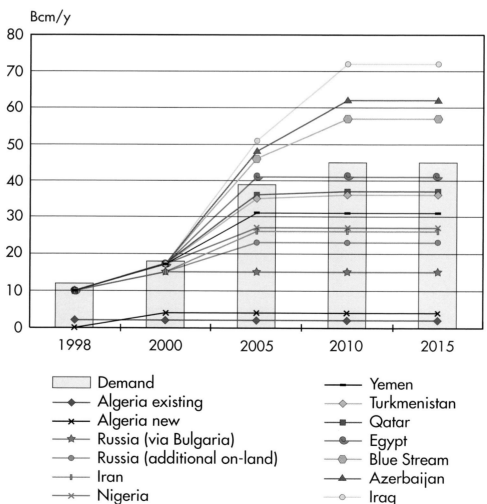

■ Botas is negotiating with Abu Dhabi and Oman for the delivery of LNG.

■ Imports from Iraq are being considered.

The chart above demonstrates how coveted the Turkish market is. There is little doubt about the future growth of Turkish gas consumption, albeit about the rate of growth. Gas contracts tend to be long-term and leave little room for flexibility or acceptance of new entrants in saturated markets. That's why many existing or potential gas suppliers to Turkey are bracing to secure an early market share, well knowing that the Turkish market may not grow enough to absorb all the proposed gas.

Natural Gas Infrastructure

Gas infrastructure in Turkey is limited, but is expected to develop quickly due to the planned increase in demand and imports. Investment decisions are negotiated between the MENR and Botas. Botas receives loans from international institutions and plans to attract foreign capital to participate in future investments (See Map 3: Black Sea Gas Transport Infrastructure).

Transmission and Import Pipelines

The main transmission line runs from the Bulgarian border to Istanbul (the largest industrial region of Turkey), and further on to Izmit, Bursa, Eskisehir and Ankara. Its length is 1,257 km and its total capacity is 8.6-8.7 bcm /year. Capacity can be expanded up to 14/15 bcm/year. In 1994, the first LNG terminal at Marmara Ereglisi near Istanbul was completed. The terminal import capacity is 3.5 bcm/year and is expected to expand to 6 bcm/year. It has also a storage capacity of 0.26 bcm of regasified gas.

Major gas infrastructure developments in Turkey are as follows:

■ The Aegean transmission line will link Bursa to Izmir. Its total length will be 534 km. The first 208 km section (Bursa-Can) was completed in 1996.

■ The southern gas transmission line (1,084 km) will run from Ankara to Iskenderun. The pipeline will also supply the towns of Kayseri and Konya.

■ The main import pipeline is also being expanded from Izmit to Karadeniz Eregli (Northern Anatolia). Iron and steel industries in this region shifted to natural gas in 1996.

Gas import pipeline plans are as follows:

■ In order to import gas from Iran, a 1,174 km pipeline is being built between Tabriz and Ankara. In Turkey, the pipeline will link Erzurum, Sivas and Ankara.

■ Botas is studying capacity expansion of the existing gas import pipeline from Russia. Studies to increase the capacity of Malkoclar metering station and Kirklareli compressor station are underway A second compressor station in Pendik is under construction and studies have started for a third compressor station.

■ A subsea gas pipeline project would link Russia directly to Turkey across the Black Sea ("Blue Stream"). Its total length will be 1,170 km.

■ The Trans-Caspian pipeline to move Turkmen gas from Turkmenistan through the Caspian Sea, Azerbaijan and Georgia to Turkey is promoted by the US, Turkish and Turkmen governments, as well as by the PSG consortium (Shell, Bechtel, GE). A memorandum was signed for this pipeline at the OSCE summit in Istanbul in November.

■ Another proposed route would skirt the Caspian by passing through Iran and/or Armenia. This pipeline would be linked in Turkey to the pipeline that should be built for the Iranian gas imports. In the longer term, Turkey plans to be a transit country for Turkmen gas to Europe. The proposal is for a gas pipeline whose capacity including the gas supplied to Turkey would increase gradually to 40 bcm/year by 2010.

■ Two new LNG terminals are planned to receive new LNG supplies when contracts with potential suppliers are signed. A feasibility study for new LNG terminals in Iskenderun and Izmir was undertaken by M.W. Kellogg. These plants will be built by Botas in a joint venture with international companies under BOT schemes and would supply CCGTs (see Chapter on Electricity).

■ A gas pipeline through Georgia to import gas from Russia to the eastern part of Turkey has been studied. A possible extension of this line to Israel has been discussed.

Distribution

Natural gas is distributed in four main towns in the western part of the country: Ankara (since 1989), Istanbul (since January 1992), Bursa (since December 1992) and Eskisehir (since October 1996). Izmit is planned to be connected to the grid. Natural gas distribution has been carried out by municipality-owned companies in Ankara (Ego) and in Istanbul (Izgas), and by Botas in Bursa and Eskisehir.

The Turkish Gas Ltd. Co. was established within Botas to distribute and market natural gas and to build LNG import terminals and gas-fired power plants. The company plans to create joint ventures with other enterprises.

Gas Regulations and Pricing

Botas is the legal monopoly for gas imports and transport and is responsible for operation and construction of new pipelines. It also sets all gas prices, except in the cities, where gas is distributed by municipality-owned companies. However, to clear the way for foreign investment, the government is considering removing this monopoly by freeing natural gas imports and allowing third-party access in transport. No decision has yet been taken on whether to privatise Botas.

Distribution can be carried out by any private company, but the shares of the different shareholders have to be approved by the Council of Ministers. Distribution companies have no obligation to supply natural gas in their areas.

Botas sets the price of natural gas it sells to end-users as well as the price of natural gas sold by producers to industries[1]. Botas sets the prices for consumers (with annual consumption below 100 million m³, i.e. power generation, industries and distribution companies) Prices to consumers with annual consumption over 100 million m³ are negotiated between Botas and the consumers.

Tariffs set by Botas to industrial customers vary as a function of the volume of natural gas, the mode of use (interruptible or un-interruptible) and the type of industry. Prices favour

---

1. Since 1993, natural gas produced in Turkey has been sold directly to industrial consumers without using Botas' infrastructure.

larger and interruptible consumers. Combined cycle power plants are charged more than distribution companies, the latter being charged more than the other industries. Fertiliser plants are charged the least.

Although Botas has the right to differentiate the prices to the LDCs, the price is now the same for all companies and varies according to the international price of oil products. Gas prices to LDCs take into account import prices, transportation costs and profits. Until February 1997, the prices charged by the LDCs were not allowed to exceed by more than 30% the prices paid by the LDCs to Botas. In February 1997, this limit was increased to 70%. Within this limit, LDCs set their prices according to their marketing strategies. The Ministry of Energy and Natural Resources approves prices for industries and households set by distribution companies.

To ensure the penetration of natural gas into the market, natural gas prices are mostly set below the level of competing fuels. In some sectors such as residential, the price of natural gas is too low to reflect the full cost of supply. Transmission costs are not differentiated according to distance.

Lower taxes on natural gas than on competing fuels allow Botas and distribution companies to set higher pre-tax prices on gas.

On average, in the Turkish industrial sector, the full price of natural gas is comparable or slightly higher than that of heavy fuel oil, but still much lower than that of steam coal. In the residential sector, the full price of natural gas is higher than that of lignite and much lower than that of light fuel oil. Natural gas for electricity generation is sold at a level slightly below that of heavy fuel oil and at a higher level than lignite.

ELECTRICITY

Electricity Demand and Generation

Electricity consumption in Turkey has been growing very rapidly. In 1997, it increased 8.8% and reached 103.2 TWh, which is over eight times higher than in 1973. In 1997, hydro-power was the largest contributor to total electricity generation (38.5%), followed by coal-fired (mainly lignite) plants (32.8%) and gas-fired plants (21.3%). Oil provided 7% of electricity generation, predominantly peak load.

The industrial sector accounted for almost 52% of total electricity consumption, a higher share than the IEA average. MENR forecasts that industry's share will further increase.

Turkey had 21,247 MW of installed capacity by year-end 1998. Of this, 43% was hydro-power, 32% was fuelled by lignite or hard coal, 18% by natural gas, and 7% by fuel or diesel oil.

To cope the expected increase in electricity consumption, electricity generation capacity must increase from 21.9 GW in 1997 to 28.1 GW in 2000, 45.6 GW in 2005, and 65.8 GW in 2010, mostly from natural gas and hydro plants. The share of hydro-power, which accounted for about 43% of capacity in 1998, is expected to dip to 40% in 2000 and to 27.5% in

2020. The use of natural gas for power generation is projected to rise from from about 26% in 2000 to 31% in 2020. The use of lignite will decline to 15% and imported coal to 8% by 2010. Annual load is expected to grow at about 14%. Consumption is expected rise from 103 GWh in 1997 to 134 GWh in 2000 and 290 GWh in 2010.

Electricity Transmission

The long distances between the main consuming areas and the main electricity generation areas require significant infrastructure investments and impose energy losses. The main consuming centres – where consumption is also increasing the fastest – are in the Northwest, whereas the main generating plants are in the north and Southeast. As a consequence, transmission is mainly designed to handle large power flows to the Northwest. By the end of 1995, there were 11,100 km of 380 kV lines, 85 km of 220 kV and 25,000 km of 154 kV lines. In 1995, electricity losses in transmission and distribution amounted to 16% of gross consumption in comparison with 12% in 1990.

Electricity Trade

Between 1990 and 1996, Turkey was a small net exporter of electricity, mainly to Azerbaijan (Nakhichevan). Since 1997, the country has become a net importer again, importing 2.4% of its electricity in 1998. There are few links with neighbouring countries (see table below), and the Turkish system is not integrated for synchronous operation with neighbouring systems.

Turkey purchases some 40 MW from Iran and 350 MW from Bulgaria. An agreement was signed with Georgia in spring 1999 for the purchase of 45 GWh during 13 months from Georgia.

An agreement was signed in 1989 to build a regional grid between Turkey, Syria, Egypt, Jordan and Iraq, which would be completed by the beginning of the next century. The initial phase of the project linking the Turkish, Syrian and Jordan was completed in 1998. Overall costs of the project are pegged at $590 million at 1994 prices. There are also studies for a 400 kV line with Greece.

Existing and Planned International Electricity Interconnections

Existing	kV
Babaeski-Dimodichev (Bulgaria)	400
Hopa-Batumi (Georgia)	220
Kars-Leninakan (Armenia)	220
PS3-Zao (Iraq)	400
Aralik-Sederek (Azerbaijan)	34.5
Igdir-Babek (Azerbaijan)	154
Dogubeyazit-Bazargan (Iran)	154
Cagcak-Kamisli (Syria)	66
Planned	
Karakaya-Khoy (Iran)	400
Cizre-Kesek (Iraq)	400
Birecik-Halep (Syria)	400
Hamitabat-Thessaloniki (Greece)	400

Source: TEAS.

Electricity Industry Structure

The State Sector

Electricity generation, transport and distribution are primarily dominated by large public enterprises. In 1994, the Turkish Generation, Transport and Distribution Company (TEK) was separated into two different companies, the Turkish Electricity Generation and Transmission Corporation (**TEAS**) and the Turkish Electricity Distribution Corporation (**TEDAS**). TEK's assets included 18,478 MW of generation capacity, mostly lignite-fired plants. Both TEAS and TEDAS report to the MENR. In 1995, TEAS owned about 74% of electricity generation capacity[1], all 380 kV lines and 92% of 154 kV lines. TEDAS owns and manages the main distribution lines.

The General Directorate for State Hydraulic Works (DSI), which reports to the Ministry of Energy and Mineral Resources, is in charge of the planning, design and building of hydro plants as well as flood protection, irrigation and land drainage works. Once the plants are commissioned, responsibility for their operation is handed over to TEAS. The General Directorate for Electrical Power Resources Survey and Development Administration (EIEI) supplements DSI by taking over the research and design of small hydro plants.

Independent Power Producers

In 1995, the private sector generated about 6.5% of total electricity. By mid-1999, only 658 MW of capacity was in private hand – about 3% of total installed capacity, which amounted to 21,247 MW at year-end 1998. There is no doubt that the role of the private sector must grow. Much of the 88,000 MW capacity, that Turkey is estimated to need by 2020, will have to be built by private operators. Private players are companies, which have been authorised to generate, transport, distribute and trade electricity. Such operators include:

- Cukurova Elektrik[2] (580 MW, i.e. six hydro units totalling 480 MW and one oil power plant totalling 100 MW) in the Adana area;

- Kepez Elektrik (which operates three hydro plants totalling 261 MW and a 47 MW unit under construction, plus some 1,200 km of transmission lines) in the western Mediterranean region;

- Kayseri Civari Elektrik.

Foreign investors include:

- Trakya Electrik (Enron 50%, Cinergy Global Power 15.5%, Western Resources 9%, Gama Endustri 10%) put a 478 MW CCGC plant in Marmara into commercial service in June 1999. The plant operates under a BOT regime.

- Edison Mission Energy (8)%) and Doga Enerji (20%) started commercial service from their 180 MW gas-fired cogeneration plant in Esenyurt in June 1999.

Distribution concessions have been given to small electricity distributors in a few areas covering about 6% of consumption. Private generators can be allowed to build their distribution lines to supply their customers.

---

1. The remaining is owned by private enterprises or under the control of the Privatisation Office.
2. The state which had a minority stake took control in 1995, after the company had financial problems.

Electricity Regulation and Tariffs

Every year, TEAS and TEDAS investment plans are submitted to the MENR for approval. Programmes are then submitted to the State Planning Organisation (SPO), which discusses them with the two companies.

Electricity tariffs are not formally set by the administration, but prices set by TEAS and TEDAS have been influenced by government policies. Private power utilities can apply to sell electricity directly to customers at a negotiated price. Private distributors set their tariffs in compliance with TEDAS tariffs.

The selling price of electricity does not allow TEAS and TEDAS to make the necessary investments. This is exacerbated by the fact that more than 7% of electricity consumption is not paid for by customers, and this proportion is growing. The government has set up a restructuring programme, sponsored by the World Bank, to improve the performance of the state-owned electricity enterprises, to better adapt the tariff system and to reduce their energy losses.

The Treasury has given capital endowment to TEAS and TEDAS. The building of dams are financed by the DSI, and the state guarantees TEAS' and TEDAS' investments. Since the beginning of the 1990's, TEAS' investments and expenses have fallen considerably. TEDAS' investments have fallen from $341 million in 1992 to $280 million in 1995.

Turkey has implemented privatisation programmes (BOT/BOO Programmes) which also aim to attract foreign capital. The major reasons for this are that TEAS and TEDAS have not had adequate financial strength to fund the expansion of the electricity supply and that public funds have been declining. The SPO estimates that the share of the private sector in future investments will amount to 42% of the total. As part of the privatisation programme, the government is transferring operating rights of TEAS. In the longer term, the government plans to create a market for electricity. It is also considering setting up an independent regulator in charge of implementing regulations, controlling the functioning of the sector and setting tariffs for transmission and distribution.

Future Investments

The August 1999 amendments to the Constitution are changing the status of power generation and removing many of the impediments to foreign IPP. In January 2000 the government passed implementing legislation providing access to international arbitration for foreign investors, thereby removing a further significant hurdle. These actions may accelerate investment covering over 10 GW of private power projects currently in development or planned. According to government counts, 135 energy projects are planned in Turkey. These include 46 contracts worth $7.2 billion that have already been signed. The expected growth in generation capacity will spur commercial demand for gas.

The Ministry of Energy and Natural Resources forecasts that electricity consumption will continue to grow at about the same pace and will reach 130.4 TWh in 2000 and 271.5 TWh in 2010. To provide enough electricity, TEAS calculates that generation capacity will have to rise from 22 GW in 1997 to 28.1 GW in 2000 and 45.6 GW in 2010. Most of the increase will be hydro, followed by lignite and gas. A 3,000 MW nuclear power plant is planned to be commissioned at Akkuyu around 2005-06. It is expected to cover up to 10% of the country's electricity needs.

New capacities will be built mainly near consuming areas. The State Planning Organisation, which planned a large expansion in lignite-fired plants, is revising this programme. Turkey is also involved in the Southeastern Anatolian Project (GAP) in the eastern part of the country to increase hydro production and irrigated areas.

New power plants to be completed before the year 2000 have a total capacity of less than 5 GW (including 10 plants with a total capacity of 1.4 GW being built under BOT programmes, i.e. much less than would be needed to meet the expected demand by 2000). However, tenders are being offered to private companies for new generating plants.

Power Plants to be Commissioned before 2000

	Number of Plants	**Total Capacity (GW)**
TEAS	24	3.5
of which lignite	*2*	*0.5*
of which natural Gas	*1*	*1.4*
of which hydro	*21*	*1.6*
BOT	10	1.4
of which natural Gas	*4*	*1.4*
*of which hydro**	*6*	*0.04*
Total	**34**	**4.9**

* The 672 MW Birecik dam is to be completed in 2002 as part of the Southeastern Anatolian Project.
Source: MENR.

Research and Development

In May 1998, the Energy Technology Study Group issued a report on the "National Energy Technology Policy". The report recommends strengthening R&D in the following areas:

■ The new technology policy should aim to enhance energy conservation and the promotion of efficient end-use energy technologies. As a consequence, an Energy Efficiency Law is to be discussed at parliament, a Committee for Energy Efficient Technologies aiming to introduce energy efficient technologies in the market is planned to be set up together with the National Energy Conservation Center which is envisaged to be the secretariat of this committee.

■ Turkey should promote environmentally friendly technologies for energy production.

■ Turkey should promote renewable energy sources, through increased efforts on R&D as well as adapted subsidies.

The Planned Akkuyu Nuclear Plant

Turkey is planning a nuclear power plant at Akkuyu on the southern coast, 45 km South-west of the town of Silifke. According to the original schedule – which is already more than two years' late –, the plant's two 600 MW reactors were to become operational in 2006 and 2008 respectively.

Three consortia submitted in an international tender in 1997:

■ Atomic Energy of Canada Ltd (AECL), Kvaerner-John Brown (UK), Korea Electric Power Corp and Hanjung (Korea), and Hitachi (Japan);

- Nuclear Power International – a partnership of Siemens (Germany) and Framatome (France).

- Westinghouse (US) and Mitsubishi (Japan).

The winner was to be announced in June 1998. But none of the successive governments has dared to make a decision on the controversial plant ever since. Before the April 1999 elections, it was announced that the winning consortia would be announced after the elections. In July 1999, the official word was that the decision would be made in October 1999, which hasn't happened. Opponents to the Akkuyu plant contend that the plant's exposure to earthquakes has not been properly gauged – an argument, which the government will find has to dispute in the aftermath of the August 1999 earthquake.

The Turkish Atomic Energy Authority (TAEA) is in charge of nuclear R&D, regulatory issues and control concerning all activities in the nuclear field. Its budget is decided annually by Parliament and, for 1997, it will amount to TL 1 600 billion. With regard to the nuclear programme, TAEA is in charge of Turkish nuclear policy, evaluating and inspecting security conditions of nuclear power plants and issuing related licences. This body may review the documents prepared for the tender procedure as to safety and licensability and will ensure that the correct procedures during the construction phase and during the functioning of the plant are followed.

IX. GREECE[1]

GREECE AT A GLANCE

Population	10.5 million (1997)
Area	131,957 sq km
Capital	Athens
President	Konstantinos Stephanopoulos
Currency	$ = 328 drachma (late 1999)

The government has embarked upon a structural reform, which will introduce competition in the electricity sector and gas distribution and foresees part-privatisation of the state petroleum company. Having little energy resources of its own, Greece imports more than 90% of its energy requirements. Its energy balance is dominated by oil (60% of TPES) and coal (33%). Gas, as a significant fuel source, appeared only in 1996 on the Greek market, with the inauguration of an import pipeline for Russian gas, followed by LNG imports from Algeria. Gas is expected to account for 7% of TPES in 2010. Greece has a relatively small electricity supply system among IEA countries. About two-thirds of electricity generation is fuelled by lignite. Greece is playing an increasingly important role in energy inter-connections in Southeastern Europe. A pipeline allowing FYROM to import oil via Greece is being built. Electricity inter-connections already exist with its northern neighbours, and are being developed to Italy and Turkey.

ECONOMIC OUTLOOK

The Greek economy has improved steadily since the mid-1990s. GDP grew at 3.5% in 1998 and is likely to grow by 3 to 3.5% in 1999-2000. This economic performance is largely due to tighter budget discipline – the budget deficit was reduced from 15% of GDP in 1990 to below the Maastricht ceiling in 1998. The OECD expects that the budget deficit will further contract in 2000. Following the considerable nominal convergence, Greece stands good chances joining the European Economic and Monetary Union at the beginning of 2001. Inflation has been brought down from around 20% in 1990 to less than 3% in 1999 and is projected to decline further. It is likely to meet the government's 2% target by end of 1999.

Both public investment supported by the EU and private investment grew strongly in 1998. Investment remains the main source for demand growth, led by a booming public sector investment programme, supported by EU structural funds.

Since late 1998, slackening growth in the EU and in Central and Eastern Europe has been reflected in declining exports. The Kosovo crisis had a limited impact on Greece, principally

---

1.   The country summary is based on the IEA's *Energy Policies of IEA Countries, Greece, 1998 Review,* and updates where necessary.

affecting trade with trade partners in the Balkans. The 1998 exports boost by a currency devaluation was counter-balanced in 1999 by an appreciation of the drachma and slackening growth in the EU and in Central and Eastern Europe.

The OECD expects economic activity to slow somewhat in 1999, largely reflecting sluggish export growth, but then to rebound in 2000 as a result of public investment, lower interest rates and sustained private consumption. Public investment will continue to be the engine of growth, increasing by about 10% in real terms in 1999 and at a somewhat slower pace in 2000.

Since 1990 Greece has pursued a policy of structural reform to improve the functioning of product, labour and financial markets, to trim down the state sector and to enhance the efficiency of public administration. Restructuring and partial privatisation of public sector corporations, mainly in telecommunication and energy, and introduction of competition into former state monopoly sectors have been key elements of this policy. The agenda will increasingly affect the role of the state in energy markets.

Over the past decade, the state-enterprise sector has received an increasing amount of financial assistance from the EU and national sources – equivalent to about 3.5% of GDP in 1998 – and has also accumulated large liabilities. Moreover, almost all public enterprises have been burdened with ill-designed public service obligations.

Main Economic Indicators

	Unit	1997	1998	*1999	*2000
GDP growth	%	3.2	3.5	3.0	3.5
GDP	$ billion	120	121	n.a.	n.a.
GDP per capita	$ per person	11340	11359	n.a.	n.a.
Industrial gross output	%	1.6	7.3	4.0	5.0
Unemployment rate	%	10.3	10.1	10.2	10.1
Consumer Price (end year)	%	5.5	4.8	n.a	n.a
Foreign Direct Investment[1]	US $ billion	2.62	2.81	n.a.	n.a.

Source: OECD.
* Estimate.
1. Net entrepreneurial capital inflows. Source: Bank of Greece, Balance of payments.

THE ENERGY SECTOR

Energy Policy Objectives

In 1999 the government expected to finalise the legal framework for introducing competition in electricity supply, finalise arrangements for regional gas distribution companies, select firms for the franchises and implement a partial privatisation of the state petroleum company. All of this activity is taking place in the context of an overall government policy of structural reform. The government's openness towards market reform and the greater role of private capital is laudable. The EU Operational Programme for Energy (1994-1999) provides substantial investment subsidies for energy-related projects in Greece, which have or will receive close to $1 billion from the programme.

Greece's key energy policy challenges are:

■ Introduction of competition in the electricity sector;

- Completion of the legal and regulatory framework for natural gas distribution;
- Reduction of the direct role of the State in energy markets;
- Development of institutions for more transparent regulation of energy markets.

Energy Balance

Greece's energy balance is dominated by oil (59.9% of TPES in 1997), followed by coal (33%) and renewables (3.7%). No other fuel accounts for more than 1.5% of the overall TPES. Greece has little energy resources of its own and had to import almost 92% of TPES in 1997. The only significant domestic fuel is coal, which provides 30% of TPES. Almost 90% of coal production is used at thermal power plants.

Transport is the largest final energy consumer (39% of TFC in 1997), followed by the residential-commercial-agricultural sector (35%) and industry (24.6%).

Main Energy Indicators

		1996	**1997**
TPES	mtoe	24.77	25.56
Net Imports	mtoe	19.04	19.48
Net Oil Imports	mtoe	17.86	18.39
Net Gas Imorts	mtoe	0.01	0.13
Electricity Production	GWh	42,411	43,292
TPES/GDP	toe per thousand 1990 $ PPP	0.27	0.27
TPES/Population	toe per capita	2.36	2.44
CO_2 Emission from Fuel Comb.	mt of CO_2	77.53	80.62
CO_2/TPES	t CO_2 per toe	3.16	3.15
CO_2/GDP	t CO_2 per 1990 $ PPP	0.70	0.71
CO_2/Population	t CO_2 per capita	7.40	7.69

Source: IEA.

Figure 23   Greece Energy Balance (1997)

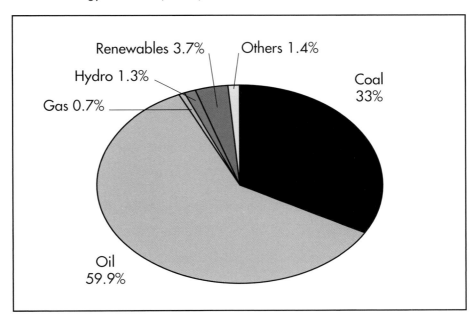

Source: IEA.

Energy Administration and Industry

The Ministry of Development has primary responsibility for energy policy matters. In 1996, the former Ministry of Industry, Energy and Technology was placed under the umbrella of the Ministry of Development. The Ministry of Environment, Physical Planning and Public Works and the Ministry of National Economy also contribute to formulation and implementation of energy-related policies.

The energy market is dominated by state-owned energy firms:

- **Hellenic Petroleum Corporation** (HP, formerly known as DEP) has a market share of about 60% of refined product sales; its exploration and production subsidiary is responsible for all domestic oil and gas production;

- natural gas development has, to date, been led entirely by the Public Gas Corporation (DEPA);

- the Public Power Corporation (PPC) owns about 98% of total electricity generation capacity;

- lignite production is almost entirely in the hands of the Public Power Corporation.

Major Public Energy Companies

Initials	Name	Greek Name	Founded	Notes
PPC	Greek Public Power Corporation	ΔΕΙ	1950	to be re-organised in 1998 or 1999 98% share of electricity market
HP	Hellenic Petroleum Corporation	ΕΛΠ	1975	20% privatised 1998 60% share of domestic refined products market
DEPA	Greek Public Gas Corporation	ΔΕΠΑ	1988	after HP privatisation, owned by State (85%) and HP (15%) 100% share of developing gas market

Source: IEA.

Privatisation and Competition

The energy sector is not spared in the government's overall economic reform programme. In oil, gas, and electricity, the policy goal is to reduce the role of the state, introduce private capital and competition at a rate consistent with market growth, and improve the functioning of state-owned enterprises. Over time, the state will no longer be a participant in the energy market and limit its role to that of a regulator.

Privatisation to-date has been unsteady and often delayed. In early 1998 the government stated its intention to privatise ten public utilities or corporations by the end of the year. In June 1998, a 20% share of DEP was sold on the Greek stock exchange. The partial privatisation of PPC has been discussed in the context of electricity market liberalisation, although there are at present no firm plans for privatisation. Although gas transmission remains in the hands of DEPA, private participation in the gas distribution companies is sought.

The market for oil products was opened in 1992. The EU Directive on Electricity was accepted in December 1996 and requires Greece to open its electricity market by 1 January 2001. The EU Directive on Gas provides a ten-year derogation for the competitive opening of emergent gas markets, of which Greece is considered one, and Greece does not have plans to proceed faster than allowed by the directive.

No agreement has been reached yet. Ownership, finance, and tariff issues have delayed the project. It is one of several alternate Bosphorus by-passes being explored. The three countries re-affirmed their support for the project in a memorandum of understanding signed in December 1997.

THE GAS SECTOR

Gas Market Development

Greece introduced natural gas into its energy balance in November 1996, when first Russian gas was delivered via a new pipeline. The 511 km high-pressure pipeline and portions of the medium-pressure system were officially inaugurated on 14 January 1997. This represented an important milestone in the Greek energy policy, which aims at increasing the share of gas in primary energy supply to at least 7% by 2010. The small domestic production of natural gas from the South Kavala field (in Thrace, northeastern Greece) had ceased in 1995. Natural gas supplies are now based on import of Russian gas and Algerian liquefied natural gas (LNG). Gas imports are expected to reach 3.8 bcm by 2005.

The Russian pipeline route to Greece traverses Ukraine, Moldova, Romania, and Bulgaria. The main components of the natural gas supply project are the high-pressure transmission trunkline and branches, an LNG terminal at the islet of Revithousa near Athens, a metering/operations station at the Greek/Bulgarian border and three operations centre along the main pipeline route. The full system, comprised of high-pressure gas lines, intermediate-pressure lines in the regions of Attiki, Thessaloniki, Larissa and Volos and the LNG terminal were expected to be commissioned by the end of 1999. Most of the low-pressure lines remain to be built.

The largest single use of natural gas will be in electricity generation, both in converted oil-fired stations and new combined-cycle gas turbine power plants. The Public Power Corporation has contracted to purchase 1.3 bcm/year for use in its Keratsini boiler steam-electric plant and its two combined-cycle power plants at Lavrio. It intends to purchase another 0.4-0.5 bcm/year for a combined-cycle power plant in Komotini. The potential for gas-fired power generation is large, because of the present high reliance on lignite-fired power. Ammonia production will be the second largest consumer in the near term, at 0.3 bcm/year. Over the period 1997 to 2001, the expected gas consumption shares are 57% for power generation, 15% for ammonia production, 21% for industrial heating use, and 7% for commercial and domestic use. In industry, natural gas will displace mainly fuel oil and liquefied petroleum gases (LPG) used for heating.

Many large industrial users have access at short distances from the main trunkline or will have access as soon as branch lines to major consumption centres are complete. Several branches are planned to serve large industrial or power customers, notably branches to Komotini, Kavala, the EKO refinery, and Volos.

The residential and commercial market for natural gas is limited compared to many other IEA member countries, because of Greece's relatively mild climate. With the exception of Athens, which switched its 550 km distribution network to natural gas in January 1998, networks for domestic natural gas use must be developed from scratch. Development of low-pressure networks is the main constraint in introducing natural gas to the commercial and domestic sectors. It is expected that it will take up to 11 years for smaller commercial companies to switch to natural gas and up to 20 years for the average household user to begin using it.

Projections for natural gas use in the longer term vary considerably. The government conservatively estimates that gas could account for 7% of TPES by 2010. The Greek Public Gas Corporation DEPA estimates this could reach 15% by 2020, based upon an annual consumption of 7 to 8 bcm. The capacity of the existing gas pipeline would possibly be sufficient to carry this amount, depending on the completion of certain upgrades and on gas delivery pressure.

Main Components of the Greek Natural Gas Grid

Component	Total Length (km)	Operating Pressure (bar gauge)
Main trunkline	511	70
High-pressure branches	450	70, 40, 30
Intermediate-pressure grids	400	19
Low-pressure distribution	6800	4
of which: Attiki (Athens area)	5100	4
Thessaloniki	1000	4
Thessalia	700	4

Source: DEPA, Ministry of Development.

Major Natural Gas Consumers

Plant	Use	Annual gas use (bcm)	Size (MWe)	Year in service
Power Plants				
PPC St. George 8&9 (Keratsini)	boiler power plant	0.48	360	1998
PPC Lavrio (small)	CCGT power plant	0.23	180	1998[1]
PPC Lavrio (large)	CCGT power plant	0.59	570	1999
PPC Komotini	CCGT power plant	0.40-0.50	370-480	2001
Industrial and Chemicals				
EKO and VFL chemicals	ammonia production	0.23		1998
Thessaloniki industrial users		0.65		1997
Larissa industrial users		0.41		1996
Inofyta industrial users		0.32		1998
Platy industrial users		0.31		1998

Source: DEPA, PPC.

A variety of pipeline extension, storage, and LNG terminal projects have been studied or are under consideration.

■ A "Western Branch" extension of the high-pressure pipeline to Albania. The 164 km line would begin at Tikala Imathias (South-west of Thessaloniki) and would be sized to transport approximately 1 bcm annually. Potential project partners are Gazprom, Prometheus Gas,

Tenneco, El Paso and PPC. PPC use of gas along this pipeline extension would be pivotal to its financial viability, particularly since there are substantial uncertainties about the potential gas market in Albania. This project was included in the list of EU-funded Trans-European Network Projects.

- A subsea pipeline from Greece to Italy to import western European gas. The route would be from Igoumenitsa in Greece to Otranto in Italy. DEPA and Snam (Italy) agreed to conduct studies on the pipeline in December 1997. Their preliminary economic evaluation concluded that the project would be viable if it transported a minimum of 3.5 bcm/year. The project could be an extension of the Western Libya gas project, which will supply gas to southern Italy.

- Supply from Turkmenistan via a pipeline through Turkey. Shell and DEPA are cooperating on a feasibility study.

- A new LNG terminal. The interest in this would be greater if the subsea pipeline from Italy is not pursued.

- A liquefaction terminal at Kavala (in Thrace, northeastern Greece) to export gas as LNG. This was proposed by Prometheus Gas but is not under active consideration.

- The expansion of the terminal at Revithousa to increase storage and peak delivery capacity. DEPA is currently conducting a pre-feasibility study.

- New underground gas storage facilities. DEPA is currently evaluating underground storage options.

- Development of LNG supply to Crete for a power generation plant using up to 0.1 bcm annually. DEPA's initial feasibility study concluded this would be a viable project.

Gas Industry Structure and Regulation

The Greek State has assumed the role of developing the natural gas system through the Greek Public Gas Corporation (DEPA), a subsidiary of the state-owned Hellenic Petroleum (HP). DEPA was created as 1988 and given the responsibility of carrying out feasibility studies, project planning, and executing the natural gas pipeline project. DEPA was transferred to direct ownership of the state, when its parent company HP was partially privatised in 1998. HP retains a 15% share in DEPA.

DEPA has the right to study, construct, own, and realise revenues from the national gas transmission system. It has, during the initial operation of the system, the exclusive right to import and trade natural gas. Following the re-negotiation of the gas supply agreement with Russia (see below), Russia's Gazprom gained the right to sell to customers within Greece beyond DEPA's contractual gas quantities and to re-export any quantities of gas.

Gazprom is present in the Greek gas market through its 50-50 joint venture Prometheus Gas, which it co-owns with the Copelouzos Group (50%), a private Greek company. Prometheus Gas was established in 1991. Prometheus has special rights of access to the gas market due to the provisions of the Russian-Greek gas supply agreement. It also has the right to participate in several large turnkey construction contracts awarded by DEPA and the Public Power Corporation.

There are three gas distribution companies, one each in the Attiki (Athens) area, in Thessaloniki, and in Thessalia. These were formed as wholly owned subsidiaries of DEPA in 1995, after previous plans to form them jointly with municipalities did not advance. The government gave the responsibility to develop the distribution network to DEPA, a task it considered critical for the timely development of the gas market beyond large industrial consumers.

The 1995 Gas Law (2364/95) (as amended by laws 2436/96 and 2528/97) provides the basic legal framework for the development of the natural gas supply system. Its main articles govern:

- import, transmission, trading, and distribution of natural gas;

- privileges, formation, and ownership of gas distribution companies;

- incorporation of DEFA into the Attiki gas distribution company;

- miscellaneous tax and commercial provisions.

The Gas Law conveys to DEPA the exclusive right of developing and exploiting the natural gas transmission system in Greece. DEPA is entitled to sell gas directly to consumers using more than 100 GWh (gross calorific value) per year, or about 10 million m^3/year; to consumers using gas for vehicles; and to gas distribution companies. DEPA has the right of first refusal for the purchase of any gas produced domestically. Seven and one-half years after DEPA's first gas deliveries (which were in November 1996; i.e. in May 2004), the Ministry of Development can issue licences to other companies to develop and operate transmission lines if DEPA chooses not to develop those lines itself. Ten and one-half years after first gas deliveries (i.e. in May 2007), the Ministry can grant licenses to companies other than DEPA for gas imports and sales to either DEPA or wholesale consumers located in a non-DEPA service area. The conditions and procedures for obtaining either license must be defined by presidential decree.

Gas distribution companies have, within their own areas, the exclusive right to distribute and sell gas through the low- and medium-pressure gas distribution systems for a period of 25 to 35 years, based on a licence granted by the Ministry of Development. They may sell to customers consuming up to 100 GWh per year. Ten years after the start of operation of the national transmission network, the Ministry may also issue gas distribution licences to companies other than those formed by DEPA in areas not covered by a gas distribution company already established by DEPA. The terms of the licence granted to the distribution companies will include provisions regarding:

- standards of performance;

- restrictions on tariff setting;

- required development of the distribution networks;

- supply obligations to consumers.

Gas Supply and End-User Contracts

Greece has developed its natural gas system based on long-term gas supply agreements with the Soviet Union and Algeria in 1988. Annual gas volumes from Russia now represent 80% of nominal contractual quantities. Gazprom is responsible for supplying gas supplies and acquired certain other rights under an amendment to the interstate agreement between the Russia and Greece.

Gas Supply Contracts

Source	Russian	Algeria
Nominal annual quantity (bcm)	2.4 ± 0.6[a]	0.57
Minimum annual purchase (bcm)	80% of nominal	0.51
Year of first delivery	1997	1999[b]
End year	2016	2020[c]
Take-or-pay clause	yes	yes

Source: DEPA.
Notes: a. Russian contract quantities are expressed in billion cubic metres at 20°C and 1.013 bar. The quantity increases over time to reach a plateau level;
b. Projected;
c. Deliveries are not guaranteed after 2015.

Gas Pricing

The government has not yet developed pricing principles for gas transmission or supply. As a general principle, the Gas Law specifies that the rate of return on investment will be used to guide DEPA's mark-up. There will be no price regulation for bulk purchasers, who will negotiate prices directly with DEPA. Prices for industrial consumers are, in general, formulated in relation to the price of heavy fuel oil. Prices to domestic consumers will be allowed to vary for each gas supply company taking into account cost of supply factors such as load factor. Specific pricing requirements will be part of the tender package for potential investors in the gas supply companies. Natural gas is subject to the current VAT applicable on liquid fuels (18%), but is exempted from other taxes up to 31 December 2010.

DEPA's single largest contract is with the Public Power Corporation for a plateau consumption of 1.3 bcm/year. The price PPC pays for natural gas is established on the basis of the border price plus a transmission fee. The price calculation is updated quarterly.

ELECTRICITY

Electricity Supply

Greece has a relatively small electricity supply system among IEA countries. In 1997 the Greek system had a gross production of 43.3 TWh from a total installed capacity of 9,800 MWe. 1998 consumption was 40.3 TWh.

Lignite is the primary energy source for electricity production, accounting for roughly two-thirds of total generation. Thermal power plants (lignite- and oil-fired) have a total capacity of 6,822 MW. The total capacity of hydro-plants is 2,977 MW. Hydro-plants and oil-fired plants are primarily used for peak and intermediate load. Natural gas became available only in 1997. To make use of this new fuel, several gas-fired plants are being commissioned, in construction, or planned. Lignite-fired stations are located close to the Ptolemaida-Aminteo and Megalopolis lignite centres. PPC projects lignite-fired generation to decrease to 64% by the year 2000, due to the introduction of natural gas.

Greece's electricity supply system consists of an interconnected grid, which encompasses all mainland areas and a number of islands connected by underwater cables, as well as independent island systems. Crete and Rhodes have the largest isolated systems. The rate of growth in electricity demand has been moderate on the interconnected system, but the island systems have consistently shown growth rates of more than double that of the mainland. This difference is due to the rapid development of the tourism industry on the islands in comparison with the steadier economic growth of the mainland. On Rhodes over half of electricity sales are in the commercial sector, reflecting tourism's economic importance there. On Crete, PPC has struggled to meet peak summer loads because of the rapid growth and local opposition to new power plants on the island. The independent island systems depend almost exclusively on heavy fuel oil and diesel oil for power generation.

PPC and other Generators

The Public Power Corporation (PPC) is the state-owned monopoly utility responsible for generation, transmission, and distribution throughout Greece. It accounts for over 98% of total generation and capacity. PPC was created in 1950 and subsequently acquired the Athens generation company and many small private companies generating and supplying electricity throughout Greece. It is the largest corporation in Greece and wields substantial commercial and political influence.

The company has a special relationship with the state. Until 1991, it was a legal entity of private law, not subject to legislation governing public sector enterprises excepting some provisions that were defined in Decree 3785/57. In 1991, a presidential decree fully transformed PPC into a corporation under private law, while still maintaining the financial and operational responsibility of the state. The Government exercises control of PPC through power of appointment to the board of directors, top management, and a Representative Assembly of Social Control. The Ministry of National Economy approves the company's financing programmes and the Ministry of Development is responsible for co-ordinating PPC's development plans with state energy policy.

PPC's investments in generating capacity have increased rapidly in recent years. From 1992 to 1997 the company's investment in thermal, hydro, and other generating assets at an average real annual rate of 11%. PPC intends to proceed with major new power plant projects for the interconnected system, including a 570 MWe combined cycle plant in Lavrio, a 370-480 MWe combined-cycle plant in Komotini, a 330 MWe lignite-fired plant in Florina, a 100 MWe hydro plant at Platanovryssi, and a 161 MWe hydro plant at Messochora. The Komotini plant and hydro plants are under construction.

Greece and PPC have effectively leveraged European Union funds for improvements in generation and transmission facilities. The EU has committed ECU117 million for the Italy-Greece interconnection project and is supporting projects to strengthen Greece's transmission network and to connect nine islands to the mainland system.

Electricity Trade and Interconnections

Greece has no direct electricity connections with IEA member countries. It is an UCTE member, but is not connected to the Western European electrical network. It is connected to Albania and FYR of Macedonia, to Bulgaria and Romania. The table below lists the rated capacities and 1995 net imports of these direct electricity links. The links are used primarily for economic exchanges between Greece and neighbouring countries, maintaining hydroelectric reserve, and providing back-up supply in case of system failures. Net imports in 1995 represented only about 2% of electricity supply.

Development of a direct current sub-sea cable linking Oporto Badisco in Italy and Aetos in Greece began in 1990. Construction of some of the land-based facilities began in 1996, but

Electricity Interconnections

Interconnected system	Capacity Rating MVA	Energy Rating GWh	Net Import, 1998 GWh
Albania	1538	2140	−804
Bulgaria	1400	1200	1,035
FYR of Macedonia	1538	3000	−1,389
Total	4476	6340	−1,158
Italy (under development)	500	4000	

Source: 1995 Annual Report of the Hellenic Power System, PPC, UCTE.

work on the Italian side had been on hold for almost three years due to local opposition. The Italian Government decided to re-route the land-based portion in late 1997. The European Commission estimated that the link could displace production from low-sulphur oil-fired power plants in Italy by natural gas-fired combined-cycle plants operating in Greece during at least 3,000 hours per year.

Two new interconnection projects are under study. One is an upgrade of an existing line with FYR of Macedonia, and the second is a new interconnection with Bulgaria. Interconnections with Turkey have been discussed periodically, with no result to date.

Electricity Pricing

Greece has industrial electricity prices lower than most IEA member countries, whereas household electricity prices range close to the IEA average. In real terms, the price of electricity supplied both to industry and households has consistently fallen since 1987, except in 1990. Average household prices have decreased by over 30% since 1987. This is at least partly because the government has tended to restrain electricity price hikes as an element of macro-economic policy designed to control inflation.

Tariffs are differentiated according to voltage, peak power demand, time of day, and type of use (domestic, agricultural, industrial, and general) according to their long-run marginal cost of supply. The Ministry of National Economy and an Inter-ministerial Committee on Prices and Income control tariff setting, generally at the level of total revenue. PPC's tariff publication notes that pricing is "affected by national policies, for social and development reasons". For example, there are special reduced agricultural and industrial tariffs designed to encourage activity among some types of users.

In principle, tariffs in individual customer classes are the same throughout Greece, even in island systems, where supply costs are generally much higher due to the use of petroleum products for fuel supply and the small size of generating plants. Uniform tariffs imply substantial cross-subsidies from users of the interconnected system to users of isolated systems. This pricing policy has been maintained in order to encourage habitation and economic activity on the many Greek islands, where living costs are generally higher.

Electricity Reform

A series of laws and ministerial decisions since 1985 have aimed to encourage private investment in electricity supply and introduce combined heat and power and renewables. The first law defined exceptions to PPC's exclusive generation rights over limited instances. Plants were connected to the national grid only if they served to provide back-up for PPC supply failure, if they were based on renewables (various cases), or in case PPC were unable to provide the capacity. Otherwise, autonomous plants (not connected to the grid) were permitted if PPC chose not to extend the national network to a consumer's installation. In no case were sales to third parties permitted. The 1995 Law did not define contractual conditions between PPC and other generators. These conditions were established later by ministerial decree.

A 1990 amendment to the 1985 law provided an additional avenue for establishing non-PPC plants, with PPC's consent, without altering the provisions available to non-PPC producers established in the earlier law. Grid-connected power plants were generally possible as long as a mutually agreeable contract could be negotiated between PPC and an independent producer. This law paved the way for negotiations on what was to be Greece's first independent private power project, a gas-fired combined-cycle plant in Lavrio. Although a power purchase agreement was negotiated between PPC and the Belgian company Tractebel in 1993, the project did not come to fruition.

Law 2244/94 (1994) defined new provisions for non-PPC generators and to improve electricity purchase prices. Three types of generators are defined in the law: auto-producers, who normally consume all of their own production; independent producers; and co-generators. All generators must rely either on renewable energy sources or gas-fired co-generation, with various provisions relating to whether or not the plant is connected to the grid, type of renewable energy source, project ownership (municipality ownership or not), and geographic region. Reimbursement for electricity sold to PPC varies according to these provisions.

The general terms of agreement between co-generators and PPC were further defined in 1996 by Ministerial Decision 8907. This allows for a consortium to establish a co-generation station, with the use of the national grid to transport electricity to consortium members if they are located within 10 km of the station. Otherwise, as with previous regulations, any electricity not consumed by consortium members can be sold only to PPC. In the absence of a defined electricity transport tariff, 10% of the electricity transported is charged for use of the grid. The Decision established minimum efficiency standards for the station: total design point energy efficiency (electricity plus heat) of 65% on an annual basis, 60% on a monthly basis.

The EU Electricity Directive was agreed in December 1996 and will require most EU member countries to develop national legislation to comply with it by 19 February 1999. Due to the "specific technical characteristics of their electricity system", Greece was granted a two-year extension (till 2001) to develop national legislation.

A 1996 study examined the options for introducing competition into electricity supply. Following this study, a draft law was prepared and is under discussion. A draft law was submitted to Parliament for debate in late 1999. The key features of the current draft bill are as follows:

■ PPC will remain owner of its current generation, transmission, and distribution assets. It will own and develop all new transmission and distribution facilities. The accounts for each segment will be unbundled;

■ PPC will remain under the control of the state;

■ An independent system operator will be responsible for plant dispatching;

■ A form of competitive market for generation will be established. The system operator will determine the operation of generating plants on the basis of daily bids for hourly periods;

■ All captive customers (non-eligible for third-party purchases) will be supplied by PPC. Other customers may conclude contracts directly with independent producers;

■ A regulatory authority will be established to oversee the application of all relevant rules, ensure competition in generation, monitor pricing, and issue licenses and authorisations.

PPC has begun planning for the opening of the electricity market to competition. It intends to implement a major reorganisation leading to the creation of four business units handling generation, transmission, distribution, and lignite mining.

Lignite Supply and Use

Lignite provides roughly 80% of Greece's indigenous energy production and 70% of electricity supply. It is Greece's only proven long-term energy source, as domestic oil and gas production has been declining for some years. Over the last two decades lignite consumption has grown at an average annual rate of over 6%, although growth slowed down to just over 1% annually in the 1990's. The use of lignite was vigorously developed after the 1970's oil shocks in order to reduce PPC's fuel bill for then-baseload oil-fired power stations. In this regard, lignite can be seen as the main factor of Greek energy diversification away from oil use. All but 1% of lignite consumption is for power production.

The Greek State has exclusive rights to develop and exploit lignite deposits. Except for a few private lignite mining operations, the State has assigned its rights at no charge to PPC. PPC has priority in the development and exploitation of all coal fields, even if another party has expressed interest before PPC. The Institute of Geological and Mineral Exploration has been assigned the right to explore for lignite and other mineral deposits in Greece.

The quality of lignite is poor. Currently exploited lignite has a 55-60% water content and 15-18% ash content. All power plants using lignite are located adjacent to the mines. The level of sulphur is relatively low (0.5%) in the largest deposits of western Macedonia. In

Production and Reserves of Major Lignite Fields

Mining Area	Location	1997 Production (mt)	Estimated economic reserves (mt)
Ptolemais	Western Macedonia	38.1	1600
Amyndeon	Western Macedonia	6.8	300
Megalopolis	Peloponesus	11.5	300
Florina	Western Macedonia	n.a.	250
Drama	Eastern Macedonia	n.a.	900
Elassona	Western Macedonia	n.a.	150
Komnina	Western Macedonia	n.a.	100
Privately owned mines (est.)		2	200
Total		58.4	3800

Source: PPC, IEA Coal Information 1996.
Note: Fields at Florina, Drama, Elassona, and Komnina have not been commercially developed.

addition, the ash in these lignite deposits contains lime, a natural sulphur sorbent that fixes a portion of the sulphur in the solid ash during combustion. According to PPC, this keeps sulphur emissions from power plants located next to the Ptolemaida-Amyndeon mining centres below the current EU limit for sulphur emissions from new power plants (400 mg/Nm^3). The lignite mined at the Megalopolis centre has over 3% sulphur and no natural lime content. PPC operates pollution monitoring stations in lignite-mining regions at Kozani, Florina and Megalopolis.

X. MAPS

Map 1: **Black Sea Oil Transport Infrastructure**

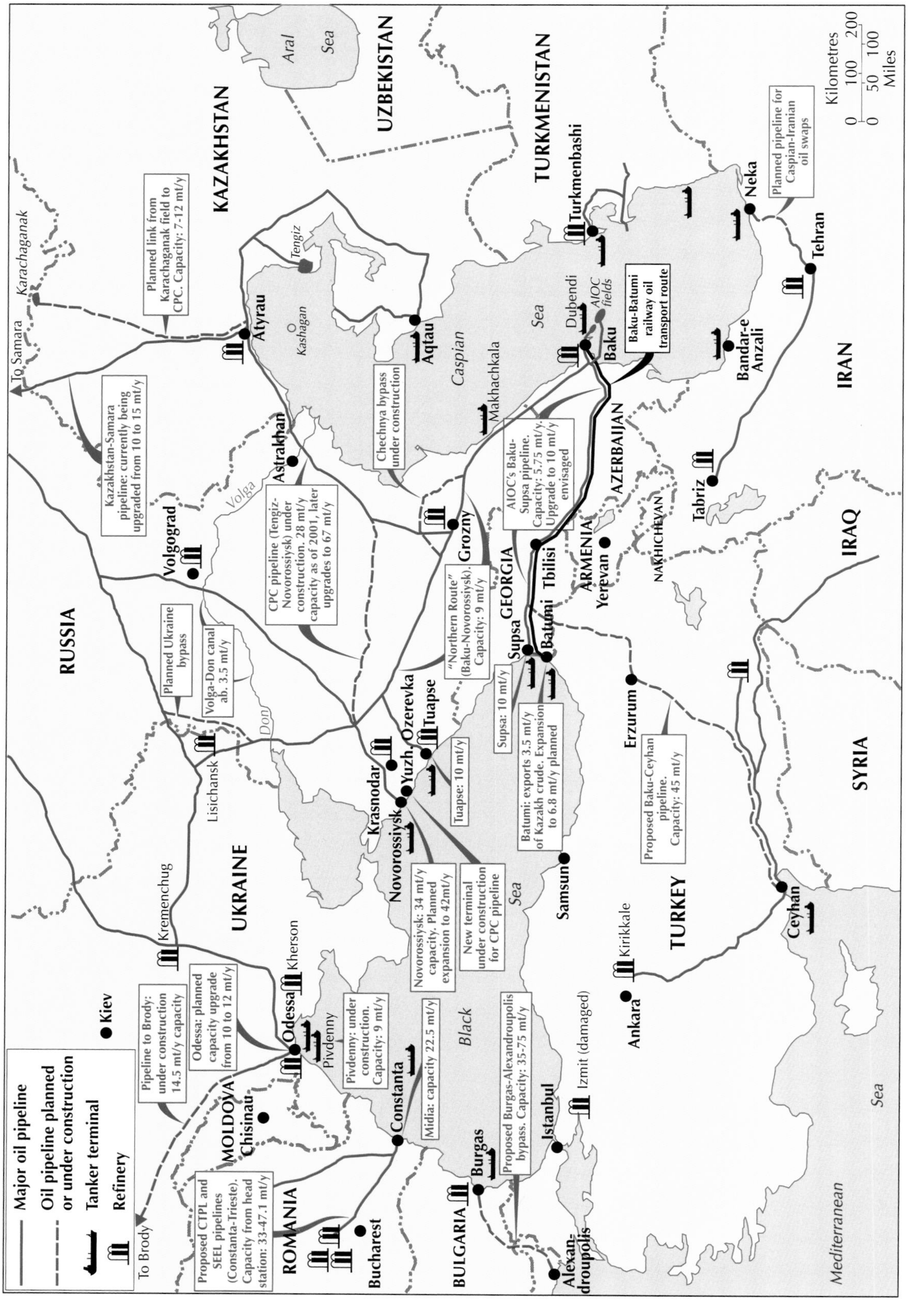

Legend:
— Major oil pipeline
– – Oil pipeline planned or under construction
Tanker terminal
Refinery

Kiev

KAZAKHSTAN

UZBEKISTAN

TURKMENISTAN

RUSSIA

UKRAINE

MOLDOVA

ROMANIA

BULGARIA

TURKEY

SYRIA

IRAQ

IRAN

ARMENIA

AZERBAIJAN

GEORGIA

NAKHICHEVAN

Aral Sea

Caspian Sea

Black Sea

Mediterranean Sea

Planned pipeline for Caspian-Iranian oil swaps

Planned link from Karachaganak field to CPC. Capacity: 7-12 mt/y

Kazakhstan-Samara pipeline; currently being upgraded from 10 to 15 mt/y

Chechnya bypass under construction

Baku-Batumi railway oil transport route

AIOC's Baku-Supsa pipeline. Capacity: 5.75 mt/y; Upgrade to 10 mt/y envisaged

CPC pipeline (Tengiz-Novorossiysk) under construction. 28 mt/y capacity as of 2001, later upgrades to 67 mt/y

Planned Ukraine bypass

Volga-Don canal ab. 3.5 mt/y

"Northern Route" (Baku-Novorossiysk). Capacity: 9 mt/y

Supsa: 10 mt/y

Tuapse: 10 mt/y

Batumi: exports 3.5 mt/y of Kazakh crude. Expansion to 6.8 mt/y planned

Proposed Baku-Ceyhan pipeline. Capacity: 45 mt/y

Novorossiysk: 34 mt/y capacity. Planned expansion to 42mt/y

New terminal under construction for CPC pipeline

Pipeline to Brody: under construction 14.5 mt/y capacity

Odessa: planned capacity upgrade from 10 to 12 mt/y

Pivdenny: under construction. Capacity: 9 mt/y

Midia: capacity 22.5 mt/y

Proposed Burgas-Alexandroupolis bypass. Capacity: 35-75 mt/y

Proposed CTPL and SEEL pipelines (Constanta-Trieste). Capacity from head station: 33-47.1 mt/y

To Samara

Karachaganak

Tengiz

Kashagan

Atyrau

Aqtau

Makhachkala

Grozny

Astrakhan

Volgograd

Volga

Don

Kremenchug

Lisichansk

Kherson

Odessa

Pivdenny

Constanta

Midia

Burgas

Alexandroupolis

Istanbul

Izmit (damaged)

Ankara

Kirikkale

Samsun

Erzurum

Ceyhan

Tbilisi

Batumi

Supsa

Yerevan

Baku

Dubendi

AIOC fields

Turkmenbashi

Neka

Tehran

Bandar-e Anzali

Tabriz

Krasnodar

Novorossiysk

Yuzh. Ozerevka

Tuapse

Chisinau

Bucharest

Kiev

To Brody

Kilometres
0 100 200
Miles
0 50 100

Map 2: **Black Sea Oil Trade Flows**

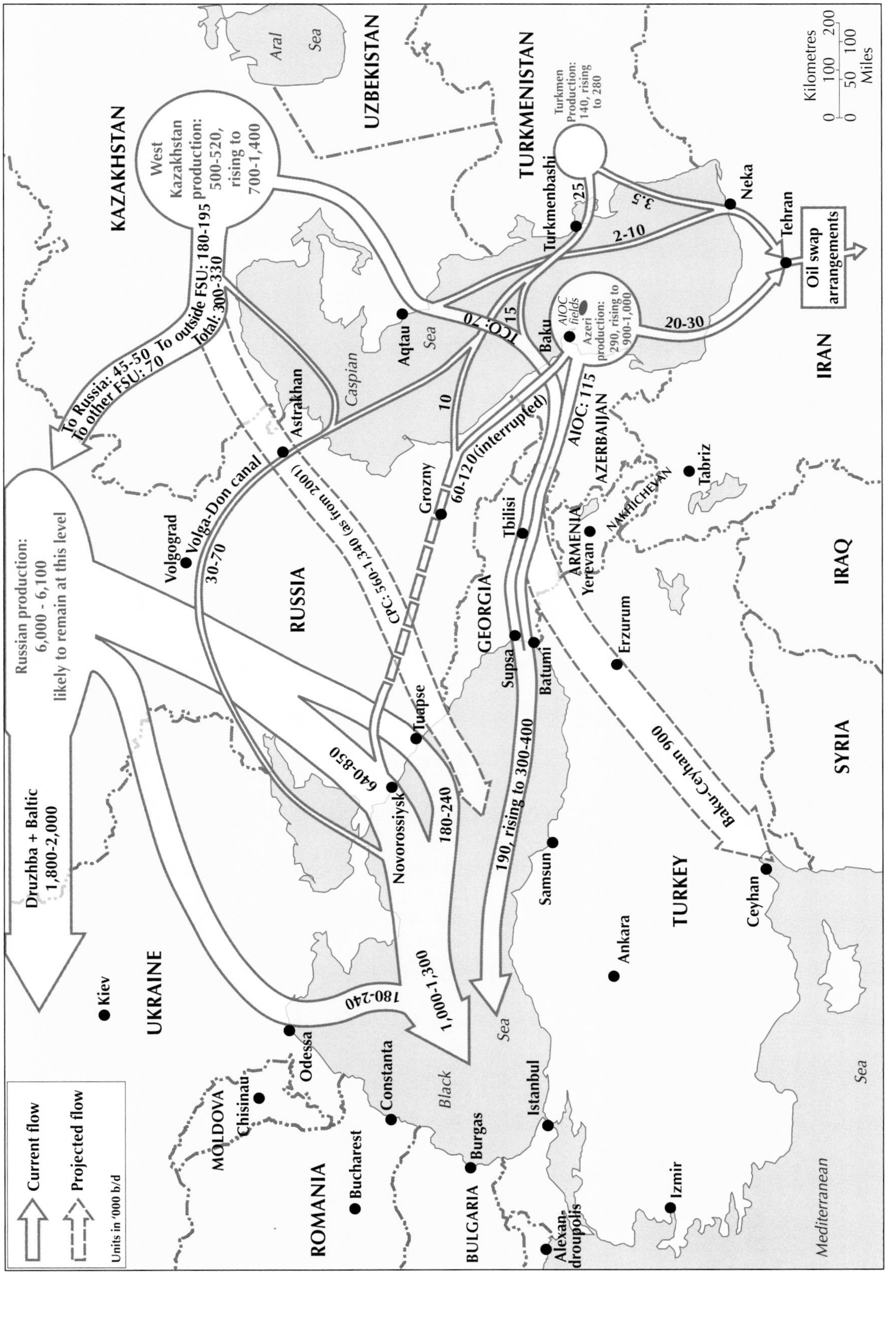

Legend:
- Current flow
- Projected flow

Units in '000 b/d

Russian production: 6,000 - 6,100 likely to remain at this level

Druzhba + Baltic 1,800-2,000

West Kazakhstan production: 500-520, rising to 700-1,400

To Russia: 45-50
To other FSU: 70
To outside FSU: 180-195
Total: 300-330

Turkmen Production: 140, rising to 280

Azeri production: 290, rising to 900-1,000

AIOC fields

AIOC: 115

Oil swap arrangements

30-70

Volga-Don canal

CPC: 560-1,340 (as from 2001)

640-850

180-240

1,000-1,300

180-240

190, rising to 300-400

Baku-Ceyhan 900

60-120 (interrupted)

10

TCO: 70

15

25

2-10

3.5

20-30

KAZAKHSTAN
UZBEKISTAN
TURKMENISTAN
IRAN
RUSSIA
AZERBAIJAN
ARMENIA
NAKHICHEVAN
GEORGIA
TURKEY
SYRIA
IRAQ
UKRAINE
MOLDOVA
ROMANIA
BULGARIA

Aral Sea
Caspian Sea
Black Sea
Mediterranean Sea

Neka
Tehran
Turkmenbashi
Baku
Aqtau
Astrakhan
Volgograd
Grozny
Tbilisi
Tabriz
Yerevan
Erzurum
Supsa
Batumi
Tuapse
Novorossiysk
Samsun
Ankara
Ceyhan
Izmir
Istanbul
Burgas
Alexan-droupolis
Constanta
Odessa
Chisinau
Bucharest
Kiev

Kilometres
0 100 200
Miles
0 50 100

Map 3: **Black Sea Gas Transport Infrastructure**

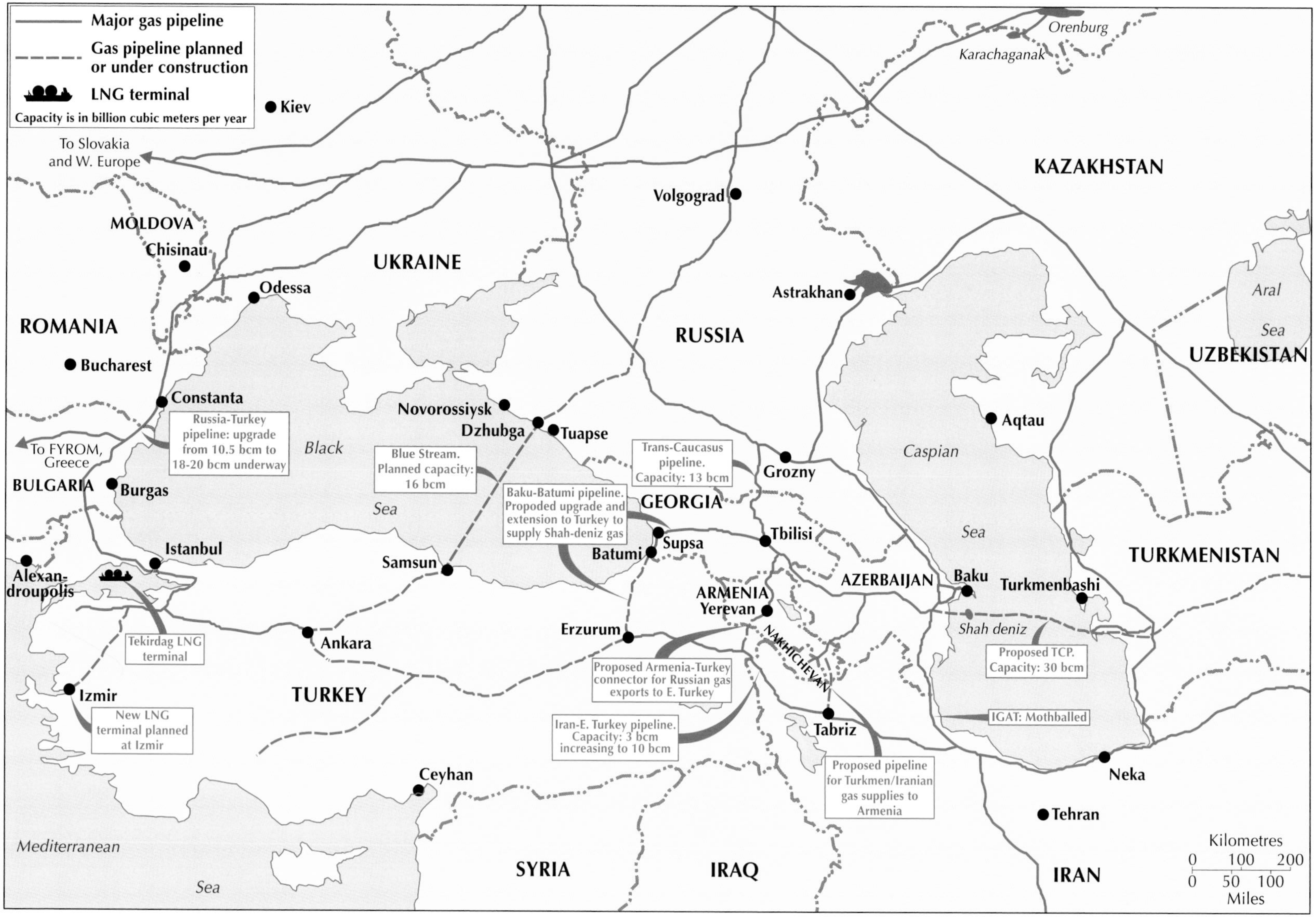

Legend:

— Major gas pipeline

--- Gas pipeline planned or under construction

● LNG terminal

Capacity is in billion cubic meters per year

● Kiev

To Slovakia and W. Europe

Labels and annotations on map:

Aral Sea

UZBEKISTAN

TURKMENISTAN

Orenburg

KAZAKHSTAN

Karachaganak

Aqtau

Caspian Sea

Baku

Turkmenbashi

Shah deniz

Neka

Tehran

IRAN

Proposed TCP. Capacity: 30 bcm

IGAT: Mothballed

Proposed pipeline for Turkmen/Iranian gas supplies to Armenia

Astrakhan

Volgograd

RUSSIA

Grozny

Tbilisi

AZERBAIJAN

Tabriz

NAKHICHEVAN

ARMENIA

Yerevan

GEORGIA

Supsa

Batumi

Trans-Caucasus pipeline. Capacity: 13 bcm

Baku-Batumi pipeline. Proposed upgrade and extension to Turkey to supply Shah-deniz gas

Proposed Armenia-Turkey connector for Russian gas exports to E. Turkey

Erzurum

Iran-E. Turkey pipeline. Capacity: 3 bcm increasing to 10 bcm

IRAQ

SYRIA

Tuapse

Dzhubga

Novorossiysk

Samsun

Blue Stream. Planned capacity: 16 bcm

Black Sea

Ankara

TURKEY

Ceyhan

UKRAINE

Odessa

Constanta

Russia-Turkey pipeline: upgrade from 10.5 bcm to 18-20 bcm underway

Burgas

Istanbul

Tekirdag LNG terminal

Izmir

New LNG terminal planned at Izmir

MOLDOVA

Chisinau

ROMANIA

Bucharest

BULGARIA

To FYROM, Greece

Alexandroupolis

Mediterranean Sea

Scale:

Kilometres
0 100 200

0 50 100
Miles

Map 6: **Trans-Caucasus Power System**

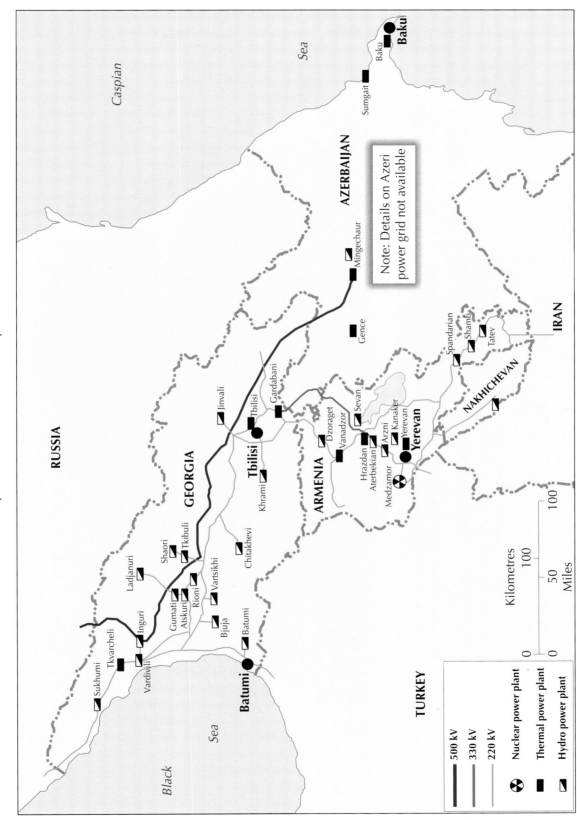

Map 7: **Bulgaria, Romania - Oil and Gas Infrastructure**

Map 8: **Bulgaria, Romania - Power System**

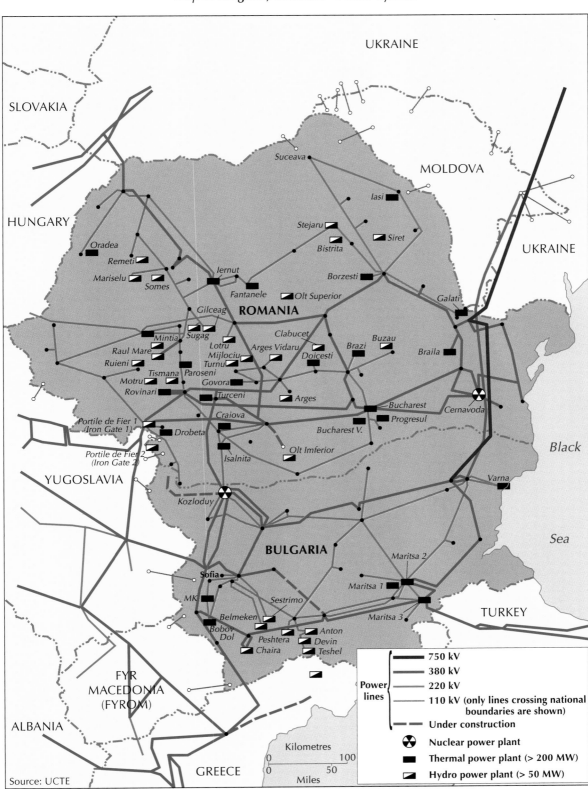

XI. GLOSSARY

bbl	Barrel
bcm	Billion cubic meters
b/d	Barrel per day
CHP	Combined heat and power plant
EBRD	European Bank for Reconstruction and Development
FDI	Foreign direct investment
GDP	Gross domestic product
GW/GWh	Gigawatt/Gigawatt-hour
HFO	Heavy fuel oil
HPP	Hydro-power plant
HV	High voltage
IMF	International Monetary Fund
IPP	Independent power project
LNG	Liquefied natural gas
LPG	Liquefied petroleum gas
mb/d	Million barrels per day
MIT	Ministry of Industry and Trade
MOFE	Ministry of Fuel and Energy
mt	Million tons
mtoe	Million tons of oil equivalent
MW	Megawatt
NPP	Nuclear power plant
PPP	Purchasing power parity
PSA	Production-sharing agreement
SHPP	Small hydro-power plant
TJ	Terajoule
TPES	Total primary energy supply
TPP	Thermal power plant
TWh	Terawatt-hour
UCTE	Union for the Coordination of Transmission of Electricity

XII. STATISTICAL TABLES

AZERBAIJAN

Units: ktoe (unless indicated otherwise)	1991	1992	1993	1994	1995	1996	1997	1998E
Supply								
Hard coal, net imports	67	12	2	0	3	3	3	na
Hard coal, total supply	67	12	3	4	3	3	3	na
Crude + NGL + Feedstocks, indigenous production	11801	11620	10671	9610	9207	9145	9066	na
Crude + NGL + Feedstocks, net imports	78	−1955	−816	857	62	0	−40	na
Crude + NGL + Feedstocks, total supply	11879	9666	9855	10467	9269	9145	9026	na
Crude oil, indigenous production	11801	10749	10346	9355	8991	8934	9045	11558
Crude oil, net imports	78	−1955	−816	857	62	0	−201	−2010
Crude oil, total supply	11879	8795	9530	10212	9053	8934	9246	9548
Natural gas, indigenous production	7023	6378	5513	5168	5383	5108	4829	4528
Natural gas, net imports	6622	3495	2037	2115	430	19	0	na
Natural gas, total supply	13645	9873	7550	7283	5813	5128	4829	na
Natural gas, indigenous production (million m³)	8668	7872	6805	6379	6644	6305	5960	5590
Natural gas, net imports (million m³)	8174	4314	2514	2611	531	24	0	na
Natural gas, total supply (million m³)	16842	12186	9319	8990	7175	6329	5960	na
Electricity, net imports	−146	−44	9	22	34	38	69	17
Electricity, indigenous production (GWh)	23356	19673	19100	17571	17044	17088	16800	17900
Electricity, net imports (GWh)	−1703	−513	100	260	399	442	800	200
Electricity, total supply (GWh)	21653	19160	19200	17831	17443	17530	17600	18100
Electricity produced from hydro-power	151	150	206	157	134	132	131	129
Electricity produced from hydro-power (GWh)	1758	1747	2400	1829	1556	1538	1520	1500
Electricity produced from gas (GWh)	21598	17926	16600	3143	3084	3100	3045	na
Electricity produced from liquid fuels (GWh)	0	0	100	12599	12404	12450	12235	na
TPES	23300	16750	15454	16196	12999	12240	11987	na
Total net energy imports	4326	−1400	−939	1256	−1726	−2146	−2041	na
Consumption								
Industry sector	683	384	4525	5227	4204	2808	2779	na
Transport sector	1399	1644	1805	1914	1646	1437	1089	na
Other sectors	10969	9058	3606	3647	3043	3287	3182	na
Non-Energy use	0	1206	155	208	46	69	69	na
TFC	13051	12291	10091	10996	8939	7601	7118	na
Indicators								
Self-sufficiency (Indigenous energy production/TPES)	0.81	1.08	1.06	0.92	1.13	1.18	1.17	na
TPES/GDP (toe/'000 $90 PPP)	1.13	1.25	1.50	1.86	1.72	1.60	1.52	na
TPES/Population (toe/capita)	3.22	2.28	2.09	2.17	1.73	1.62	1.58	na
Electricity consumption/population (kWh/capita)	2585	2233	2081	1924	1795	1819	1816	na

na: not available; E: estimation.

ARMENIA

Units: ktoe (unless indicated otherwise)	1991	1992	1993	1994	1995	1996	1997	1998E
Supply								
Hard coal, net imports	131	63	1	16	1	2	2	2
Hard coal, total supply	131	63	1	16	1	2	2	2
Crude + NGL + Feedstocks, net imports	4388	2430	1221	393	280	155	155	na
Natural gas, net imports	3593	1519	658	706	1143	891	1110	1088
Natural gas, total supply	3593	1519	658	706	1143	891	1110	1088
Natural gas, net imports (million m³)	4435	1875	812	872	1411	1100	1370	na
Natural gas, total supply (million m³)	4435	1875	812	872	1411	1100	1370	na
Electricity, net imports	135	24	10	1	1	0	0	0
Electricity, indigenous production (GWh)	9516	9004	6295	5658	5561	6214	6021	6200
Electricity, net imports (GWh)	1572	283	114	16	13	0	0	0
Electricity, total supply (GWh)	11088	9287	6409	5674	5574	6214	6021	6200
Nuclear, indigenous production	0	0	0	0	79	606	598	598
Electricity produced in nuclear plants (GWh)	0	0	0	0	304	2324	2300	2300
Electricity produced from hydro-power	133	262	369	302	165	135	138	138
Electricity produced from hydro-power (GWh)	1546	3044	4293	3514	1919	1572	1600	1600
Electricity produced from gas (GWh)	2670	2060	1456	1508	2913	2191	2905	na
Electricity produced from liquid fuels (GWh)	5300	3900	546	636	425	127	127	na
TPES	8381	4298	2260	1420	1671	1790	1804	na
Total net energy imports	8248	4036	1890	1117	1425	1048	1267	na
Consumption								
Industry sector	1759	801	490	237	354	207	206	na
Transport sector	1279	829	503	122	91	57	55	na
Other sectors	2745	1485	634	636	743	392	487	na
Non-Energy use	312	45	45	35	25	14	14	na
TFC	6094	3160	1672	1030	1213	669	762	na
Indicators								
Self-sufficiency (Indigenous energy production/TPES)	0.02	0.06	0.16	0.21	0.15	0.41	0.30	na
TPES/GDP (toe/'000 $90 PPP)	1.25	1.35	0.83	0.49	0.54	0.55	0.54	na
TPES/Population (toe/capita)	2.32	1.17	0.61	0.38	0.44	0.47	0.48	na
Electricity consumption/population (kWh/capita)	2610	1835	1077	916	899	1024	1260	na

na: not available; E: estimation.

GEORGIA

Units: ktoe (unless indicated otherwise)	1991	1992	1993	1994	1995	1996	1997	1998E
Supply								
Hard coal, indigenous production	310	89	36	20	19	10	2	na
Hard coal, net imports	93	91	91	48	12	22	0	na
Hard coal, total supply	403	180	128	67	32	32	2	na
Crude + NGL + Feedstocks, indigenous production	182	101	101	74	47	129	135	na
Crude + NGL + Feedstocks, net imports	1720	675	208	201	0	−114	−105	na
Crude + NGL + Feedstocks, total supply	1920	776	309	275	47	15	30	na
Crude oil, indigenous production	182	101	101	74	47	129	135	101
Crude oil, net imports	1720	675	208	201	0	−114	−105	na
Crude oil, total supply	1920	776	309	275	47	15	30	na
Natural gas, indigenous production	40	31	41	8	8	2	2	2
Natural gas, net imports	4366	3927	2972	1990	729	631	765	871
Natural gas, total supply	4407	3957	3012	1998	737	634	767	873
Natural gas, indigenous production (million m³)	50	38	50	10	10	3	3	3
Natural gas, net imports (million m³)	5389	4847	3668	2456	900	779	944	1075
Natural gas, total supply (million m³)	5439	4885	3718	2466	910	782	947	1078
Electricity, net imports	194	87	61	69	58	7	16	0
Electricity, indigenous production (GWh)	13376	11520	10150	6803	6900	7226	7172	8100
Electricity, net imports (GWh)	2252	1016	711	800	670	86	191	−600
Electricity, total supply (GWh)	15628	12536	10861	7603	7570	7312	7363	7500
Electricity produced from hydro-power	606	560	605	405	457	520	520	516
Electricity produced from hydro-power (GWh)	7041	6515	7034	4713	5310	6041	6044	6000
Electricity produced from gas (GWh)	3000	4577	2835	1900	1500	1105	1119	na
Electricity produced from liquid fuels (GWh)	3335	428	281	190	90	80	9	na
TPES	10212	6241	4626	2958	1469	2112	2295	na
Total net energy imports	8950	5398	3788	2407	903	1466	1664	na
Consumption								
Industry sector	602	468	1964	870	644	386	487	na
Transport sector	1336	482	313	111	86	558	526	na
Other sectors	7488	4867	2072	1568	886	1265	1351	na
TFC	9426	5817	4349	2549	1616	2209	2364	na
Indicators								
Self-sufficiency (Indigenous energy production/TPES)	0.11	0.13	0.18	0.18	0.39	0.33	0.30	na
TPES/GDP (toe/'000 $90 PPP)	0.60	0.61	0.75	0.54	0.26	0.34	0.33	na
TPES/Population (toe/capita)	1.87	1.14	0.85	0.55	0.27	0.39	0.42	na
Electricity consumption/population (kWh/capita)	2293	1785	1532	1088	1084	1151	1142	na

na: not available; E: estimation.

BULGARIA

Units: ktoe (unless indicated otherwise)	1991	1992	1993	1994	1995	1996	1997	1998E
Supply								
Hard coal, indigenous production	72	140	149	98	110	78	58	92
Hard coal, net imports	2800	2272	2619	2078	2135	2296	2296	3463
Hard coal, total supply	2797	2419	3033	2370	2123	2168	2516	3555
Brown coal, indigenous production	4628	4916	4701	4671	5006	5092	4838	4838
Crude + NGL + Feedstocks, indigenous production	59	54	44	37	44	32	28	30
Crude + NGL + Feedstocks, net imports	4492	2246	5824	7041	8085	7094	5970	5678
Crude + NGL + Feedstocks, total supply	4568	2453	5776	7057	8105	7051	6049	5744
Crude oil, indigenous production	59	54	44	37	44	32	28	30
Crude oil, net imports	4492	2246	5824	7041	8085	7094	5970	5678
Crude oil, total supply	4568	2453	5776	7057	8105	7051	6049	5744
Natural gas, indigenous production	8	30	55	45	40	33	28	21
Natural gas, net imports	4496	4060	3776	3737	4561	4729	3851	2855
Natural gas, total supply	4616	4066	3801	3819	4583	4676	3699	2876
Natural gas, indigenous production (million m³)	10	38	69	57	50	42	35	26
Natural gas, net imports (million m³)	5658	5109	4757	4712	5748	5959	4856	3600
Natural gas, total supply (million m³)	5808	5116	4790	4815	5775	5893	4664	3626
Electricity, net imports	183	233	9	–6	–14	–39	–305	–17
Electricity, indigenous production (GWh)	38917	35610	37997	38133	41789	42716	42803	41698
Electricity, net imports (GWh)	2124	2705	110	–72	–160	–449	–3550	–200
Electricity, total supply (GWh)	41041	38315	38107	38061	41629	42267	39253	41498
Electricity produced in nuclear plant	3436	3011	3641	4000	4504	4718	4633	1505
Electricity produced in nuclear plant (GWh)	13184	11552	13973	15335	17261	18082	17751	17500
Electricity produced from hydro-power	210	177	96	70	107	144	146	na
Electricity produced from hydro-power (GWh)	2441	2063	1942	1468	2314	2919	2936	na
Electricity produced from coal (GWh)	19055	18016	17398	17148	17561	17397	18408	na
Electricity produced from natural gas (GWh)	2885	2766	3040	2556	3210	2983	2439	na
Electricity produced from liquid fuels (GWh)	1352	1213	1644	1626	1443	1335	1269	na
TPES	22144	20517	21867	21025	22904	22598	20616	na
Total net energy imports	13643	11903	13169	11847	13301	12949	10944	na
Consumption								
Industry sector	7030	6318	5984	6187	6914	7067	6498	na
Transport sector	1539	1550	1767	1629	1691	1574	1146	na
Other sectors	3992	3645	3925	3724	3564	3863	3382	na
Non-Energy use	210	73	98	74	62	11	9	na
TFC	12772	11585	11774	11614	12231	12514	11035	na
Indicators								
Self-sufficiency (Indigenous energy production/TPES)	0.39	0.41	0.40	0.43	0.44	0.46	0.48	na
TPES/GDP (toe/'000 $90 PPP)	0.44	0.44	0.48	0.45	0.48	0.52	0.51	na
TPES/Population (toe/capita)	2.57	2.40	2.58	2.49	2.73	2.70	2.48	na
Electricity consumption/population (kWh/capita)	4136	3907	3934	3950	4310	4391	3999	na

na: not available; E: estimation.

ROMANIA

Units: ktoe (unless specifically indicated in other units)	1991	1992	1993	1994	1995	1996	1997	1998E
Supply								
Hard coal, indigenous production	1496	1598	477	532	448	516	683	780
Hard coal, net imports	1783	3472	1600	2421	2823	2403	3149	2111
Hard coal, total supply	3382	4709	2198	2858	3285	3031	3697	2891
Brown coal, indigenous production	4944	5929	6665	6778	6915	7014	5546	4174
Brown coal, net imports	377	224	94	34	5	126	0	0
Brown coal, total supply	5422	6079	6853	6875	6887	6902	5450	4174
Crude + NGL + Feedstocks, indigenous production	6593	6651	6752	6796	6773	6676	6579	na
Crude + NGL + Feedstocks, net imports	8153	6380	7360	7885	8404	6947	6063	5669
Crude + NGL + Feedstocks, total supply	14784	12823	14067	14820	15283	13547	12655	na
Crude oil, indigenous production	6593	6422	6517	6540	6521	6433	6327	6103
Crude oil, net imports	8153	6380	7360	7885	8404	6947	6063	5669
Crude oil, total supply	14784	12593	13832	14562	15033	13303	12408	11790
Natural gas, indigenous production	20052	17607	16755	14819	14442	13760	11905	11070
Natural gas, net imports	3739	3582	3615	3734	4793	5653	4029	3219
Natural gas, total supply	23791	21189	20370	18554	19235	19413	15934	14289
Natural gas, indigenous production (million m³)	24807	21782	20737	18511	18043	17249	14965	13855
Natural gas, net imports (million m³)	4626	4452	4493	4641	5958	7026	5007	4028
Natural gas, total supply (million m³)	29433	26234	25230	23152	24001	24275	19972	17883
Electricity, net imports	606	361	161	62	26	69	–7	63
Electricity, indigenous production (GWh)	56803	54195	55476	55136	59266	61350	56885	52485
Electricity, net imports (GWh)	7047	4203	1873	725	299	807	–83	732
Electricity, total supply (GWh)	63850	58398	57349	55861	59565	62157	56802	53217
Electricity produced by nuclear plant	0	0	0	0	0	361	1407	456
Electricity produced by nuclear plant (GWh)	0	0	0	0	0	1386	5400	5300
Electricity produced by hydro-power	1224	1006	1098	1122	1436	1355	1506	na
Electricity produced by hydro-power (GWh)	14234	11700	12768	13046	16693	15755	17509	na
Electricity produced from coal (GWh)	15613	18522	19208	19738	20800	20793	17281	na
Electricity produced from gas (GWh)	20468	19470	17997	16566	15971	16713	10084	na
Electricity produced from liquid fuels (GWh)	6134	4446	5434	5786	5799	6703	6863	na
TPES	50341	46367	45121	42292	45669	49114	44109	na
Total net energy imports	14303	13481	11954	10634	13986	14399	14186	na
Consumption								
Industry sector	19821	15231	13625	13906	14624	14747	13071	na
Transport sector	3776	3725	3240	3343	3324	4229	4272	na
Other sectors	10458	10421	8943	8297	8540	13071	11678	na
Non-Energy use	1270	873	497	523	620	682	713	na
TFC	35326	30250	26305	26069	27107	32729	29735	na
Indicators								
Self-sufficiency (Indigenous energy production/TPES)	0.70	0.73	0.73	0.74	0.70	0.70	0.70	na
TPES/GDP (toe/'000 $90 PPP)	0.72	0.73	0.70	0.63	0.64	0.66	0.63	na
TPES/Population (toe/capita)	2.17	2.03	1.98	1.86	2.01	2.17	1.96	na
Electricity consumption/population (kWh/capita)	2501	2320	2273	2235	2329	2432	2227	na

na: not available; E: estimation.

TURKEY

Units: ktoe (unless specified otherwise)	1991	1992	1993	1994	1995	1996	1997
Supply							
Hard coal, indigenous production	1827	1727	1722	1635	1319	1382	1347
Hard coal, net imports	4663	4130	4045	3950	4346	5889	7016
Hard coal, total supply	6272	6254	5827	5498	5889	7358	8450
Brown coal, indigenous production	9997	10389	9960	10472	10765	10889	11771
Brown coal, net imports	56	4	0	2	3	0	37
Brown coal, total supply	11415	10935	10059	10385	10679	11131	12291
Crude + NGL + Feedstock, indigenous production	4460	4370	3978	3777	3593	3577	3525
Crude + NGL + Feedstock, net imports	18020	19741	22459	22302	25237	24757	23849
Crude + NGL + Feedstock, total supply	23072	23755	26134	25451	27789	26978	27534
Crude oil, indigenous production	4460	4370	3978	3777	3593	3577	3525
Crude oil, net imports	18020	19741	22459	22302	25237	24757	23849
Crude oil, total supply	23096	23701	26077	25438	27801	27020	27554
Natural gas, indigenous production	167	163	165	164	150	170	208
Natural gas, net imports	3321	3652	4077	4371	5664	6840	8172
Natural gas, total supply	3487	3814	4239	4519	5785	6984	8339
Natural gas, indigenous production (million m³)	203	198	200	199	182	206	253
Natural gas, net imports (million m³)	4035	4437	4954	5313	6881	8039	9584
Natural gas, total supply (million m³)	4237	4634	5150	5493	7029	8214	9800
Electricity, net imports	22	−11	−32	−46	−60	−6	191
Electricity, indigenous production (GWh)	60246	67342	73808	78321	86247	94862	103296
Electricity, net imports (GWh)	253	−125	−376	−539	−696	−73	2221
Electricity, total supply (GWh)	60499	67217	73432	77782	85551	94789	105517
Electricity produced from hydro-power	1951	2285	2920	2630	3057	3481	3424
Electricity produced from hydro-power (GWh)	22683	26568	33951	30586	35541	40475	39816
Electricity production from hard coal (GWh)	998	1750	1738	1926	1596	1877	2323
Electricity produced from gas (GWh)	12589	10813	10788	13822	16579	17174	22086
Electricity produced liquid fuels (GWh)	3294	5273	5174	5548	5772	6540	7157
TPES	53496	54978	58103	56783	62203	67653	71273
Total net energy imports	25853	28068	32536	32028	37343	41535	43341
Consumption							
Industry sector	13255	13651	13762	12763	14456	16851	18094
Transport sector	9204	9447	11245	10887	12197	12891	12209
Other sectors	17261	18028	18480	17892	19490	20126	21155
Non-Energy use	1263	1254	1836	1311	1599	1897	2158
TFC	40983	42379	45323	42853	47743	51765	53616
Indicators							
Self-sufficiency (Indigenous energy production/TPES)	0.48	0.48	0.45	0.46	0.42	0.40	0.39
TPES/GDP (toe/'000 $90 PPP)	0.16	0.15	0.15	0.16	0.16	0.16	0.16
TPES/Population (toe/capita)	0.93	0.94	0.98	0.94	1.01	1.08	1.12
Electricity consumption/population (kWh/capita)	924	997	1062	1089	1164	1259	1364

GREECE

Units: ktoe (unless indicated otherwise)	1991	1992	1993	1994	1995	1996	1997
Supply							
Hard coal, net imports	914	1386	869	975	916	1045	749
Hard coal, total supply	998	1246	944	934	962	945	749
Brown coal, indigenous production	6903	6997	7165	7407	7508	7192	7709
Brown coal, net imports	0	–2	0	0	0	0	–3
Brown coal, total supply	6753	6927	7212	7575	7416	6996	7687
Crude + NGL + Feedstocks, indigenous production	856	703	575	544	468	527	476
Crude + NGL + Feedstocks, net imports	13692	16083	13789	14640	17200	18653	18705
Crude + NGL + Feedstocks, total supply	14893	15956	13867	16206	17327	19451	19082
Crude oil, indigenous production	806	667	548	511	444	493	445
Crude oil, net imports	11929	13780	11286	12751	15006	17632	18126
Crude oil, total supply	13082	13705	11425	14302	15174	18307	18556
Natural gas, indigenous production	136	126	93	48	44	46	45
Natural gas, net imports	0	0	0	0	0	8	129
Natural gas, total supply	136	126	93	48	44	49	171
Natural gas, indigenous production (million m³)	116	109	81	38	36	38	38
Natural gas, net imports (million m³)	0	0	0	0	0	9	160
Natural gas, total supply (million m³)	116	109	81	38	36	42	194
Electricity, net imports	55	52	70	33	69	116	197
Electricity indigenous production (GWh)	35813	37410	38395	40623	41551	42567	43506
Electricity, net imports (GWh)	644	605	809	382	797	1350	2294
Electricity, total supply (GWh)	36457	38015	39204	41005	42348	43917	45800
Electricity produced from hydro-power	267	189	196	224	303	374	334
Electricity produced from hydro-power (GWh)	3171	2389	2541	2842	3782	4504	4096
Electricity produced from coal (GWh)	133	1338	214	146	266	438	282
Electricity produced from gas (GWh)	93	79	84	80	75	78	332
Electricity produced from liquid fuels (GWh)	8847	8186	7837	8011	8860	8534	8300
TPES	22349	22903	22641	23488	23671	24766	25556
Total net energy imports	15910	18000	17486	15983	18448	19035	19478
Consumption							
Industry sector	4038	3911	3762	3702	4051	4353	4419
Transport sector	6122	6293	6419	6595	6580	6713	6879
Other sectors	4673	4694	4728	4858	5030	6074	6251
Non-Energy use	435	393	377	395	418	414	409
TFC	15268	15291	15285	15550	16079	17554	17957
Indicators							
Self-sufficiency (Indigenous energy production/TPES)	0.39	0.38	0.38	0.38	0.38	0.37	0.38
TPES/GDP (toe/'000 $90 PPP)	0.21	0.22	0.22	0.22	0.22	0.22	0.22
TPES/Population (toe/capita)	2.18	2.22	2.18	2.25	2.26	2.36	2.44
Electricity consumption/population (kWh/capita)	3276	3424	3487	3629	3747	3881	4003

Order Form

OECD CENTRES

Please send your order by mail, fax, or by e-mail to your nearest OECD Centre

OECD BONN OFFICE

c/o DVG mbh (OECD)
Birkenmaarstrasse 8
D-53340 Meckenheim, Germany
Tel: (+49-2225) 926 166
Fax: (+49-2225) 926 169
E-mail: oecd@dvg.dsb.net
Internet: www.oecd.org/bonn

OECD MEXICO CENTRE

Edificio INFOTEC
Av. Presidente Mazarik 526
Colonia: Polanco
C.P. 11560 - Mexico D.F.
Tel: (+52-5) 281 38 10
Fax: (+52-5) 280 04 80
E-mail: mexico.contact@oecd.org
Internet: www.rtn.net.mx/ocde

OECD TOKYO CENTRE

Landic Akasaka Building
2-3-4 Akasaka, Minato-ku
Tokyo 107-0052, Japan
Tel: (+81-3) 3586 2016
Fax: (+81-3) 3584 7929
E-mail: center@oecdtokyo.org
Internet: www.oecdtokyo.org

OECD WASHINGTON CENTER

2001 L Street NW, Suite 650
Washington, D.C., 20036-4922, US
Tel: (+1-202) 785-6323
Toll-free number for orders:
(+1-800) 456-6323
Fax: (+1-202) 785-0350
E-mail: washington.contact@oecd.org
Internet: www.oecdwash.org

I would like to order the following publications

PUBLICATIONS	ISBN	QTY	PRICE*	TOTAL
☐ Black Sea Energy Survey	92-64-17652-7		$100	
☐ Caspian Oil and Gas	92-64-16095-7		$100	
☐ China's Worldwide Quest for Energy Security	92-64-17648-9		$100	
☐ World Energy Outlook: 1999 Insights	92-64-17140-1		$120	
☐ Energy Policies of IEA Countries – Greece – 1998 Review	92-64-16136-8		$50	
☐ Coal Information 1998	92-64-17087-1		$200	
☐ Electricity Information 1998	92-64-17089-8		$130	
☐ Natural Gas Information 1998	92-64-17088-X		$150	
☐ Oil Information 1998	92-64-05863-X		$150	
☐ South East Asia Gas Study	92-64-17174-6		$50	
			TOTAL	

*Postage and packing fees will be added to each order.

DELIVERY DETAILS

Name _____ Organisation _____

Address _____

_____

Country _____ Postcode _____

Telephone _____ Fax _____

PAYMENT DETAILS

☐ I enclose a cheque payable to IEA Publications for the sum of $ _____ or FF _____

☐ Please debit my credit card (tick choice). ☐ Access/Mastercard ☐ Diners ☐ VISA ☐ AMEX

Card no: ⌐_ _ _ _ _ _ _ _ _ _ _ _ _ _ _ _ _¬

Expiry date: ⌐_ _ _ _ _ _¬

Signature:

International Energy Agency, 9 rue de la Fédération, 75739 Paris CEDEX 15
PRINTED IN FRANCE BY CHIRAT
(61 00 03 1 P) ISBN 92-64-17652-7 - 2000